talking
the
TALK
Italian

ALWENA LAMPING

Series Editor: Alwena Lamping

Published by BBC Active, an imprint of Educational Publishers LLP, part of the Pearson Education Group, Edinburgh Gate, Harlow, Essex CM20 2JE, England.

First published 2017.
5 4 3 2 1

ISBN 978-1-4066-8469-8

Publisher: Debbie Marshall
Development editor: Liviana Ferrari
Layout: Reality Premedia Services
Cover design: Two Associates
Cover photograph: © iStock.com/mrdoomits
Illustrations: © Mark Duffin
Project editor: Emma Brown
Proofreading: Daniela Nava
Contributor: Siân Stratton-Brown
Audio producer: Colette Thomson, Footstep Productions Ltd.

Printed and bound by Neografia, Slovakia.

The Publisher's policy is to use paper manufactured from sustainable forests.

contents

introduction

Talking the TALK Italian is BBC Active's latest addition to the bestselling **TALK** series. It is about social conversation: not just small talk but getting to know people and their lives, sharing information, opinions and anecdotes, making plans, talking about aspirations and obligations – and more.
An **audio component**, which is available for you to download from www.bbcactivelanguages.com/TTI, complements the book.

Who is it for?

It's for people of all ages who are learning Italian or who are familiar with the basics, and whose ambition is to be able to chat to people in Italian, whether someone they've just met, a business contact, extended family, a fellow enthusiast, a neighbour ... or anyone else.
The contents are also ideal for someone who has followed a course but would like to update their Italian and extend the range of what they can say.

How does it work?

It is based on the principles of successful conversation.
Everyday conversation hangs on a relatively small number of **core linguistic structures** which provide the framework for what we want to say.
The potential of this framework is realised by building on it, so **personalised vocabulary building** is a priority. This book contains hundreds of examples, using **varied and contemporary language**.
Conversation works better if you have the **strategies to keep it flowing**. And it's easier when you have the confidence that what you're saying sounds **natural and up to date**, and when you know that you'll be **readily understood**.

Is it easy to use?

The approach is hands-on, to enable you to adapt what you're learning so that it's **personal and relevant** to you.
Content is presented in **manageable steps**, with page headings showing clearly what the focus is. Core linguistic structures are generously illustrated

and explained with the hallmark **TALK** clarity. Focused wordbanks, placed just where you need them, allow you to practise, adapt and **personalise the language structures**: there are frequent suggestions on how you might do this.

The design allows learning Italian to fit into a busy lifestyle: this is a book that can be dipped into a page or two at a time. The pages are grouped into 12 chapters, each of which ends with conversations that bring the language you're learning to life and a checkpoint which serves as revision and as an aid to remembering the contents.

How does the audio fit in?

The Italian presenters of the audio have clear aims:

- **helping you to pronounce Italian correctly**, since conversation is more enjoyable when both sides understand each other without endless repetition. They guide you through the sounds of Italian, focusing on the ones that English speakers often struggle with. They do this with material selected from each chapter, **reinforcing the core language structures**. They're supported in the book by how to sound Italian, a guide to the sounds and stress patterns of Italian.

- **developing your listening skills**, since conversation is as much to do with listening as talking. Each chapter ends with informal conversations between the presenters; these are printed in your book on the Talking the TALK page, and the Audio Support Pack offers suggestions on how to make the most of them.

How do I access the audio?

To download the audio, go to www.bbcactivelanguages.com/TTI.

For maximum flexibility, you can download the complete script including the conversations, or you can download the conversations separately, entirely in Italian, for intensive listening.

The **Audio Support Pack** is also available from www.bbcactivelanguages.com/TTI. It includes full transcripts plus guidance and activities on how to make the most of the conversations.

> BBC Active would like to thank all the language tutors who contributed to the planning of Talking the TALK. The concept is based on your suggestions and feedback.

the basics

grammar terms

To get to the point when you can hold your own in a conversation, you don't need to know complex and detailed grammatical terminology. But familiarity with the basic terms can fast-track you to that point because it allows you to make sense of explanations of how Italian works.

The ten definitions on this page will take you a very long way. You don't have to learn them all now: just remember they're here for quick reference. When you decide you'd like to know more, there's a fuller list on pages 175–177.

Nouns are the words for living beings, things, places and abstract concepts: *boy, Rachel, engineer, mosquito, computer, house, Rome, time, strategy*.

Articles are *the* and *a/an*.

A **pronoun** is used instead of a noun, and saves having to repeat that noun. *Where's Theo? He's with a friend; I saw them earlier.*

Adjectives are words used to describe a noun or a pronoun: *good wine; strong red wine; my wine; that wine; it is English; it was superb*.

Verbs are words like *eat, live, sleep, go, listen, have, want, be, die*, which relate to doing and being. In English you can put *to* in front of a verb: *to eat*.

In a dictionary, Italian verbs are listed in the **infinitive**, the equivalent of *to eat*. Nearly all Italian infinitives end in -**are**, -**ere** or -**ire**: **arrivare** *to arrive*, **spendere** *to spend*, **finire** *to finish*.

The -**are**, -**ere** and -**ire** at the end of infinitives are called – understandably – **verb endings**. They're significant in Italian: they change because they can carry a variety of information.

The **tense** of a verb refers to when it's happening, e.g. present tense, future tense. The perfect and imperfect tenses refer to the past.

Most verbs, nouns and adjectives follow patterns: these are defined as **regular**. Ones that deviate from the patterns are called **irregular** and have to be learnt separately. English, too, has irregularities, e.g. *boy/boys* but *child/children*; *work/work**ed*** but *speak/spoke*.

the main differences between Italian and English

There are many similarities between Italian and English, and some essential differences too. It helps to be prepared for those.

- One conspicuous contrast is the way adjectives often come after nouns in Italian: **parco nazionale** *national park*, **asparagi freschi** *fresh asparagus*. Also, words like *it, us, her, them* usually come before a verb, not after it: **lo rispetto** *I respect him*.

- Italian has three everyday words for *you*, **tu**, **lei**, **voi**, depending on who you're talking to. So every sentence or question containing *you* can be phrased in three slightly different ways.

- Every single Italian noun — not just the words for people and animals — is either **masculine (m) or feminine (f)**. There's no sense of *it*, not even for things like cars, food, sport or days of the week. Nouns end in a vowel, with many masculine nouns ending in -**o** and feminine nouns in -**a**.

- In the **plural**, i.e. when there's more than one, you don't add -**s** as in English. Instead, the end vowel of the noun changes: **un adulto** *one adult*, **due adulti** *two adults*; **un cappuccino**, **due cappuccini**.

- Words linked to a noun have to be masculine or feminine to **agree** with it: **il risotto** (m) *the risotto*, but **la musica** (f) *the music*. An adjective in a dictionary has the masculine singular ending, but it changes to agree: when welcoming a man you say **benvenuto**, a woman **benvenuta**, and a group of people **benvenuti**.

- Italian has seven versions of *the*, depending on the noun that comes after it. Since *the* combines with *at, from, of* and *in*, the result is a number of small words such as **al**, **alla** *at the*, **dal** *from the*, **dello** *of the*, **nella** *in the*, which can be rather distracting at first.

- In the English *Do you speak other languages? Yes, I speak Russian*, the verb *speak* in the question is repeated in the answer. In the Italian equivalent **Parli altre lingue? Sì, parlo russo**, the verb has a different ending in the answer because the ending of a verb depends on who is carrying it out.

- Because it's clear from its ending who's implementing the verb, the words *I, we, you, s/he, it, they* aren't essential and are omitted more often than not. This can sound quite strange until you get used to it.

how to
sound Italian

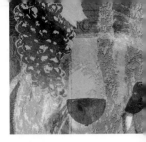

The sounds and rhythm of Italian are not the same as English but, with the right knowledge and focused practice, it's entirely feasible for an English speaker to speak Italian with an accent easily understood by native speakers, regardless of where in Italy they come from.

The starting point is listening, to as many different voices and accents as possible. There are different levels of listening: more often than not you're listening in order to understand **what**'s being said, but you can also train yourself to listen in order to hear **how** something is being said. It doesn't matter that you don't understand everything; what you're doing is getting a feel for the rhythm and overall sound of Italian. When you hear many Italians speaking English, you'll recognise that same rhythm — and this is what you're aiming to recreate.

Italian sounds are not difficult for English speakers if you
- know how to pronounce the letters of the Italian alphabet and key combinations of letters. This takes relatively little time because the sounds don't vary from one word to the next, unlike English;
- practise and keep practising until what you say is what you hear. It's not enough to say things in your head; you need to say them out loud so that your jaw, facial muscles, mouth, tongue, vocal cords and lips are working and adapting to Italian sounds.

The **Talking the TALK** audio download, available from www.bbcactivelanguages.com/TTI, is there to support you. But before sampling the audio, have a look at the next few pages, which summarise the fundamentals of pronunciation, stress and rhythm.

vowels

In English, vowels sound different according to which word they're in, e.g.
a: cart, care, paw, woman
o: one, bone, done, gone

This doesn't happen in Italian; the five Italian vowels are consistent sounds:
a as in the English cat and cart: a sound that comes right from the back of the throat.
e in some words e has an open sound as in penny, net; in others a closed sound similar to the a in chaos.
i as in bee, machine, yet.
o in some words o is open as in pour, in others closed as in the English *not* without the *t*; this is how to pronounce **No** in Italian.
u blue, crude: a sound made in the front of the mouth with the lips rounded.

The vowels are sounded cleanly and crisply, with nothing added: **bravo** is *bra·voh*, never *bravow*.

They retain their individual sound when in combination with others:
> **aerobico** *ah·eh·roh·bee·coh*
> **aiuto** *help, ah·ee·oo·toh*
> **idea** *ee·deh·ah*

Almost all Italian words end in a vowel, the vast majority in **a**, **e**, **o** or **i**. These are never swallowed or mute, which means that words that look identical to English words are pronounced quite differently, e.g.
ape *bee* is pronounced *ah·peh*
grave *serious* is pronounced *grah·veh*
guide *guides* is pronounced *gwee·deh*
olive *olives* is pronounced *olee·veh*
pausa *pause, interval* is pronounced *pow·sah*
per *for* is pronounced like *per* in *periscope*, never like *purr*
produce *produces* is pronounced *pro·doo·cheh*
sublime *sublime* is pronounced *soo·blee·meh*

consonants

Most consonants sound similar in Italian and English, but a few are different. A double consonant always has twice the value of a single.

c + most letters sounds like the English *k*: **Chi**anti, **caffè**, **chi**lo; but when it's followed by **e** or **i**, it sounds like the English *ch* in *chess*: **c**entrale is pronounced *chen-tra-leh*, **ci**nema *chee-neh-mah*.

g + e/i sounds like the English *j*: **gelato**, **formaggio.**
g + n sounds like *ny*: **bolognese** *boh·loh·ny·ay·seh*, **gn**occhi *ny·oh·kee*.
g + li sounds like *lli* in *million*: **tagliatelle** *tah·lee·ah·tell·eh*.
g + other letters is like a hard English *g*: **grammo**, **spaghetti**, **ragù.**

h is not pronounced: it has no sound of its own in Italian.

s between two vowels has a *z* sound: **rosa** *roh·zah*.
s + ce/ci sounds like the English *sh*: **pros**ciutto *proh·shoot·oh*.
s + c + other letters sounds like *sk*: **Lambrusco**, **bruschetta** *broo·skeh·tah*.
z sounds like the English *dz* in some words and *tz* in others: **zucchini**, **pizza.**

r is worth a special mention — getting it right will make all the difference to your Italian. It's often not sounded at all in English, even when there are two together: as in *barn*, *world*, *storm*, *purr*. When **r** is sounded, in words like *rock*, *green* or *marry*, the tongue is towards the centre of the mouth. For the Italian **r**, the tip of the tongue is higher and further forward; it vibrates against the top front of your mouth, practically on the back of the teeth, which produces a distinct rolled sound, very similar to the Scottish **r**. Say *Grrrr* fiercely then tone it down and try familiar words such as **arrivederci** and **grazie**. Focus on what your mouth is doing: this is the characteristic posture of the mouth for Italian.

Another useful tip is to focus on how you say words beginning with **p, t** and hard **c**. At the beginning of an English word, these are aspirated, i.e. accompanied by a little puff of air — but not so in Italian. With your hand right in front of your mouth, say *pin* followed by *spin* and feel the difference. Now say **pasta** without producing the puff of air.

stress

Knowing where the stress falls in Italian words can be tricky. Some words have an accent showing that you stress the final vowel:

- **là** *over there*, **dà** *gives*, **papà** *dad*, **sarà** *it will be*, **velocità** *speed*;
- **è** *is*, **caffè** *coffee*;
- **benché** *even though*, **perché** *why, because*, **trentatré** *33*;
- **lì** *there*, **lunedì a venerdì** *Monday to Friday*, **tassì** *taxi*;
- **casinò** *casino*, **perciò** *therefore*, **però** *however*, **sarò** *I will be*;
- **laggiù** *down there*, **più** *more*, **tivù** *tv*.

Getting the stress right can be critical for a few of these words: without accents, **casino** means *brothel* or *mess* and **papa** means *pope*.

As a general rule, the stress is on the last syllable but one, often a different place from the English equivalent: **adulto** *adult*, **conversazione** *conversation*, **italiano** *Italian*, **nazionale** *national*, **presidente** *president*.

There are many exceptions to this rule and no ready means of identifying them — the position of the stress is learnt by listening.

Most of the exceptions have the stress on the third syllable from the end, e.g. **automobile** *car*, **cardiologo** *cardiologist*, **domenica** *Sunday*, **giovane** *young*, **macchina** *car*, **telefono** *telephone*, **economico** *economic*. In this category are verbs after *they*: **vivono** *they live*, **vivevano** *they were living*.

In **Talking the TALK**, exceptions have the stressed vowel underlined, including the stressed **i** in words such as **farmacia** *chemist's*. In most words ending in **-ia**, the stress is on the preceding syllable: **aria** *air*, **memoria** *memory*.

intonation/rhythm

Pronunciation is about more than individual words. It involves the rhythm and intonation of whole sentences: how the voice rises at the end of a question and falls in an exclamation; how it varies for different emotions.

Getting this right is largely a matter of listening and imitating. When actors are learning an accent, after mastering the key sounds they focus on the rhythm of a language. They also watch how mouths and faces move, and what gestures people make with their hands and shoulders when they speak. When they themselves start speaking, they exaggerate the sounds and gestures, with a view to toning them down later.

uno
first impressions

Although less formal than in the past, Italy retains a sense of occasion: doing things properly is valued, especially when done with style. Italians care about creating a good impression; they tend to put effort into image and looking cool — and they appreciate it in others. They call it **fare bella figura**.

While **fare bella figura** undeniably involves appearance, it's more than skin-deep; it's an attitude towards life in general, including language. Levels of formality are built right into Italian; for example, it's important to choose the right version of *you* so that you don't get off on the wrong foot.

As in most languages, the way you communicate with people in Italian is affected by social context, age, hierarchy and respect. Using the right greetings and forms of address is integral to **le buone maniere** *common courtesies*; a casual **ciao** works only in informal situations.

First impressions matter.

tu, lei or voi?

Unlike English, which has only one word for *you*, Italian has three: **tu**, **lei** and **voi**, and they're not interchangeable.

tu	someone you know well and call by their first name; people you've just met informally who are about your age or younger. Children are all **tu**. It's to do with being casual, familiar and informal.
lei	a stranger; somebody you've already met but don't know particularly well; a person who's clearly older than you are, who's in a senior position in work or towards whom you want to appear respectful. This is the one for more formal situations.
voi	more than one person. However, in southern Italy or among older people, you might also hear **voi** used instead of **lei**.

The use of **lei** dates back to when important people were addressed in the third person. Words like *Your Excellency* and *Your Grace* are feminine in Italian, which is why **lei** *you* is the same word as **lei** *she*.

The verb changes according to whether you're using **tu**, **lei** or **voi**:

	How are you?	*What time are you arriving?*
tu	**Come stai?**	**A che ora arrivi?**
lei	**Come sta?**	**A che ora arriva?**
voi	**Come state?**	**A che ora arrivate?**

Widespread use of **tu** is becoming more acceptable, and is the norm on social media and among groups of young people. But if you use **tu** straightaway with an older person or an official, they might perceive it as over-familiarity or lack of respect.

Bear in mind that you don't necessarily use **tu** with someone who's calling you **tu** – it all depends on who that person is.

If you're starting a conversation and you're not sure whether to use **tu** or **lei**, opt for **lei**. If **tu** is more appropriate, someone will soon suggest **Possiamo darci del tu?** or **Diamoci del tu?** *Let's use tu, let's not be so formal.*

addressing someone properly

Formality isn't confined to a choice of **tu** or **lei**; titles too communicate respect and there's a range in everyday use.

Signor/signora + name equate to *Mr* and *Mrs,* but **signore** and **signora** are also in everyday use without a name after them. It's considered a basic courtesy to add them when addressing people — something which has no equivalent in English: **Buongiorno signore; Grazie signora.**

wordbank

Professional titles such as the following take precedence over **signore/signora**, and not only in a professional setting:

architetto for an architect

avvocato for a lawyer, solicitor or barrister

comandante or **capitano** for an airline pilot; **comandante** for a ship's captain

direttore for a manager or a director

dottore for any **laureato** *graduate* as well as for medical doctors

ingegnere for a qualified engineer

ispettore for an inspector in any context

maestro for a primary school teacher as well as for an eminent musician

ministro for a minister

preside for a headteacher or principal

professore for a teacher in high school as well as university

ragioniere for an accountant

ranks in the police and the armed forces, such as **comandante** *commander*, **maggiore** *major,* **commissario** *commissioner*, **ispettore** *inspector.*

In Italian, as in English, gender can be a delicate issue. Feminine versions of professions exist in Italian, many ending in **-essa** or **-trice**, but their use is less prevalent than it used to be. While **maestra, professoressa** and **dottoressa** are still in regular use, **avvocatessa**, for example, is contentious, with women lawyers tending to use **avvocato.**

At the same time, historically male roles, which had a masculine version only, are being feminised, for example **chirurgo/a** *surgeon* and **architetto/a**. There's little consensus on how to address a woman in some roles and you might well come across **il ministro** or **la ministra** for a woman minister, and **il sindaco** or **la sindaca** for a woman mayor.

greeting people with confidence

hello

Buongiorno. *Hello. Good morning.*
Buona sera. *Hello. Good afternoon. Good evening.*
Salve. *Hello.*
Ciao. *Hi.*

Buongiorno is suitable for **tu, lei** or **voi** until mid-afternoon, when **Buona sera** takes over. **Salve** can also be used with anyone at any time, whereas **Ciao** is more casual.

Greetings tend to be followed by a title or a name. Titles ending in **-ore**, such as **signore, professore** or **dottore** lose the final **-e** when they're followed by a name, but the stress stays on the **-o-**:
Buongiorno signore, signora.
Salve signor Barbieri.
Buongiorno professor Rinaldi.
Buongiorno commissario.
Salve ingegnere.
Buona sera dottore.
Ciao ragazzi. *Hi guys.*
Ciao bello/bella! *Hi gorgeous!*

how are you?

Come stai/sta/state? *How are you?*
Come va? Tutto bene? *How's it going?*
Come vanno le cose? *How are things going?*
Bene, grazie. *Fine, thank you.*
      ... e tu/lei/voi? *... and you?*

While **Bene** is a perfectly adequate reply, there are plenty of other options:
Benissimo. *Really well.*
Tutto bene. *All's well.*
Sto da Dio. *Amazing lit. I'm feeling like God.*
Sono al settimo cielo. *I'm on cloud nine.*
Non c'è male, grazie. *Not so bad, thanks.*
Così così. *So-so.*
Un po' giù oggi. *A bit down today.*
Sono a pezzi. *I'm shattered.*

farewells

Arrivederci. *Goodbye.*
Arrivederla. *Goodbye.*
Ciao. *Bye.*
Buona notte. *Goodnight.*
Sogni d'oro. *Sweet dreams.*
Stammi bene! *Take care!*

Arrivederci can be used with anyone at any time of day. Its literal and original meaning is *until we see each other again.* **Arrivederla** is more formal; its literal meaning is *until I see you* (**lei**) *again.*

Buongiorno and **Buona sera** can be used to say *goodbye,* in the sense of *Have a good day/evening.* **Buona giornata** and **Buona serata** too mean *Enjoy your day/your evening.*

Arrivederci signora. Buona notte.
Ciao Anna. Buona giornata.
Arrivederci. Vi auguro una buona giornata. *Goodbye. I hope you all/both have a good day.*
Arrivederci dottor Biondi. Arrivederla avvocato.
Buona notte, cara. Sogni d'oro.

> **terms of endearment**
> The Italian equivalent of *darling* is **caro** or **carissimo** for a man, **cara** or **carissima** for a woman. Many terms of endearment are the same for a man, woman or child: you'll hear **amore mio** *my love,* **tesoro mio** *my treasure* and **gioia mia** *my joy.*

see you ...

A **domani.** A **più tardi.** *See you tomorrow. See you later.*
A **presto.** *See you soon.*
Ci vediamo ... *See you ...*
       ... in ufficio. *... in the office.*
       ... a/dopo pranzo. *... at/after lunch.*
       ... a/dopo cena. *... at/after dinner.*
       ... stasera. *... this evening.*
       ... fra poco/pochissimo. *... soon/very soon.*
Va bene. D'accordo. *OK.*
Ci sarò. *I'll be there.*

meeting people

The key words come from the indispensible verb <u>e</u>ssere *to be*.

io	sono	*I am*	noi	siamo	*we are*
tu	sei	*you are*	voi	siete	*you are*
lei	è	*you are*	loro	sono	*they are*
lei	è	*she is*			
lui	è	*he is*			
	è	*it is* (**esso/essa** *it* m/f exist but are rarely used)			

The words in blue are the important ones; **io, tu, lei**, etc. are used much less than in English, usually only for emphasis:
Lui è inglese ma io sono scozzese. *<u>He</u>'s English but <u>I</u>'m Scottish.*
I'm not is **non sono**, and the others work in the same way: **non è** *he's not/she's not.*

introducing yourself

(Io) sono Jon. *I'm Jon.*
Sono inglese/irlandese. *I'm English/Irish.*
Sono qui in vacanza/per lavoro. *I'm here on holiday/for work.*
Mi chiamo Meg Riley. *My name is/I'm called Meg Riley.*
Il mio nome è Meg Riley. *My name's Meg Riley.*
Il mio cognome è Riley. *My surname is Riley.*

finding the right person

Tu sei M<u>o</u>nica? *Are you Monica?*
Lei è il dott<u>o</u>r Amato? *Are you Dottor Amato?*
Lei è Gianni D'Orazio, vero? *Gianni D'Orazio, I believe?*
Voi siete i MacLeod? *Are you the MacLeods?*

introducing other people

Ti/le/vi presento ... *Let me introduce ...* (*to you* **tu/lei/voi**).
Questo è Antonio/Questa è Sara. *This is Antonio/Sara.*
Ecco ... *Here is, Here are ...*

responding

Piacere. *Pleased to meet you.*
Che piacere. *What a pleasure.*
Molto lieto/lieta. *Good to meet you.* (male/female speaking)
Lieto/a di con<u>o</u>scerti. *Nice to meet you.* **tu**
Molto lieto/a di con<u>o</u>scerla. *Delighted to meet you.* **lei**

how to spell names

You never know when you might be asked to spell your name, and you might want to know how someone else spells theirs. The key question is **Come si scrive?** which literally means *How is it written?*

When face to face, you can just say **Si scrive così** *It's written like this* and write your name down. Otherwise, you'll need to spell it out.

how to say the letters in Italian

a *ah*	b *bee*	c *chee*
d *dee*	e *eh*	f *effeh*
g *gee*	h *acka*	i *ee*
j *ee lunga*	k *kappa*	l *elleh*
m *emmeh*	m *enneh*	o *oh*
p *pee*	q *coo*	r *erreh*
s *esseh*	t *tee*	u *oo*
v *voo*	w *voo doppia*	x *iks*
y *ipsilon/ee greca*	z *dzehtah*	

Mi chiamo Iris: si scrive ee · erreh · ee · esseh. *My name's Iris: it's spelt ...*
Sono Jake: ee lunga · ah · kappa · eh. *I'm Jake: ...*

For *double* you can either repeat the letter or use **doppia**:
Il mio nome è Henry ma preferisco Harry: si scrive acka · ah · erreh · erreh · ipsilon / acka · ah · doppia erreh · ipsilon. *My name's Henry but I prefer Harry, spelt ...*

With letters that are easily confused, such as **b, p** and **v**, people sometimes use **come** *like* + an Italian city: **b come Bologna, p come Padova, v come Venezia.**
Mi chiamo Niamh; è un nome irlandese, si scrive enneh come Napoli · ee · ah · emmeh come Milano · acka. *My name's Niamh; it's an Irish name, written ...*

> It's worth working out how to spell out your own name in Italian and committing it to memory.

introductions

When meeting for the first time, Italians shake hands in formal situations. When introduced informally by a friend, women, and a man and a woman, might exchange two kisses, one on each cheek, but this very much depends on the context. In the main, kisses tend to be for family and close friends.

You can introduce a person with **questo/questa** è or with ecco *here is, here are* which works for any number of people.

My is normally **il mio** or **la mia**, but **il** and **la** are dropped with a family member — unless there's information added on, such as *ex*, *step*, *great* or an adjective, e.g. *younger*, *favourite*.

Ecco mio fratello, Roberto. *Here's my brother, Roberto.*
Questa è la mia zia preferita. *This is my favourite aunt.*
Questa è la mia cara amica Marta. *This is my great friend Marta.*
Ecco Matteo, il mio amico d'infanzia. *Here's Matteo, my childhood friend.*
Questo è il mio collega Jack. *This is my colleague Jack.*
Questo è Giacomo, il mio vicino di casa. *This is Giacomo, my neighbour.*
Questa è Mona, la mia compagna/partner. *This is my partner Mona.*
Ecco la mia fidanzata Federica. *Here's my girlfriend/fiancée Federica.*

A more formal way of introducing is with **ti presento**, literally *to you I introduce*. When *you* is **lei**, you use **le presento**, and for **voi** it's **vi presento**.

Ti presento mia madre. *Let me introduce my mother.*

Ti presento Fabio, il mio fratello minore/maggiore. *Let me introduce Fabio, my younger/older brother.*

Vi presento Aldo, la mia dolce metà. *Let me introduce Aldo, my other half/ my beloved/my significant other.*

Le presento la mia collega Sofia. *Let me introduce my colleague Sofia.*

Ti presento mio zio: Zio Antonio è il fratello di mia madre. *Let me introduce my uncle: Uncle Antonio is my mother's brother.*

> In Italian, there's no equivalent of the English *'s*: you use **di** *of* instead; *my son's partner* becomes *the partner of my son*:
> **Questo è Leo, il compagno/partner di mio figlio.** *This is Leo, my son's partner.*

When introducing more than one person, **ecco** and **ti/le/vi presento** don't change, but **questo/questa è** become **questi/queste sono**. The plural of **mio** is **i miei** while **mia** becomes **le mie**.

Questi sono i miei figli. *Here are my sons/my children.*

Ti presento i miei genitori. *Let me introduce my parents.*

Le presento le mie figlie. *Let me introduce my daughters.*

Ecco le mie amiche, Giada e Laura. *Here are my friends, Giada and Laura.*

> **Parenti** means *relatives*, not *parents*: **un parente stretto** and **un familiare** both mean *a close relative*. **I miei**, literally *mine*, means *my family, my folks*.

Practise introducing members of your family and circle of friends. Photos are useful props: you can point at people and say who they are.

Include some detail, such as *my little sister, my brother's girlfriend, my father's cousin, my favourite uncle*. Remember to match questo and questa to the right genders and to use mio/il mio as appropriate.

It's much more effective if you do this out loud rather than in your head. When you've finished, write down two or three of your introductions. Make sure you can introduce yourself too and spell your name.

basic courtesies

tu **Scusa.**
lei **Scusi.** *Excuse me.*
voi **Scusate.**

Per favore, per cortesia, per piacere all mean *please.*
Italians don't tend to use *please* as much as English speakers do. This is because it's often implicit in the tone of a sentence. If you're not sure, use it anyway.

Grazie. *Thank you.*
Molte grazie. *Thank you very much.*
Mille grazie. *Thank you so much.*
Grazie a te/lei/voi. *Thank you.*

A response such as **Prego** *You're welcome* or **Di niente** *Think nothing of it* is expected after **Grazie**.
Prego is also used in the sense of *please do, of course, after you.*
Permesso? *Excuse me, May I?* e.g. come in, squeeze past, reach over.
Prego. *Of course.*

Figurati tu/Si figuri lei are also used in response to **grazie**, as well as in all sorts of other situations:
Grazie mille dell'aiuto. *Thanks a lot for your help.* **Si figuri.** *My pleasure. Think nothing of it.*
Mi dispiace. *I'm sorry.* **Figurati.** *Don't worry about it.*
La disturbo? *Am I disturbing you?* **Si figuri.** *Not at all.*
Posso? *Can I? May I?* **Figurati.** *Be my guest.*
Mi puoi aiutare? *Can you help me?* **Figurati.** *Sure, of course, no problem.*

When you're eating with other people, it's customary to wish everyone **Buon appetito** *Enjoy your meal.* You'll also hear the more specific **Buona colazione** *Enjoy your breakfast*, **Buon pranzo** *Enjoy your lunch* and **Buona cena** *Enjoy your dinner*. The response to all of them is **Altrettanto** *You too.*

You can make people feel at home and comfortable with:
tu **Accomodati.**
lei **Si accomodi.**
voi **Accomodatevi.**

talking the talk

The Talking the Talk page towards the end of each chapter sets out the transcript of the informal conversations between Daniela and Renzo on the audio.

Listen to the conversation first – at least a couple of times – before you read it here. Assuming that you have worked through the chapter, you'll probably be able to get the gist and pick out some details. At the same time you'll be getting familiar with the rhythm of Italian.

Don't stop at that. You'll find practical ideas in your Audio Support Pack on how to make the most of these conversations, how to use them to develop your listening skills.

Renzo	Carla, ti presento mio cugino Gianni e sua sorella Giada.
Carla	Piacere.
Renzo	Mia nonna ...
Nonna	Piacere.
Carla	Molto lieta di conoscerla, signora. Si accomodi, prego.
Renzo	Ed ecco mio nonno. Ciao Nonno!
Angelo	Questa è Ambra, mia figlia.
Carla	Ciao Ambra. Tutto bene?
Renzo	Vi presento mio zio ... E questa è la mia cara amica Marta. Marta, ti presento Carla.
Marta	Piacere.
Signora	Renzo – ecco Leo, il compagno di mio figlio.
Renzo	Leo! Che piacere. Come vanno le cose?
Leo	Benissimo! E tu?
Marta	Scusa Renzo, dov'è Angelo?

checkpoint 1

1   What would you say when trying to make your way out of a crowded lift?

2   Would you use **tu**, **lei** or **voi** when speaking to a close friend's elderly grandmother?

3   When being introduced to a woman, does a man say **Molto lieto** or **Molto lieta**? When you're being introduced to a couple, do you say **Lieto/Lieta di conoscerti**, **conoscerla** or **conoscervi**?

4   To introduce yourself, what's the word that you use before your name? How do you make that word negative?

5   If you're addressing a man whose status you're not very sure about, which of these is the safest option? **ispettore, maestro, direttore, dottore, signore**

6   What could you add to **grazie** to say *thank you very much*? List two ways you might respond to **grazie**.

7   If someone replied to your **come stai** with **a pezzi**, would it be more appropriate to commiserate or give them a high five?

8   What's the Italian for *Excuse me* when talking to more than one person?

9   **Dove abitate? Dove abita?** and **Dove abiti?** all mean *Where do you live?* Which would you use with **lei**?

10 What's the Italian for *See you this evening* and *See you after lunch*?

11 Fill the gap to ask *Are you* (**tu**) *on Facebook?* .... **su Facebook?**

12 At what time of day do you use **Salve**?

13 Which of these are younger than you? **figlia, zia, madre, nuora, nonna**

14 How would you invite a couple to sit down and make themselves at home?

15 Based on **attore** *m*/**attrice** *f actor* and **lavoratore/lavoratrice** *worker*, work out the missing forms of **autore/** .... *author;* ....**/traduttrice** *translator;* **traditore/** .... *traitor.*

16 What do **professore, preside** and **maestro** have in common?

17 Given that **Di dove sei?** is the way to ask one person (**tu**) where he/she is from, how would you ask more than one person?

18 What are the two meanings of **sono**?

due
getting to know people

Italians tend on the whole to be sociable and genuinely interested in people's personal and family circumstances – and comfortable talking about them.

Getting to know people implies that you'll be telling them about yourself, so it's worth becoming thoroughly familiar with the words you need to do this, as well as practising some complete sentences.

But a conversation is a two-way process, and to find out about the lives of the Italian people you meet, you're going to be asking questions. A good conversation relies heavily on asking the right questions. Closed questions such as *Do you work here?* or *Have you been there before?* tend to lead to *yes* or *no*, at which point the conversation grinds to a halt. To elicit more information, you can ask open questions, using words like **dove** *where?*, **quando** *when?*, **perché** *why?*

You'll probably need to establish that you're keen to speak Italian, otherwise people may be equally keen to practise their English on you.
Ti/Le/Vi dispiace se parlo italiano? *Do you mind if I speak in Italian?*
Sto imparando l'italiano. *I'm learning Italian.*
Sto studiando l'italiano. *I'm studying Italian.*
Vorrei un po' di pratica. *I'd like some practice.*
Ho bisogno di fare pratica. *I need to practise.*

breaking the ice

To meet people and put your Italian into practice you might want to start a conversation, possibly with someone staying next door, attending the same business meeting or sporting event, standing in a queue or a lift, sitting next to you in a concert or restaurant or by the pool, admiring the same view.

Icebreakers usually involve a question, and the simplest way of forming a question is to make your voice go up inquiringly at the end of a statement, just as you can in English. Try it with **Sei qui in vacanza.** *You are on holiday.* **Sei qui in vacanza?** *Are you on holiday?*

Lei è qui per lavoro? *Are you here on business?*
Sei qui per il campionato/la fiera/la mostra? *Are you here for the championships/the trade fair/the exhibition?* **(tu)**
È la prima volta che vieni/viene qui? *Is this the first time you've been here?*
Stai/Sta qui da molto tempo? *Have you been here long?* **(tu/lei)**
Siamo nello stesso albergo, no? *Aren't we at the same hotel?*

Adding **no? vero?** or **giusto?** to your question is like adding an English question tag such as *isn't it? does she? aren't you? won't they? haven't we? didn't it?*

Lavori qui, no? *You work here, don't you?*
Non lavori qui, vero? *You don't work here, do you?*
È la guida, giusto? *She's the guide, right?*

Bel posto, vero? *Isn't this a beautiful place?*
Che panorama! *What a view!*
È sempre così affollato? *It is always this crowded?*
Come si chiama quell'edificio? *What's the name of that building?*
Sai/Sa dove si trova l'uscita? *Do you know where the exit is?* **(tu/lei)**
Sai/Sa a che ora apre lo stadio? *Do you know what time the stadium opens?*

Che tempo stupendo, vero? *Isn't the weather amazing?*
Posso aiutarti/aiutarla/aiutarvi? *Can I lend a hand?*
Le dispiace se mi siedo qui? *Do you mind if I sit here?*
È un programma interessante, vero? *It's an interesting programme, isn't it?*

asking questions

Open questions are based on question words such as **dove** *where* or **chi** *who*. The verb follows them directly without words like *do/does/did*: **Quando arriva?** *When does he arrive? When is he arriving?*

Chi è il Direttore Generale? *Who's the CEO?*
Chi sono quelle persone laggiù? *Who are those people over there?*
Di chi sono queste chiavi? *Whose are these keys?*

Che vuoi? Cosa vuoi? Che cosa vuoi? *What do you want?*
Cosa facciamo? *What shall we do?*
Che succede? *What's the matter? What's happening?*
Che cosa vi porta qui? *What brings you here?*

Quando partono? *When are they leaving?*
Fino a quando è qui? *Until when are you here? Until when is he/she here?*

Di dove sei? Di dov'è? Di dove siete? *Where are you from?* (**tu/lei/voi**)
Dove sei nato? *Where were you born?*
Dove volete andare stasera? *Where do you want to go this evening?* (**voi**)

Perché stiamo aspettando? *Why are we waiting?*
Perché no? *Why not?*

Come vanno le cose? *How are things going?*
Come si dice ... in italiano? *How do you say ... in Italian?*
Come mai conosci Angelo? *How come you know Angelo?* (**tu**)

Quanto pesa? *How much do you, does he/she/it weigh?*
Quanta roba hanno? *How much stuff have they got?*
Quanti figli avete? *How many children do you have?* (**voi**)
Quante volte è successo? *How many times did it happen?*

Quale lato preferisci? *Which side do you prefer?* (**tu**)
Quali attività sono previste? *What (which) activities are planned?*

Quale vuoi? Quale? *Which one do you want? Which one?* (**tu**)
Qual è il tuo/suo/vostro? *Which one is yours?*
Quali sono i tuoi/suoi/vostri? *Which ones are yours?*

sharing information

As you get to know people, the more information you tend to share and the more detail you get into. In English, the words *Scottish, Australian, Cornish* or *Californian* don't change depending on who they're referring to — but in Italian they do, as does any other adjective, e.g. *funny, tall, stuck-up, sunny.*

word bank

Adjectives are listed in a dictionary with their masculine singular ending, which is nearly always -o or -e.

americano *American*
australiano *Australian*
canadese *Canadian*
cinese *Chinese*
finlandese *Finnish*
francese *French*
gallese *Welsh*
giapponese *Japanese*

inglese *English*
irlandese *Irish*
italiano *Italian*
polacco *Polish*
scozzese *Scottish*
spagnolo *Spanish*
sudafricano *South African*
tedesco *German*

When you're talking about someone who *isn't* masculine singular (yourself included), the dictionary ending changes:
- for a female, -o changes to -a; -e doesn't change.
- for more than one male and for mixed company, -o and -e both change to -i.
- for more than one female, -a becomes -e, while -e becomes -i.

Sono gallese. *I'm Welsh.*
Mia madre è scozzese. *My mother is Scottish.*
Il mio ex/La mia ex è americano/a. *My ex is American.*
Sua nonna era italiana. *His/Her grandmother was Italian.*
I miei bisnonni erano irlandesi. *My great-grandparents were Irish.*
Nostra nuora è polacca. *Our daughter-in-law is Polish.*
I miei suoceri sono francesi. *My in-laws are French.*
Sei italiano/a? *Are you Italian?*

For more on adjectives, see page 179.

An Italian is as likely to say **Sono toscano/a** *Tuscan*, **sardo/a** *Sardinian* or **calabrese** *Calabrian* as **Sono italiano/a**. Cities too have their adjectives: **romano** *Roman*, **fiorentino**, *Florentine*, **napoletano** *Neapolitan*, **bolognese** *from Bologna*. There are no Italian words for e.g. *Aberdonian*: you say **Sono di Aberdeen.** However, you can say **Sono londinese** *I'm from London*.

How much personal detail you divulge in a conversation obviously depends on you and on the circumstances, but it's worth knowing a range of vocabulary so that you understand words when you hear them.

Terms you'll come across include:

single *single*
impegnato *in a relationship*
fidanzato *engaged*
sposato *married*
unito civilmente *in a civil partnership*
separato *separated*

divorziato *divorced*
vedovo *widowed*
etero *straight*
gay *gay*
lesbica *lesbian*
bisessuale *bisexual*
transessuale *transgender*

Hai/Ha/Avete figli? *Do you have any children?*
Hai/Ha fratelli? *Do you have any brothers and sisters?*

Ho/Abbiamo ... *I/we have ...*
    ... un fratello, una sorella. *... a/one brother, sister.*
    ... quattro fratelli. *... four brothers/siblings.*
    ... un figlio/una figlia. *... a son/a daughter.*
    ... tre figli. *... three sons/three children.*
    ... tre bambini. *... three young children.*
    ... due femmine e un maschio. *... two daughters and a son.*
    ... due figlie adottive. *... two adopted daughters.*
    ... tre figli adulti. *... three grown-up children.*
    ... un nipote/una nipote. *... a grandson/a granddaughter.*
    ... cinque nipoti. *... five grandchildren.*
Sono figlio/a unico/a. *I'm an only child.*
Siamo genitori affidatari. *We're foster parents.*
Non ho/abbiamo figli. *I/We don't have children.*

Nipote translates *nephew, niece, grandson* and *granddaughter*. *Niece* and *granddaughter* are **la nipote**, *nephew* and *grandson* **il nipote**. So, **Ecco mio nipote** can mean both *This is my grandson* and *This is my nephew*. Young grandchildren are usually referred to as **i nipotini**.

avere *to have*

Avere, one of the most used verbs in Italian, translates *have, has (got)*. It also has uses where the English equivalent doesn't mention *have*.

io	ho	*I have (got)*	noi	abbiamo	*we have*
tu	hai	*you have*	voi	avete	*you have*
lei	ha	*you have*	loro	hanno	*they have*
lei	ha	*she has*			
lui	ha	*he has*			
	ha	*it has*			

It's used in the widest sense of *to have* or *to own:*

Ho due biglietti per stasera. *I have two tickets for this evening.*
Hai il binocolo? *Have you got the binoculars?*
Ha gli occhi azzurri. *She has blue eyes.*
Ha una casa grande con giardino ... *She's got a large house with a garden ...*
 ... ma non ha un terrazzo. *... but it doesn't have a terrace.*
Non hanno animali domestici. *They don't have any pets.*

Avere is also used to talk about age, literally translating *to have ... years:*
Quanti anni hai? *How old are you?*
Ho quindici anni. *I'm 15.*
Mia madre ha sessant'anni. *My mother is 60.*
Quanti anni ha il bambino? *How old is the little boy?*
Ha tre anni ... ma ne dimostra di più. *He's three ... but he looks older.*
Mio nonno ha novantadue anni. *My grandfather's 92.*
Davvero? Non li dimostra. Li porta benissimo. *Really? He doesn't look it. He carries them (the years) very well. (i.e. He looks amazing.)*

Italian often uses **avere** + noun where English uses *to be* + adjective, e.g.
avere fame *to be hungry,* **avere paura** *to be frightened* lit. *to have fear.*
Io non ho sete. *I'm not thirsty.*
Abbiamo vergogna. *We're ashamed.*
Hai ragione tu. *You're right.*
Avete caldo/freddo? *Are you hot/cold?*
Marisa ha sonno. *Marisa's sleepy.*
Hanno torto. *They're wrong.*

Avere is used when talking about physical wellbeing. **Che hai?** means *What's up with you?* (**tu**). **Che ha?** can mean *What's the matter with you?* (**lei**) or *What's wrong with him/her?* and the answer starts with **ho** for yourself or **ha** to talk about somebody else.

Ho mal di testa/di gola/di schiena/di pancia. *I have a headache/a sore throat/backache/tummy ache.*
Ho la nausea. *I feel sick.*
Ho le vertigini. *I'm having dizzy spells.*
Ho il raffreddore/la febbre *I've got a cold/a temperature.*
Ha la febbre da fieno. *He has hayfever.*
Ha lo stomaco scombussolato. *She's got an upset stomach.*
Ha i postumi di una sbornia. *He's got a hangover.*
Il bambino ha il singhiozzo. *The baby's got hiccups.*
Hanno la febbre. *They've got a temperature.*
Non so che cosa ho/ha. *I don't know what's wrong with me/with him/her.*

---

wordbank

Avere also features in dozens of everyday expressions, many of which don't use *have* in their English equivalent:

> **avere bisogno di** *to need*
> **avere del fegato** *to be brave/gutsy* lit. *to have liver*
> **avere fretta** *to be in a hurry*
> **avere le mani bucate** *to spend money like water* lit. *to have holes in the hands*
> **avere il pelo sullo stomaco** *to be ruthless* lit. *to have hair on the stomach*
> **avere qualche rotella fuori posto** *to have a screw loose*
> **avere voglia di** *to feel like, to fancy*
> **avere una cotta per** *to have a crush on*
> **avere un debole per** *to have a weakness for*
> **avere i grilli per la testa** *to have crazy ideas*
> **avere la luna storta** *to be in a bad mood* lit. *to have the crooked moon*

Ho bisogno della password. *I need the password.*
La mia sorella minore ha le mani bucate. *My little sister spends money like water.*
I miei genitori hanno sempre fretta. *My parents are always in a rush.*
Avete voglia di un aperitivo? *Do you fancy an aperitif?*

describing people

Com'è Nicolò? Com'è Irene? *What's Nicolò/Irene like?*
Com'è la tua dolce metà? *What's your other half like?*
Come sono i tuoi colleghi? *What are your colleagues like?*
Nicolò è gentile e premuroso. *Nicolò's kind and thoughtful.*
È simpatica Irene. *Irene's nice.*
I gemelli sono timidi. *The twins are shy.*
I miei colleghi sono abili. *My colleagues are competent.*

Com'è fisicamente? What does he/she look like?
Che aspetto ha? What does he/she look like?
È alto. È alto due metri/un metro e novanta. *He's tall. He's 2 m/1 m 90 tall.*
... mentre lei è robusta e alta un metro e settanta. *... while she's well built and 1 m 70 tall.*
Pesa 70 chili più o meno. *He/She weighs about 70 kg.*
Ha gli occhi neri/marroni/azzurri. *He/She has black/brown/blue eyes.*
Ha i capelli lunghi/corti/ricci/lisci. *He/She has long/short/curly/straight hair.*

You can bring your descriptions to life by
* slotting in **molto** *very*, **poco** *not very*, **davvero, veramente** *really*, **abbastanza** *quite*, **piuttosto** *rather*, **un po'** *a bit*, **estremamente** *extremely*, **così** *so*, **super** *super*.
* replacing the final vowel of many adjectives with **-issimo**, which has to agree with what it's describing.

Ha i capelli foltissimi. *He's/She's got really thick hair.*
Lei è molto simpatica, gentilissima. *She's very nice, extremely kind.*
È poco ambizioso. *He's not very ambitious.*
I gemelli sono abbastanza timidi. *The twins are quite shy.*
Non sono molto entusiasti. *They're not particularly keen.*
Gianluca è un po' tranquillo. *Gianluca's a bit quiet.*
Sei davvero bravo a golf. *You're seriously good at golf.*
Raffaele sembra super egoista. *Raffaele seems incredibly selfish.*
Alice è bellissima ma così magra! *Alice is very attractive but so thin!*
Mia moglie? È paziente ... pazientissima! *My wife? She's patient ... incredibly patient!*

wordbank

 Try describing a few people – family, friends or celebrities. Use these adjectives and/or look others up in a dictionary. Use extras like piuttosto, molto, (non) li porta bene, and add -issimo/a to at least one adjective.

alto *tall*
tarchiato *stocky, thickset*
massiccio *solid, burly*
sovrappeso *overweight*
bello *beautiful, handsome*
elegante *smart*
calvo *bald*

basso *short*
allampanato *gangly, lanky*
magro *thin,* **snello** *slim*
minuto *petite*
ordinario *plain, ordinary*
sciatto *scruffy*
bruno/biondo *dark-haired/blonde*

Ha una memoria da elefante. *He's/She's got a memory like an elephant.*
È un tesoro/un(a) rompiscatole. *He's/She's a treasure/a pain in the neck.*
Mi dà sui nervi. *He/She gets on my nerves.*

abile *capable, talented*
capace *able, competent*
simpatico *nice, pleasant*
cordiale *open, friendly*
sicuro *confident*
sereno *calm, serene*
premuroso *thoughtful*
educato *polite*
prudente *cautious, careful*
discreto *tactful, diplomatic*
tirchio *tight-fisted*
serio *dependable*
sensibile *sensitive*
paziente *patient*
diligente *hard-working*
ingenuo *naïve*
ottimistico *optimistic*

scemo/sciocco *dumb, stupid*
sbadato *scatterbrained, careless*
antipatico *unpleasant, disagreable*
furbo *canny, shrewd*
timido, riservato *shy, reserved*
ansioso *anxious*
indelicato *tactless*
maleducato *rude*
impetuoso *rash, impetuous*
diretto *outspoken*
generoso *generous, kind-hearted*
irresponsabile *irresponsible*
insensibile *insensitive*
testardo/ostinato *stubborn*
rilassato *laid-back,* **pigro** *lazy*
scaltro *streetwise*
pessimistico *pessimistic*

Bravo *clever, skilled, good at* needs either **a** or **in** before a noun:
bravo a calcio/a suonare la chitarra *good at football/at playing the guitar;* **bravo in matematica/in filosofia** *good at maths/philosophy.*

talking about places

Dove <u>a</u>biti/<u>a</u>bita/abitate? *Where do you live?*
Dove vivi/vive/vivete? *Where do you live?*
Dove sei di casa? *Where do you live?*
Dove in Inghilterra si trova? *Whereabouts in England is it?*
È grande la città? *Is it a big town/city?*
Com'è il paesaggio? *What's the landscape like?*
Com'è la regione? *What's the region like?*

Abitare and **v<u>i</u>vere** both mean *to live*. You can use both to talk about where you live and who you live with but only **v<u>i</u>vere** in the wider sense of living as opposed to dwelling/residing.
Dove <u>a</u>biti/vivi? *Where do you live?*
<u>A</u>bito/vivo **a Bologna.** *I live in Bologna.*
Abitiamo **in un casale.** *We live in a farmhouse.*
<u>A</u>bito/vivo **vicino alla stazione.** *I live near the station.*
Vivo solo. *I live alone.* **Vivevo con <u>E</u>lena.** *I used to live with Elena.*
Viviamo insieme. *We're living together.*
Vivo bene. *I live well.*
Io vivo **e lascio vi<u>v</u>ere.** *I live and let live.*

To say where you used to live, you replace <u>a</u>bito/abitiamo with abitavo/abitavamo and vivo/viviamo with vivevo/vivevamo.

Dove alloggi/alloggia/alloggiate? *Where are you staying?*
Siete in albergo/in un appartamento? *Are you in a hotel/an apartment?*
In quale hotel stai/sta/state? *Which hotel are you staying at?*
Dove si trova il campeggio? *Where's the campsite?*
Quant'è grande il complesso? *How big is the complex?*
Com'è il villaggio/la città/l'albergo? *What's the village/town/hotel like?*

c'è *there is*, **ci sono** *there are*:
C'è una piscina/un campo da tennis? *Is there a pool/a tennis court?*
C'è un parco giochi per bambini? *Is there a play area for young children?*
Quali servizi/attrezzature ci sono? *What services/facilities are there?*
Non c'è una piscina; non ci sono ristoranti. *There's no swimming pool; there are no restaurants.*

La zona dove viviamo è ... *The area we live in is ...*

 ... nel nord est del Regno Unito. *... in the north east of the UK.*

 ... in Cornovaglia/nello Yorkshire occidentale. *... in Cornwall/in West Yorkshire.*

 ... remota/urbana/montuosa. *... remote/urban/mountainous.*

La mia città si trova ... *The town where I live is ...*

 ... fra Cambridge e Londra. *... between Cambridge and London.*

È una località ... *The place is ...*

 ... grande/abbastanza piccola. *... big/quite small.*

 ... affollata/sonnolenta. *... crowded/sleepy.*

 ... in via di sviluppo. *... up and coming.*

 ... davvero sperduta. *... a real backwater.*

È ... *It is ...* **L'albergo è ...** *The hotel is ...*

 ... accogliente e ben attrezzato. *... welcoming and well-equipped.*

 ... pulitissimo/piuttosto squallido. *... spotless/somewhat run-down.*

 ... ben tenuto/un po' trascurato. *... well kept/a bit neglected.*

Ha sicuramente vissuto giorni migliori. *It's definitely seen better days.*
Da ritornarci. *Somewhere to come back to.*
Da evitare! Pessimo posto. *Avoid! Dreadful place.*

Il campeggio/il villaggio è ... *The campsite/resort is ...*

 ... a cento metri dalla spiaggia. *... 100 metres from the beach.*

 ... soleggiato/ombreggiato. *... sunny/shaded.*

 ... sabbioso/fangoso. *... sandy/muddy.*

C'è parecchio da fare/un sacco da fare. *There's plenty to do.*
Ci sono un campo giochi e un campo da tennis. *There's a playing field and a tennis court.*

Un campo is *a field*, which is how it's translated in **campo giochi** *playing field* and **campo di combattimento** *battlefield*. But it has other translations too: **campo da calcio** *football pitch*, **campo da golf** *golf course*, **campo da basket** *basketball court*, **campo da tennis** *tennis court*. It can also mean *camp*, as in **campo estivo** *summer camp*.

Use some of these adjectives to describe places: where you live, where someone you know lives, where you last went on holiday, a place you saw in a film. Bring your descriptions to life with *molto*, *un po'*, etc. and words like *ma* but; *anche* also; *però*, *comunque* however; *inoltre* what's more.

minuscolo *tiny*, **piccolo** *small*, **stretto** *narrow, cramped*
grande *big*, **enorme** *huge*
ampio *ample, broad*, **spazioso** *spacious*, **comodo** *comfortable*

nuovo *new*, **vecchio** *old*
moderno *modern*, **antico** *ancient*, **storico** *historic*
antiquato *dated*, **decrepito** *dilapidated*

tranquillo *quiet*, **affollato** *crowded*
animato *lively*, **movimentato** *bustling*, **trafficato** *congested, busy*

rurale *rural*, **remoto** *remote*, **rustico** *rustic*
boschivo *wooded*, **collinare** *hilly*, **montuoso** *mountainous*
aspro *rugged*, **ripido** *steep*, **piatto** *flat*, **roccioso** *rocky, stony*

urbano *urban*
industriale *industrial*, **centrale** *central*, **turistico** *touristy*

soleggiato *sunny*, **ombreggiato** *shady*
arido *dry*, **fangoso** *muddy*, **sabbioso** *sandy*, **arioso** *airy*

pulito *clean*, **immacolato** *immaculate*, **lussuoso** *luxurious*
ben attrezzato *well-equipped*, **ben tenuto** *well kept*
sporco *dirty*, **spartano** *basic*, **trascurato** *neglected*, **inquinato** *polluted*

accattivante *fascinating, appealing*, **eccezionale** *superb*
grandioso *imposing*, **incantevole** *charming*, **pittoresco** *picturesque*
noioso, tedioso *boring*, **tetro** *dismal, depressing*, **scadente** *shoddy, dire*

how to remember words

It's all very well having a bank of words to refer to – but how do you remember them? The key to transferring a word to your long-term memory is to consciously *do something with it*. Try some of these suggestions and see which suit you.

Don't try and learn too many words at the same time. Aim for about seven or eight at a time, ideally with a connection between them.

- Listen to the words online. If you search for *crowded in Italian*, the first search result is likely to be a box containing **affollato.** Click on the speaker icon and listen to how it's said – as many times as you want. Try it with *steep* and *comfortable* to hear where the stress is in the Italian.

- Say the words out loud – several times. Some people swear by doing this last thing at night, then again the next morning.

- The way words look on a page can make them easier to remember. If you have a visual memory, the unusual arrangement of the words opposite should help you. If so, use a similar technique for your own notes.

- Don't always think in individual words. Sometimes a group of words, e.g. **in via di sviluppo, ha vissuto giorni migliori** can be more memorable.

- Write words down. It doesn't matter whether you write them on paper or key them in. Keep them in manageable groups rather than an endless list. Highlight words that you think will be useful (but don't discount others, since you never know what someone else is going to say).

- Learn tricky words first. You're going to remember words like **moderno, rurale** and **regione** anyway, so leave them until last.

- Use associations to help you remember words. For example, the Italian for *fascinating/appealing* is **accattivante**, so think of a really appealing cat sitting on the roof of a van.

- Use the words. Use the ones opposite as suggested, but don't stop there. When you're out and about, think of an adjective to describe the places you see. It could be factual: **piccolo, vecchio, trascurato**; or it could be subjective: **incantevole, tetro.**

talking the talk

Daniela	Chi è Angelo?
Renzo	Angelo è il mio fratello minore. Ha ventisette anni. È sposato – si è sposato molto giovane ... troppo giovane – ed è separato dalla moglie. Però i due sono in contatto perché hanno una bambina. Si chiama Ambra; è la mia unica nipote.
	Virginia, la moglie, abita nel piccolo comune di Bioglio nel nord ovest. La bambina vive con lei. Angelo vive solo: ha una casa non troppo lontano dalla moglie: quindici chilometri, venti forse. La casa è piccola, non ha un giardino; però c'è un piccolo terrazzo.
	Abitano in una bella regione: rurale, pittoresca, montuosa ... piuttosto tranquilla.
Daniela	Com'è Angelo?
Renzo	Rilassato, paziente, poco ambizioso. Molto simpatico.
Daniela	Che aspetto ha? È alto come te?
Renzo	Beh. È alto due metri; sportivo, capelli corti ... molto corti ... troppo corti!
Renzo	Tu hai fratelli, Daniela?
Daniela	No, sono figlia unica. Però ho cinque cugini, tutti maschi. Uno di loro, Beniamino, abita in un appartamento qui vicino. È molto artistico, abile ma pigro. Ha troppi grilli per la testa!

verb practice 1

1   Fill the gaps with the correct forms of **essere** *to be* (page 18), and say what the sentences mean.
    a   Io .... divorziato.
    b   Noi non .... inglesi.
    c   Cristina .... molto ostinata.
    d   Luca e suo fratello .... gemelli.
    e   Voi .... qui fino a quando?
    f   L'albergo .... pulito e comodo.
    g   Io non .... molto religioso.
    h   Il signor Bassani non .... impegnato.
    i   Loro .... simpaticissimi.
    j   Tu .... fidanzato?

2   Now do the same using **avere** *to have*.
    a   Io .... gli occhi neri ma lui .... gli occhi azzurri.
    b   Francesco non .... sonno.
    c   Quanti anni .... Camilla?
    d   Io e mia moglie .... un debole per il cioccolato.
    e   .... diciotto o diciannove anni tu?
    f   Voi .... tre figli, vero?
    g   Loro .... una piccolissima casa in centro.
    h   Lei .... fame signora?

3   How would you ask these questions in Italian?
    a   *Is she Canadian or American?*
    b   *Are Martina and Michela sisters?*
    d   *Does the hotel have a pool?*
    c   *Marco's gay, isn't he?*
    e   *Are you thirsty?* (**tu**, **lei** and **voi**)
    f   *Are there tennis courts?*

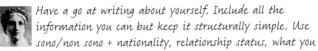

Have a go at writing about yourself. Include all the information you can but keep it structurally simple. Use sono/non sono + nationality, relationship status, what you look like; use ho and non ho with at least five nouns, e.g. siblings, children, pets, house; use abito/vivo + where/how you live.
Now make a list of the questions you would need to ask to get this information from someone else.

checkpoint 2

1 *Isn't it, is she, aren't you, didn't we* at the end of a question can all be expressed by which words in Italian?

2 Is **abita** or **vive** the right word for *lives* in **Mio figlio .... in un universo parallelo.** *My son lives in a parallel universe.*?

3 Name in Italian three recreational facilities you might expect to find in a holiday complex.

4 **dove, perché, quale, quanti, che cosa, chi, quanto, quando, come** Rearrange these question words into the order *who, which, why, what, when, where, how, how many, how much.*

5 How might you offer to lend someone a hand?

6 Work out the Italian for: *I'm thirsty. Are they cold? She's got a cold. I've got an upset stomach.*

7 Add the correct ending to these adjectives and translate the sentences: **Mio nonno è vedov_. Le mie amiche sono galles_. Mia cugina è biond_. Il mio vicino di casa è molto diligent_. Mia suocera è gentilissim_.**

8 What are the missing words in this sequence? **abito** *I live*, **penso** *I think*, **rispetto** *I respect*, **abitavo** *I used to live*, **........** *I used to think*, **........** *I used to respect.*

9 **Forte come un bue** means *as strong as an ox*. Which adjectives do you think fit into **........ come un uovo** *egg* and **........ come un mulo**?

10 If you hear someone described **Ha le mani bucate**, what sort of person would you expect him or her to be?

11 Rearrange **si Italia dove trova in** to mean *Whereabouts in Italy is it?*

12 Which of these means *awful/dreadful*: **pulitissimo, prossimo, pessimo, pessimistico**?

13 Does *a* or *in* fit in the gaps: **Luisa è molto brava .... inglese. Io non sono molto bravo .... golf.**

14 What do you need to add to **viviamo** to say *We're living together*?

15 Sort these adjectives into pairs with opposite meanings: **ampio, collinare, immacolato, movimentato, nuovo, piatto, sporco, stretto, tranquillo, vecchio**

16 How do you tell people you're learning Italian?

tre
what do you do?

What do you do? is often one of the first questions asked when people are getting to know each other. The key word in Italian is **lavoro**, which translates both *a job* and *I work*.

It's tempting to suppose that all you need is the language to say what you do and to ask some questions. But when you ask the questions, you might be confronted with a wide variety of replies, so don't be too selective in the vocabulary you learn. If you're neither a pilot nor a postman you're never going to want to say **sono un pilota** or **sono postino** ... but somebody might well say it to you.

In the workplace, hierarchy is more in evidence in Italy than in English-speaking countries. Professional titles are more prevalent; introductions are likely to consist of a surname or a full name, together with the role in the company.

Being able to chat informally in Italian with your hosts, between meetings, over a meal or in the bar, is rated highly and puts everyone at ease. However, even if the culture seems to you to be casual, it's as well not to assume that immediate informality will break the ice quickly and forge strong relationships: uninvited use of **tu** and first names may instead take some people out of their comfort zone.

saying what you do

Typical conversations about work start with questions like:
Che lavoro fa/fai? *What (work) do you do?*
Che fa/fai nella vita? *What do you do in life?*
The answer might start with **faccio il/la** or with **sono**. After **sono**, traditionally **un/una** was not used but these days you're as likely to hear it as not.

> **Faccio il/la designer**, **l'insegnante.** *I'm a designer, a teacher.*
> **Sono (un/a) terapista sportivo/a.** *I'm a sports therapist.*

wordbank

agente immobiliare *estate agent*
agente di viaggi *travel agent*
allenatore/rice *trainer*
arredatore/rice *interior designer*
autista *driver*
bagnino/a *lifeguard*
banchiere/a *banker*
calciatore/rice *footballer*
cantante *singer*
consulente *consultant, counsellor*
controllore di volo *air traffic controller*
costruttore/rice *builder*
cuoco/a, **chef** *cook, chef*
docente *lecturer*
giardiniere/a *gardener*
grafico/a *graphic designer*
idraulico/a *plumber*

impiegato/a *office worker*
infermiere/a *nurse*
informatico/a *computer scientist*
intermediario/a finanziario/a *stockbroker*
istruttore/rice *coach, instructor*
modello/a *model*
parroco *vicar*
politico/a *politician*
poliziotto/a *policeman*
pompiere *firefighter*
ricercatore/rice *researcher*
scienziato/a *scientist*
sorvegliante *security guard*
storico/a *historian*
tata *nanny*

jobs you can guess

Many Italian occuptions end in **-ista** for both men and women. Some have an English equivalent ending in **-ist**: **analista** *analyst*, **farmacista** *pharmacist*, **fiorista** *florist*, **fisioterapista** *physiotherapist*, **giornalista** *journalist*.
But not all of them: **barista** *bartender*, **elettricista** *electrician*, **estetista** *beautician*, **musicista** *musician*, **regista** *film director*.

The English ending *-ologist* generally equates to **-ologo**: **ecologo**, **geologo**, **ginecologo**, **microbiologo**, **ornitologo**, **patologo**, **psicologo**, **radiologo**, **riflessologo**, **zoologo**. You might or might not hear **-ologa** for a woman.

not the nine to five

Sono un(a) libero/a professionista. *I work freelance.*
Faccio il fotografo indipendente/freelance. *I'm a freelance photographer.*
Lavoro in proprio. *I'm self-employed. I have my own business.*
Lavoro ... *I work ...*
  ... da casa. *... from home.*
  ... a tempo parziale/part time. *... part-time.*
  ... a tempo pieno/full time. *... full-time.*

You'll hear many English words used in Italian, e.g. *freelance, part time, babysitter*. They might, however, sound different, and if you use them, it's as well to pronounce them the Italian way to make sure you're understood.

Sono (uno/una) studente/studentessa. *I'm a student.*
Sono (uno/una) stagista. *I'm a trainee/an intern.*
Sono (un/un') apprendista. *I'm an apprentice.*
Sono una mamma/un papà a tempo pieno. *I'm a stay-at-home mum/dad.*
Sono una mamma lavoratrice. *I'm a working mother.*
Sono in fase di transizione. *I'm between jobs.*
Sono disoccupato/a. *I'm unemployed.*
Sono in pensione. *I'm retired.*
Faccio volontariato. *I volunteer, do charity work.*
Mi prendo un anno di pausa. *I'm taking a gap year, a year out.*
Mi prendo un periodo sabbatico. *I'm taking a sabbatical.*
Cerco lavoro. *I'm job hunting.*
Ho accettato le dimissioni volontarie. *I've taken voluntary redundancy.*
Sono andato/a in pensione anticipata. *I've taken early retirement.*
Curiamo i nostri nipotini. *We look after our grandchildren.*
Non lavoro. *I don't work.*

 With some simple changes, you can adapt what you've learnt to talk about other people. To say what someone else does, you replace sono *with* è *and* lavoro *with* lavora: *mia sorella è fisioterapista, il mio compagno lavora in proprio. Try this out by choosing a couple of the people you described in* **Chapter 2** *and adding what they do to your description.*

how regular verbs work

The -are ending of **lavorare** shows you it means *to work*. Grammatically, it's called the infinitive.

To say that you or somebody else works or is working, you replace -are with a different ending, e.g. **lavoro** *I work*, **Gino lavora** *Gino works*, **lavorano** *they work*. Any other infinitive ending in -are behaves in the same way.

parlare *to speak*	**Parlo inglese.** *I speak English.*
curare *to look after*	**Curo i nipotini.** *I look after the grandchildren.*
cercare *to look for*	**Cercano una casa.** *They're looking for a house.*

Not all infinitives end in -are. There are two other groups, ending in -ere and -ire. Their **present tense** endings differ only slightly for each group of verbs; although a few verbs in the small -ire group add -isc (page 188).

infinitive (*to*)	-are	-ere	-ire	-ire
io *I*	-o	-o	-o	-o
tu *you*	-i	-i	-i	-isci
lei *you*	-a	-e	-e	-isce
lui/lei *he/she; it*	-a	-e	-e	-isce
noi *we*	-iamo	-iamo	-iamo	-iamo
voi *you*	-ate	-ete	-ite	-ite
loro *they*	-ano	-ono	-ono	-iscono

Once you're familiar with these endings, you can use the present tense of any regular verb to say what you **do** and what you **are doing** – and it takes surprisingly little time for the association of -**o** with *I*, -**iamo** with *we*, etc. to become hardwired in the brain.

aiutare *to help*	**aiuto** *I help*, **aiuta** *he/she's helping*
aspettare *to wait*	**aspettiamo** *we wait, we're waiting*
capire *to understand*	**capisco** *I understand*, **capisci** *you understand*
chiedere *to ask*	**chiedi**, **chiede**, **chiedete** *you ask*
dipendere *to depend*	**dipende** *it depends*
finire *to finish*	**finisco** *I finish*
partire *to leave*	**parte** *it leaves*
prendere *to take*	**prendono** *they take, they're taking*

Take care with pronunciation when you're using **loro** *they*: the stress is never on the ending itself, except for -**iscono**.

infinitives ending in -si: reflexive verbs

The infinitives of some verbs have **si** tacked on to them so that in a dictionary they end in **-arsi**, **-ersi** or **-irsi**. These are reflexive verbs: the English translation often, but not always, includes or implies *self*.

alzarsi *to get (oneself) up*
annoiarsi *to get bored*
chiamarsi *to be called*, lit. *to call oneself*
chiedersi *to wonder*, lit. *to ask oneself*
divertirsi *to enjoy oneself*
occuparsi di *to look after, to manage*, lit. *to occupy oneself with*
preoccuparsi *to worry (oneself)*
ricordarsi *to remember*, lit. *to remind oneself*
riposarsi *to rest (oneself)*
sedersi *to sit (oneself) down*
sentirsi *to feel*
sposarsi *to get married*

Si means *oneself*, and is replaced by **mi, ti, si, ci, vi** or **si** to say *myself, yourself, ourselves*, etc. **Devo sedermi.** *I need to sit (myself) down.*

When not in the infinitive, a reflexive verb loses **si** and behaves like any other verb, but with the addition of a separate **mi, ti, si, ci, vi** or **si** beforehand:

	svegliarsi *to wake (oneself) up*	
io	mi **sveglio**	*I wake up*
tu	ti **svegli**	*you wake up*
lei	si **sveglia**	*you wake up*
lui/lei	si **sveglia**	*he/she wakes up*
noi	ci **svegliamo**	*we wake up*
voi	vi **svegliate**	*you wake up*
loro	si **svegliano**	*they wake up*

Mi chiamo Claudia. *My name's Claudia.* lit. *I call myself Claudia.*
Si occupa del sito web. *He/She manages the website.*
Non si preoccupano. *They're not worrying.*

work talk

Dove lavori/lavora? *Where do you work?*
Lavoro ... *I work ...*

a *in*
a Londra *in London,* **a Roma** *in Rome,* a **Milano** *in Milan*

in *in*

un'agenzia di scommesse *a betting shop*
un asilo nido *a nursery*
un'autofficina *a repair shop/garage*
un call center *a call centre*
un'erboristeria *a herbalist's*
una fabbrica *a factory*
una fattoria *a farm*
un negozio di alimenti naturali *a health-food shop*
un negozio di animali *a pet shop*

un ospedale *a hospital*
una palestra *a gym*
una scuola superiore *a high school*
un supermercato *a supermarket*
uno stabilimento farmaceutico *a pharmaceutical plant*
uno studio medico *a surgery*
un ufficio *an office*
un vivaio *a nursery, garden centre*
una zona industriale *industrial estate*

nel settore ... *in the ... field*

nel settore agricolo *in agriculture*
nel commercio al dettaglio *in retail*
nel settore pubblico *in the public sector*
nel settore bancario *in banking*

nel settore sanitario *in the health sector*
nel settore turistico *in tourism*
nelle pubbliche relazioni *in PR, public relations*

Per chi lavori/lavora? *Who do you work for?*

per *for*
una banca internazionale *an international bank*
un'azienda vinicola *a winery*

un'organizzazione benefica *a charity*
un'azienda di software *a software company*

presso *for/at*
il Ministero dell'Ambiente *the Department for the Environment*
la NATO *NATO*

FG&S SpA *FG&S plc*
un'agenzia di stampa *a news agency*

Da quanto tempo fa/fai questo lavoro? *How long have you been doing this work/job?*

Whereas English uses *have been doing*, Italian uses *am doing* and **da**.

Faccio questo lavoro da ... *I've been doing this work/job for ...*

Faccio il doganiere da ... *I've been a customs officer for ...*

    ... sei mesi. *... six months.*

    ... un anno e mezzo. *... a year and a half.*

    ... dieci anni. *... ten years.*

    ... più anni di quanti voglia ricordare. *... longer than I care to remember!*

Lavoro qui ... *I've been working here ...*

    ... dall'anno scorso. *... since last year.*

    ... da settembre. *... since September.*

    ... dal duemilatredici. *... since 2013.*

Qual è il suo ruolo? *What's your role/position?*

Lavoro nell'ufficio stampa e comunicazione. *I work in the media office.*

Rispondo direttamente al capo. *I answer directly to the boss.*

Sono il responsabile del controllo di qualità. *I head Quality Control.*

Sono addetto alle risorse umane. *I work in HR.*

Sono l'addetto alla manutenzione. *I'm the maintenance man.*

Sono coordinatore di progetti. *I'm a projects co-ordinator.*

Sono vice direttore. *I'm deputy director/assistant manager*

Sono caporeparto. *I'm supervisor/head of department/foreman.*

Sono il/la tuttofare. *I'm the dogsbody.*

Qual è il suo campo (di competenze)? *What's your field (of expertise)?*

Sono in amministrazione. *I'm in admin.*

Sono responsabile del magazzino. *I'm in charge of the warehouse.*

Gestisco il reparto. *I run the department.*

Gestisco il sistema informatico. *I manage the IT system.*

Mi occupo della sicurezza sul lavoro. *I deal with Health and Safety.*

Mi occupo del sito web aziendale. *I look after the company website.*

The Italian words for *the* combine with **a** *at/to*, **da** *from*, **di** *of*, **in** *in* and **su** *on* (page 179). **A** + **il** becomes **al** as in **al capo** *to the boss*; **di** + **il** becomes **del** as in **del magazzino** *of the warehouse*, and **in** + **le** becomes **nelle** as in **nelle pubbliche relazioni** *in PR*. See how many other examples you can find on these two pages.

wordbank

These 60 commonly used verbs are arranged in pairs/groups to help you remember them by association. The **-ire** verbs without **-isc-** are marked *.

imparare to learn
indovinare to guess
indagare to investigate
sperare to hope
giocare to play
tifare per to support (team)
pareggiare to draw, equalise
cercare to look for, search
guardare to look at
cominciare to start
mettere to put
promettere to promise
ascoltare to listen
ridere to laugh
chiacchierare to chat
capire to understand
mentire* to lie
chiedere to ask
offrire* to offer
consigliare to advise
accettare to accept
permettere to allow
curare to look after
guidare to drive, to lead
incontrare to meet
aprire* to open
prendere to take
comprare to buy
spendere to spend
pagare to pay

insegnare to teach
calcolare to calculate
fantasticare to fantasise, daydream
confrontare to compare
segnare to score
vincere to win
perdere to lose
trovare to find
vedere to see
finire to finish
smettere to quit, stop
ricompensare to reward
sentire* to hear, to feel
sorridere to smile
chattare to chat online
chiarire to clarify
fingere to pretend
rispondere to answer
suggerire to suggest
ignorare to ignore
rifiutare to refuse
vietare to forbid
trascurare to neglect
seguire* to follow
evitare to avoid
chiudere to close
lasciare to leave
vendere to sell
cambiare to change
contrattare to haggle, negotiate

Choose ten verbs and replace the infinitive endings with other endings. Try using a few of them in a sentence. Verbs such as cercare and pagare add h before e or i so that they keep the hard sound of the c and g.

fare *to do, to make*

Not all verbs follow the regular patterns shown on page 44. **Fare** is one of the irregular ones, the one-offs. Since it's one of the most used Italian verbs, it's worth making sure you know how it works.

io	faccio	*I do*	noi	facciamo	*we do*
tu	fai	*you do*	voi	fate	*you do*
lei	fa	*you do*	loro	fanno	*they do*
lei	fa	*she does*			
lui	fa	*he does*			
	fa	*it does*			

Fare is used to talk about work:
Che lavoro fa/fai? *What (work) do you do?*
Cosa fa nella vita? *What does he/she do for a living?*
Faccio il ragioniere. *I'm an accountant.*
Fa la casalinga/la docente. *She's a housewife/a lecturer.*
Vorrei fare lo chef. *I'd like to be a chef.*

It means *do/make* in a general sense:
Cosa facciamo? *What shall we do?*
Non fa differenza. *It makes no difference.*
Devo fare il bucato. *I must do the washing.*
Fa un rumore strano. *It's making a funny noise.*

It's used to talk about the weather (page 116):
Che tempo fa? *What's the weather like?*
Fa bello/brutto/caldo/freddo/fresco. *It's lovely/awful/hot/cold/cool.*

... and in many expressions that don't use the words *make* or *do* in English,
e.g.
    fare baldoria *to party, to paint the town red*
    fare la coda *to queue*
    fare una domanda *to ask a question*
    fare un pisolino *to take a nap*
    fare lo splendido *to show off, put on airs*
    fare lo scemo *to be silly, stupid*
    Non fare complimenti! *Feel free, don't hold back.*
    fare male *to hurt, to be painful*
        Mi fa male il collo. *My neck's hurting.*
        Mi fanno male i piedi. *My feet hurt.*

talking the talk

Daniela	Che lavoro fa tuo fratello?
Renzo	Angelo? Fa il maestro in una scuola elementare.
Daniela	Anche vostro padre è maestro, vero?
Renzo	No. Mio padre lavora per un'azienda vinicola ... un'azienda che produce vino.
Daniela	Qual è il suo ruolo?
Renzo	È il responsabile del controllo qualità. Fa questo lavoro da vent'anni.
Daniela	Che tipo di vino producono?
Renzo	Il Barolo, di ottima qualità. Tutto DOCG.
Daniela	Tutto DOCG?
Renzo	Sì. Tutto Denominazione di Origine Controllata e Garantita. Ottima qualità garantita.
Daniela	Tua madre lavora?
Renzo	Lei cura i nonni. Mia nonna non sta bene.
Renzo	Tua madre lavora?
Daniela	Sì, fa la grafica.
Renzo	Per chi lavora?
Daniela	Fa la libera professionista. In questo momento lavora per un'organizzazione benefica.
Renzo	Dove lavora?
Daniela	Cambia, ma normalmente lavora da casa.
Renzo	A tempo parziale?
Daniela	Dipende. Le ore cambiano. A volte lavora ventiquattr'ore su ventiquattro, sette giorni alla settimana.
Renzo	Davvero una mamma lavoratrice!

verb practice 2

1   Add the correct present tense endings to the verbs.

   a   **aggiungere** to add   **tu** ....
   b   **cambiare** to change   **loro** ....
   c   **creare** to create   **voi** ....
   d   **durare** to last   .... (it)
   e   **mettere** to put   **noi** ....
   f   **piangere** to cry   **lei** ....
   g   **provare** to try   **io** ....
   h   **ripetere** to repeat   **lui** ....
   i   **salvare** to save   **noi** ....
   j   **succedere** to happen   .... (it)

2   Only a few verbs end in **-ire**. Fill the gaps with the correct form of
     one of these, none of which adds **-isc**: **aprire** to open, **dormire** to
     sleep, **offrire** to offer, **partire** to leave:

   a   **Non** .... **bene quando fa caldo.** She doesn't sleep well when it's
        hot.
   b   **Il suo volo** .... **stasera.** His flight leaves this evening.

     Among **-ire** verbs that do add **-isc** are: **abolire** to abolish, **costruire**
     to build, **finire** to finish, **fornire** to provide, **garantire** to guarantee,
     pulire to clean, **preferire** to prefer, **punire** to punish, **restituire** to give
     back, **unire** to join.

   c   **Se voi** .... **le norme.** If you abolish the rules.
   d   .... **la macchina ogni giorno.** He cleans his car every day.
   e   .... **alle due.** They finish at two o'clock.
   f   **Chi** .... **i dati?** Who's providing the data?
   g   .... **la vostra sicurezza.** We guarantee your safety.
   h   .... **perfettamente.** I understand perfectly.

3   Decide whether **mi, ti, si, ci** or **vi** belongs in the gap:

   a   **Come ... chiama il cane?** What's the dog called?
   b   **... occupano del magazzino.** They look after the warehouse.
   c   **Non ... alziamo molto presto.** We don't get up very early.
   d   **Lara ... annoia facilmente.** Lara gets bored easily.
   e   **... ricordi?** Do you remember?
   f   **Oggi ... sento meglio.** Today I feel better.
   g   **... divertite tutti?** Are you all having a good time?

1   Match the people with their workplace: **microbiologo, meccanico, allenatore, giardiniere, doganiere, infermiere: palestra, autofficina, studio medico, vivaio, stabilimento farmaceutico.** What does the person left over do?

2   To say what your occupation is, do you normally use **il/la** after **sono** or after **faccio**?

3   What two words do you add to **lavoro qui** .... **quindici** .... to say you've been working here for 15 years?

4   What do you think the Italian is for *meteorologist*? And what do you think a **reumatologo** an **oftalmologo** and a **mafiologo** are?

5   If you needed a driver, would you ask for a **regista, apprendista, autista** or **stagista**?

6   What's the Italian for *it makes no difference*?

7   What words do you add to **mamma** to describe a stay-at-home and a working mother?

8   How would you tell someone in Italian that your partner is self-employed?

9   Where do people employed **nel settore risorse umane, nel settore alberghiero, nel settore automobilistico** and in **una fattoria** work?

10   How would you ask someone what their role is?

11   Without necessarily knowing what they mean, decide from the verbs whether these questions relate to **tu, lei** or **voi: Vi ricordate la data? Quando finisci? Si occupa della sicurezza? Non vende francobolli?**

12   If **caporeparto** means head of department, what do you think a **capofabbrica** is?

13   Given that **gestisco** *I manage* comes from **gestire** *to manage*, what's the Italian for *We manage a factory in Milan*?

14   Rearrange these words to form a sentence, then say what it means in English: **del un'agenzia responsabile sono di web in immobiliare sito**

15   To say what you *used to be*, you replace **sono** with **ero** – so how would you say in Italian *I was a teacher*?

16   What do you think **Mio nonno era un poliziotto** means?

quattro
the art of conversation

Once you're past the stage of exchanging basic information with someone, you usually move on to more general conversation. A proper conversation flows without awkward pauses or prolonged silences; it feels comfortable and includes comments and prompts, questions and exclamations.

The general principles — showing interest in the person you're talking to, knowing when to say something, how much or how little to say — are things we do in our first language without much conscious thought, but when you're speaking in a new language and concentrating on finding the right word at the right time, it helps to think about how to achieve them.

Even if you can't always say as much as you'd like, you can still contribute just by knowing how to keep a conversation going: there are a number of strategies you can use to show you're properly engaged. Gestures, eye contact, a smile, positive body language or a nod at the right time all show that you're actively listening and following what's being said — but they're not half as satisfying as coming up with a succinct comment or an exclamation.

For the strategies to work, it's important to concentrate your energies on listening to what's being said and to resist the temptation to half listen while you work out what you're going to say next. A conversation is unpredictable and, by the time you're ready with your perfect sentence, the thread might well have moved on.

following what's being said

When you're new to a language, it can seem as if it's spoken very rapidly.
Nobody will mind if you ask for help now and again or find it necessary to
slow the conversation down so you can understand.

Scusami. *Excuse me.* tu
Mi scusi. *Excuse me.* lei
Chiedo scusa ma ... *I beg your pardon, but ...*
Scusate se interrompo ma ... *Sorry for interrupting, but ...*

Non capisco. *I don't understand.*
Non ho capito. *I haven't understood.*
Non so se ho capito bene. *I don't know if I've understood properly.*
Non sono sicuro di aver capito. *I'm not sure I've understood.*

Non ho capito ... *I haven't understood ...*
Cosa significa ...? *What does ... mean?*
... vuol dire ..., vero? *... means ..., doesn't it?*

Come hai/ha detto? *What did you say?*
Puoi/Può ripetere per favore? *Can you repeat that please?*
Puoi parlare più lentamente? *Can you speak more slowly?*
Ti dispiacerebbe spiegare? *Would you mind explaining?*
Le dispiacerebbe ripetere? *Would you mind repeating that?*

You can show you're following by echoing what's been said before
offering a relevant comment or question.
Mio cognato lavora in Cina. *My brother-in-law works in China.*
In Cina? Davvero? Dove? *In China? Really? Whereabouts?*

For emphasis you can change word order.
E anche Luca ha partecipato. *And even Luca took part.*
Luca ha partecipato? Bravo. *Luca took part? Well done.*
Ha partecipato Luca? Caspita! *Luca took part? Wow!*

making yourself understood

There will be times when you need to know if you're getting your message across.

Mi capisci/capisce/capite? *Do you understand me?* tu/lei/voi

Mi spiego? *Am I making sense?*

Mi spiego. *Let me explain/clarify.*

Mi spiego meglio. *Let me explain better.*

Non so se mi spiego bene. *I don't know if I'm explaining things very well.*

If you're struggling for a word, say so:

Ho dimenticato la parola. *I've forgotten the word.*

Non trovo la parola giusta. *I can't find the right word.*

Mi sfugge la parola. *The word escapes me.*

Ce l'ho sulla punta della lingua. *It's on the tip of my tongue.*

Come si dice ... in italiano? *What's the Italian for ... ?*

Come si chiama questo? *What's this called?* is useful if **questo** is within reach. If not, paraphrasing can be effective.

> **È il contrario di ...** *It's the opposite of ...*
> **È quadrato/rotondo.** *It's square/round.*
> **Non è ...** *He/She isn't ..., It's not ...*
> **È una specie di ...** *It's a sort of ...*
> **È un po' come ...** *It's a bit like ...*
> **Serve a misurare/calcolare.** *It's used to measure/calculate.*
> **Assomiglia a ...** *He/She/It looks like ...*
> **Non ricordo come si chiama ... il tizio che abita in Corso Umberto.**
> *I don't remember his name ... the guy who lives in Corso Umberto.*
> **Si trova a sud di Firenze, in piena campagna, remotissimo, dove ...**
> *It's south of Florence, out in the country, very remote, where ...*

You can always resort to words like **il coso** *thingy, contraption;* **l'aggeggio** *gizmo;* **l'aggeggino** *little thingummyjig;* **il tizio** *guy, bloke.*

... and, if all else fails, you can turn to gestures and mime.

Era grande così. *It was this big.*

Aveva la faccia così. *His face was like this.*

educated guesswork

Many Italian words are instantly recognisable to an English speaker, e.g. **adulto, animale, dollaro, elefante, errore, familiare, musicale, momento, elegante, maturo, moderno, natura, universale.** These are called cognates, meaning *born together* because they generally share a common ancestor.

Knowing which English words have an Italian cognate is not as straightforward, but there are pointers that raise the odds of an educated guess turning out to be correct.

Noun endings can provide clues, e.g.

-tion	-zione	attenzione, conversazione, stazione
-ty	-tà	qualità, quantità, università
-y	ia	democrazia, fotografia, infanzia, lotteria

... as can adjective endings, e.g.

-al	-ale	generale, individuale, internazionale
-ary	-ario	immaginario, ordinario, straordinario
-ic	-ico	artistico, patetico, pubblico
-ive	-ivo	conclusivo, esclusivo, repulsivo

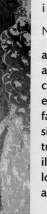

i falsi amici *false friends*

Not all words mean what they appear to mean, e.g.

attualmente *at the present time*	*actually* **in realtà**
abusivo *illegal*	*abusive* **offensivo, violento**
crudo *raw*	*crude* **volgare**
educato *polite, well-mannered*	*educated* **colto, istruito**
fastidioso *annoying*	*fastidious* **schizzinoso**
simpatico *nice*	*sympathetic* **comprensivo**
triviale *vulgar, indecent*	*trivial* **banale, di poco conto**
il gusto *taste*	*gust* **la raffica**
lo stormo *flock*	*storm* **la tempesta**
accomodare *to fix*	*accommodate* **alloggiare, ospitare**

There are enough false friends to suggest that guesswork should not be your default approach to vocabulary!

showing empathy

A well chosen interjection shows that you're listening and understanding the mood of the conversation. To endorse what's being said, you can say:

Bravo! Bene! *Well said! Hear, hear!*
Ecco! *That's just it!* **Giusto!** *That's right!*
Già! Infatti! *Indeed!*
Esatto! Assolutamente! Precisamente! *Exactly! Absolutely! Spot on!*

Like English, Italian has expressions that can equally well convey interest, admiration, incredulity, indignation, amusement, concern or horror depending on the tone of your voice and the expression on your face.

Davvero? *Really?*
Sul serio? *Seriously? For real?*
Mamma mia! Madonna! *Wow! Goodness me! Gordon Bennett!*
Oddio! *OMG!*
Ma va'! Ma dai! *Get away! You don't say! Oh, come on!*
Santo cielo! Santa pace! *Good grief! For pity's sake!*
Accidenti! Accipicchia! Caspita! *Wow! Holy smoke! Stone the crows!*
Ma pensa un pò! *Well I never! Who'd have thought it!*
Stai scherzando! *You're joking! No kidding!*
Per carità! *For goodness' sake!*
Beato te/lei! Beati voi! *Lucky you!* **Beati loro!** *Lucky them!*

Others are a bit more specific:

Macché! *As if! No way.*
Magari! *If only! I wish!*
Coraggio! Forza! *Come on, you can do it!*
Pazienza. *Ah well. Hey ho, never mind.*
Uffa! *Whatever!* (showing annoyance or impatience)

Some expressions are far removed from their literal meaning:
Miseria is *poverty* but **Porca miseria!** means *Good grief!*
Un fico is *a fig* but **Fico!** translates as *Cool! Wicked!*
Cavolo is *cabbage* but it's also used as a replacement for an expletive: **Cavolo!** *Damn!* **Ma che cavolo fai?** *What the heck are you doing?* **Col cavolo!** *No way. In your dreams. Yeah, right.*
Awesome is **imponente**, **grandioso** but *Awesome!* is **Fantastico!** or **Mitico!**, which literally means *legendary, mythical.*

commenting

It's a fallacy that long complex sentences are in some way superior: in a conversation, a simple comment is often very appropriate.

Che followed by a noun, is the equivalent of *What a ...* or sometimes *How ...*

    Che barba! Che noia! *What a bore!*
    Che confusione! Che casino! *What a mess!*
    Che delusione! *What a disappointment! How disappointing!*
    Che emozione! *What a thrill! How exciting!*
    Che figata! *How cool!*
    Che fastidio! Che seccatura! *What a nuisance!*
    Che gioia! *What a joy!*
    Che peccato! *What a pity! What a shame!*
    Che perfezione! *What perfection!*
    Che rottura! *What a drag! What a pain!*
    Che schifo! *How disgusting! Gross!*
    Che sciocchezza! *How silly!*
    Che spavento! *What a scare!*
    Che spettacolo! *What a sight! What a performance!*

You can use **che** + noun to comment on a person as well as a situation:

    Che sciocco/sciocca! *What a fool!*
    Che guastafeste! *What a killjoy, spoilsport!*
    Che primadonna! *Such a drama queen!*
    Che cervellone! *What a genius, brainbox!*
    Che cervello di gallina! *What a birdbrain!*
    Che agnellino! *What a little darling! lit. little lamb*

The combination noun + adjective can also produce a concise comment, with or without **che** or **così** *such*:

    Un vero incubo! *A true nightmare!*
    Che buona idea! *What a good idea!*
    Una risposta così inattesa! *Such an unexpected response!*
    Che bella sorpresa! *What a lovely surprise!*
    Una combinazione strana, no? *A strange coincidence, isn't it?*
    Un sollievo enorme! *A great relief!*
    Un vero peccato! *A real pity!*

wordbank

Sometimes a well-chosen adjective is all you need to show insight into what's being said and affinity with the speaker. They work on their own, with words like **molto** or **davvero**, or they too can be used with **che** *how*:

Impeccabile! *Perfect*
Così generoso. *So generous.*
Che strano. *How odd.*

Scandaloso! *Outrageous!*
Davvero bizzarro! *Seriously weird!*
Molto triste. *Very sad.*

admiration, appreciation
eccezionale *amazing, exceptional*
fantastico *fantastic*
fortunato *lucky*
impressionante *impressive*
incantevole *delightful*
meraviglioso *wonderful*
mitico *terrific*
speciale *special*
splendido *amazing*
squisito *exquisite*

concern, empathy
antipatico *unpleasant*
barboso *tedious*
deludente *disappointing*
noioso *boring*
seccante *annoying*
spiacevole *unpleasant*

horror, sympathy
catastrofico *catastrophic*
odioso *hateful*
orrendo *horrendous*
orribile *horrible*
sfortunato *unfortunate*
stressante *stressful*

terribile *terrible*
tragico *tragic*
schifoso *gross, disgusting*

astonishment, amusement
assurdo *absurd*
bizzarro *weird*
buffo *funny*
curioso *odd*
divertente *amusing*
incredibile *incredible*
pazzesco *crazy, weird*
ridicolo *ridiculous*
straordinario *extraordinary*

general interest
difficile *difficult*
efficace *effective*
emozionante *thrilling, moving*
grave *serious (situation, event)*
imprevisto *unexpected*
interessante *interesting*
opportuno *appropriate*
originale *original*
pratico *handy, practical*
sconveniente *inconvenient*
utile *useful*

Choose at least six of these adjectives and think of situations where you might use them with che, così or davvero. Say them out loud.

bello and brutto

If ever you can't think of the right adjective, consider **bello** for a positive comment and **brutto** for a negative one. Their basic meanings are *beautiful* and *ugly* but they're not confined to the physical: they cover a whole range of circumstances.

bello

Che bello! *How wonderful/beautiful/delightful/glorious/super!*
Che bella giornata. *What a lovely day.*
Che bello sentirti. *How nice to hear from you.*
Un bel guaio! *A fine mess!*
Sarebbe così bello ... *It would be so nice to ...*
Ho tanti bei ricordi. *I have so many fond memories.*
Che fai di bello? *What are you up to?*
troppo bello per essere vero *too good to be true*

brutto

Che brutto! *How dreadful/unpleasant/nasty/appalling!*
Che brutto tempo. *What awful weather.*
Che brutte notizie. *What bad news.*
Che brutta sorpresa. *What a dreadful shock.*
Che brutto affare. *Such a nasty business.*

un brutto clima *a harsh climate*
un brutto colpo *a bitter blow*
un brutto periodo *a difficult time*
una brutta situazione *an ugly situation*
una brutta fine *a sorry end*
un brutto muso *hard-faced*
il brutto anatroccolo *the ugly duckling*

avere una brutta fama *to have a bad name/reputation*
fare brutta figura *to create a bad/poor impression*

Di brutto is a slang expression meaning *big time, like crazy*:
Piove di brutto. *It's bucketing down.*
Ti sbagli di brutto. *You're so wrong.*
Spacca di brutto! *Wicked!*

prompting

Simple prompts are very effective at moving a conversation along:

E poi? *And then?*
E dopo? *And afterwards?*
A proposito della riunione ... *Talking of the meeting ...*
Riguardo a Marta ... *About Marta ...*

<table>
<tr><td>tu</td><td>

Dimmi. *Tell me.*
Dimmi cosa è successo dopo. *Tell me what happened after.*
Spiegami come sei finito lì. *Explain to me how you ended up there.*
Parlami di ... *Tell me about ...*
</td></tr>
<tr><td>lei</td><td>

Mi dica. *Tell me.*
Mi spieghi perché. *Explain to me why.*
Mi parli di ... *Tell me about ...*
Mi parli dell'incidente. *Tell me about the accident.*
</td></tr>
</table>

Open questions (page 27), even at their most basic, promote further conversation. The following can simply stand alone:

Dove? *Where?*
Quando? *When?*
Con chi? *Who with?*
Come mai? *How come?*
Quale/Quali? *Which one(s)?*
A che ora? *What time?*
Perché? *Why?*

Connectors that normally join together parts of a sentence can be used inquiringly to prompt:

e? *and?*
o? oppure? *or?*
ma? *but?*
però? *but surely?*
quindi? dunque? *and so?*
cioè? *that is?*
per esempio? *for example?*

wine talk

Sitting round the dinner table with family and friends is central to Italian life, and conversation is very much part of the experience. Wine is a frequent topic — Italy takes its wine seriously.

Questo vino è prodotto da uve di sangiovese al cento per cento. *This wine is produced from 100% sangiovese grapes.*
Questo, invece, è un vino locale. Mio suocero ha una piccola vigna a solo tre chilometri da qui. *Whereas this one is a local wine. My father-in-law has a small vineyard just three kilometres from here.*
Ancora un bicchierino? *Another little glass?*
Assaggia questa uva: così dolce ... dalla vigna di zio Vittorio. *Taste these grapes: so sweet ... from Uncle Vittorio's vineyard.*

---

word bank

L'uva è il frutto della vite. *The grape is the fruit of the vine.*
Un chicco d'uva *a single grape;* **un grappolo d'uva** *a bunch of grapes.*
Il vitigno is also translated *grape*, but refers to a defined variety of wine grape, such as **albanello**, **barbarossa**, **nebbiolo**, **sangiovese**, **trebbiano**.
L'enologia is *the science — or art — of winemaking.* **Un enologo** is *a winemaker or a wine expert.*
Un vigneto is a *vineyard*, while **una vigna** is also used for a piece of land where grapes are grown.
La vendemmia is *the grape harvest.*
L'uva passa and **l'uvetta** both mean *raisin* but **l'uva spina** is a *gooseberry*.

Many adjectives are employed to talk about wine.
Ottimo! Eccezionale! *Excellent! Exceptional!*
Davvero squisito questo. *This one is truly superb.*
È così vigoroso: pieno di sapore. *It's so vigorous: full of flavour.*
Questo qui è un vino corposo. *This one is a full-bodied wine.*
Che robusto! *How robust!*
Che sottile questo. *How subtle this one is.*
Un po' troppo giovane ancora. *A bit too young still.*
È piuttosto aggressivo, no? *It's rather acidic, isn't it?*
È molto secco? *Is it very dry?*
Alla salute. Cin cin! *Your health. Cheers!*

The Italians are always delighted to answer questions about their wines.

Che cos'è il vin santo? *What is **vin santo**?*
È un vino tradizionale toscano – un tipo di vino da dessert. *It's a traditional Tuscan wine — a type of dessert wine.*
Quindi ... è un vino dolce, giusto? *So ... it's a sweet wine, is that right?*
Giusto. Da noi è servito con i cantucci. *Indeed. We serve it with cantucci (Tuscan almond biscuits).*

Che significa IGT? *What does **IGT** mean?*
È l'acronimo di Indicazione Geografica Tipica. Significa che il vino è prodotto in una determinata zona. Mi spiego? *It's the acronym for **Indicazione Geografica Tipica**. It means that the wine is produced in a specific area. Am I explaining it properly?*

Dimmi. Cos'è lo spritz? *Tell me. What's **spritz**?*
È un aperitivo a base di prosecco, con bitter e una spruzzata di seltz. Molto rinfrescante! *It's an aperitif made with prosecco, bitters and a dash of soda water. Very refreshing!*

Questo vino è forte? *Is this wine strong?*
Guardi l'etichetta: indica la quantità di alcool presente nel vino; indica anche l'annata, la tenuta e il vitigno, cioè la varietà di vite. *Look at the label: it shows the quantity of alcohol in the wine; it also shows the vintage, the estate and the **vitigno**, i.e. the grape variety.*
Anche il produttore – una vera miniera d'informazioni! *Also/Even the producer — a real mine of information!*

Italian wines are strictly controlled and classified. The highest quality carries the label **DOCG Denominazione di Origine Controlata e Garantita** *controlled and guaranteed designation of origin*. Also subject to rigorous standards are **DOC** wines: **Denominazione di Origine Controlata** *controlled designation of origin*. The terms **Riserva**, **Classico** and **Superiore** are used only for DOC and DOCG wines.
IGT indicates that a wine is produced in a specific area. **I Super Tuscan** fall into this category: these are high quality red wines from Tuscany, but they don't qualify as DOC because they use non-traditional grape varieties.
VdT Vino da Tavola *table wine* is the lowest designation of Italian wine.

adding structure and fluency

Real conversations tend to include words like *well, besides, anyway, let's see, frankly, however, in fact*. Some of them add structure to what you say, others add emphasis, while some simply bring a natural feel to a conversation. Using them also gives you time to think.

allora ..., beh ..., bene ..., dunque ..., *well then ..., so ..., right then ...*
e *and*, **anche** *also*, **inoltre, per di più** *what's more, furthermore*
ma *but*, **però, comunque** *however*, **invece** *instead, whereas*
eppure *still, and yet*
quindi, dunque, perciò, *so, therefore*
tuttavia, in ogni caso *anyway*
chiaramente *clearly*, **ovviamente** *obviously*
addirittura *actually, even, indeed, Really?*
anzi, in effetti, in realtà *in fact, indeed*
insomma *basically, all in all, on the whole*
a dire la verità *to be honest*, **francamente** *frankly*
infatti *as a matter of fact*
per farla breve *to cut a long story short*
per esempio *for example*
cioè *that is, in other words, the thing is*
sa/sai *you know*
vediamo un po' *let's see*

È una buona idea, anzi splendida! *It's a good idea, terrific in fact!*
Che ne dici? *What do you reckon?*
Insomma ... vediamo un po'. *Well ... , let's see.*
Eppure non lo sapevo. *And yet I didn't know.*

For a more formal discussion:
in primo luogo *first of all*
in secondo luogo *secondly*
direi *I would say*
in breve *in short*
per farla breve *to cut a long story short*
da una parte *on one hand*; **dall'altra (parte)** *on the other (hand)*
in conclusione, alla fine *finally, to conclude*

talking the talk

Renzo	Sono buone le tagliatelle, no?
Daniela	Buonissime. E questo vino è ottimo.
Renzo	Hai ragione ... è pieno di sapore. (*calls waiter over*) Scusi.
Cameriere	Prego signore?
Renzo	È un vino locale questo?
Cameriere	Sì, sì.
Daniela	Renzo, guarda l'etichetta! La tenuta si trova a dieci chilometri da qui. Bello!
Daniela	Dimmi, riguardo a tuo fratello ...
Renzo	Angelo
Daniela	Sì, Angelo. Aiuta la moglie con la bambina: con Ambra?
Renzo	Ma certo. Lei è una mamma lavoratrice e lui aiuta.
Daniela	Ma ... non abita vicino.
Renzo	Vero. Comunque, normalmente i nonni aiutano quando Virginia lavora. Anche la sorella Luisa aiuta. Lei è una mamma a tempo pieno, ha tre figli giovani. Suo marito è Piero Santorio.
Daniela	Sul serio? Santo cielo! Tu sei il cognato della moglie di Piero Santorio. Pensa un po' ...
Renzo	No ... per carità ... Piero è ... Piero è il marito della sorella di mia cognata. Capisci?
Daniela	Pensa un po'! Piero Santorio ... Ma ... Piero Santorio è sposato con una cantante, no?
Renzo	Sì sì ... la cantante Luisa Aquilani.
Daniela	... che adesso si chiama Luisa Santorio. Capisco. Mitico!

checkpoint 4

1   What's the Italian for *I beg your pardon*?

2   If you think you're getting blank looks, how can you check whether you're making sense?

3   Is **Fico!** a term of admiration or disapproval?

4   What small word means *how, what* and can be used with a noun or an adjective to comment?

5   How do you ask how to say *crisis* in Italian?

6   What do you add to **semplice** to say *too simple*?

7   Which of these is the odd one out? **imprevisto, straordinario, particolare, originale, pazzo, barboso**

8   What's the difference between **capite, caspita** and **comunque**?

9   Class the following as positive or negative: **che fastidio, che sollievo, che gioia, che seccatura, che peccato**

10 How do you ask somebody if they would mind explaining?

11 Which of these are not used to say *well*? **allora, cavolo, perciò, dunque, insomma, però, bene, in breve**

12 How would you ask what **cartellino giallo** means?

13 What's *for example* in Italian?

14 What do you add to **Questa stima è .... ottimistica** to mean *This estimate is rather optimistic.*?

15 If you were prompted with **Riguardo all'incidente**, what would you talk about?

16 Does **inoltre** or **in effetti** mean *in fact*?

17 How would you say *Lucky you!* to a close friend?

18 Fill the gap to reinforce **Forse è vero, ... certamente è vero** *Maybe it's true, actually it's definitely true.*

19 Make an educated guess at the meaning of **Questo bottone serve ad aggiustare il contrasto.**

20 How do you say something's on the tip of your tongue?

cinque
been there, done that

A real conversation is unpredictable: it may at times be confined to the here and now but is more likely to weave comfortably between the present, past and future as you chat about what's going on, what your plans are, where you've been and what you've been doing.

When it comes to talking about what's just happened to you, sharing an experience or recounting an anecdote, the perfect tense is essential. It brings a whole new dimension to your Italian – and it's more straightforward than in English. Using *to play* as an example, English has *I played, I have played, I have been playing* – whereas Italian conveys all of them with **ho giocato**.

It's easy to practise talking about the past in Italian: every so often you can say to yourself what you've been doing, preferably out loud; every day spend a few minutes writing a journal. You'll be using the same structures over and over, and your vocabulary will expand exponentially as you look up any new words you need.

There does exist a single-word tense to say *I played* – **giocai** – but it's not widely used in spoken Italian outside parts of southern Italy. You might also come across this tense in some stock phrases such as **Vissero per sempre felici e contenti** *They lived happily ever after.*

what you've been doing

To talk about what you *did, have done* or *have been doing*, you use the perfect tense, which is in two parts, just like *have + played* in English.

1   the present tense of **avere** *to have:*

io	ho	noi	abbiamo
tu	hai	voi	avete
lei/lui	ha	loro	hanno

2   + past participle. In English this often ends in *-ed.* e.g. *worked, watched, sneezed;* in Italian the ending depends on the infinitive:

-are → -ato	**lavor**are *to work*	**lavor**ato *worked*
-ere → -uto	**v**e**nd**ere *to sell*	**vend**uto *sold*
-ire → -ito	**forn**ire *to provide*	**forn**ito *provided*

Ho mangiato troppo. *I ate too much. I have eaten too much.*
Ho lavorato fino alle undici. *I worked until 11 o'clock.*
Ha aggiustato il portatile. *He/She (has) mended the laptop.*
Edoardo mi ha aiutato. *Edoardo (has) helped me/has been helping me.*
Qualcuno ha lasciato un messaggio. *Someone (has) left a message.*
Abbiamo googlato/googolato il suo nome. *We (have) googled his name.*
Abbiamo chattato un po'. *We chatted online for a while.*
Avete diagnosticato il problema? *Have you diagnosed the problem?*
Stamattina hanno giocato a tennis. *This morning they played/they have played/they've been playing tennis.*

A che ora hai cominciato? *What time did you start?*
Hai mai provato il surf? *Have you ever tried/Did you ever try surfing?*
Dove avete pranzato? *Where did you have lunch?*
Ha mai visitato le catacombe? *Did you ever visit the catacombs?*
Hanno controllato il motore? *Did they check the engine?*

Non ho finito il sudoku. *I haven't finished the sudoku.*
Non ho finito il sudoku ieri. *I didn't finish the sudoku yesterday.*
Non hanno comprato niente. *They haven't bought/didn't buy anything.*

past participles

Just as English has irregular, i.e. unpredictable, past participles such as *eat* →
eaten, catch → *caught, freeze* → *frozen*, so too does Italian.

aprire *to open* → aperto
offrire *to offer* → offerto
scoprire *to discover* → scoperto
soffrire *to suffer* → sofferto
bere *to drink* → bevuto
vivere *to live* → vissuto
chiedere *to request* → chiesto
rispondere *to reply* → risposto
vedere *to see* → visto
vincere *to win* → vinto
aggiungere *to add* → aggiunto

dire *to say* → detto
leggere *to read* → letto
mettere *to put* → messo
rompere *to break* → rotto
scrivere *to write* → scritto
chiudere *to close* → chiuso
perdere *to lose* → perso
spendere *to spend* → speso
uccidere *to kill* → ucciso

Ho aperto un nuovo conto corrente. *I've opened a new current account.*
Hanno scoperto la causa? *Have they found out the cause?*

Cos'ha detto? *What did you say?*
Scusi, ho rotto un bicchiere. *Sorry, I've broken a glass.*
Hai scritto la mail? *Have you written the email?*
Ho letto i termini e le condizioni. *I've read the terms and conditions.*
Avete messo tutto in valigia? *Have you packed everything?* lit. *Have you put
everything in the case?*

Abbiamo aggiunto il suo nome. *We (have) added his/her/your name.*
Perché non hai risposto? *Why haven't you replied? Why didn't you reply?*
Come mai non l'hai visto? *How come you didn't see him?*
Chi ha vinto? *Who won?*
Abbiamo bevuto tutto il vino rosso? *Have we drunk all the red wine? Did we
drink all the red wine?*

Ha ucciso la moglie. *He (has) killed his wife.*
Qualcuno ha chiuso la finestra. *Somebody (has) closed the window.*
Abbiamo speso così tanto. *We (have) spent so much.*
Hanno perso tutto. *They (have) lost everything.*

> **Fare** is the only irregular **-are** past participle: **fare** *to do/make* →
> **fatto** *done, made.* **Cos'hai fatto?** *What did you do? What have you
> done/been doing?*

where you've been

All Italian verbs have two parts for the perfect tense but a minority replace **avere** with **essere** for the first part.

io	sono	noi	siamo
tu	sei	voi	siete
lei/lui	è	loro	sono

Most verbs relating to existence and movement belong in this group. The following are among the most common (irregular past participle in brackets).

word bank

andare *to go*
apparire *to appear* (**apparso**)
arrivare *to arrive*
cadere *to fall*
costare *to cost*
crescere *to grow (up)*
crollare *to collapse*
degenerare *to degenerate*
diventare *to become*
durare *to last*
emergere *to emerge* (**emerso**)
entrare *to enter*
esistere *to exist* (**esistito**)
essere *to be* (**stato**)
morire *to die* (**morto**)
nascere *to be born* (**nato**)
partire *to leave*
piacere *to please*

raggiungere *to reach* (**raggiunto**)
restare *to stay*
rimanere *to stay* (**rimasto**)
ritornare *to return*
riuscire *to succeed, to manage*
salire *to come, to go up*
scadere *to run out, to expire*
scappare *to run off, to escape*
scendere *to come, go down* (**sceso**)
sembrare *to seem*
sparire *to disappear*
stare *to be, to stay*
succedere *to happen* (**successo**)
tornare *to return*
uscire *to go out*
valere *to be worth* (**valso**)
venire *to come* (**venuto**)
vivere *to live* (**vissuto**)

Reflexive verbs, e.g. **divertirsi** *to enjoy oneself,* **svegliarsi** *to wake up* (page 45) also use **essere**. They behave exactly like other **essere** verbs with the addition of **mi, ti, si, ci, vi, si.**

The **past participle** of verbs taking **essere**, although formed in exactly the same way as all other verbs, changes in the same way as an adjective ending in **-o**, depending on who's involved.

Sono andato/a in città l'altro ieri. *I went to town the day before yesterday.*
Daniela è andata via in fretta. *Daniela went away/went off in a rush.*
È caduto/a sulla scala mobile. *He/She fell on the escalator.*
Perché è uscita Sara? *Why has Sara gone out? Why did Sara go out?*
Com'è diventato così ricco? *How did he become so rich?*
Il viaggio è costato oltre cinque mila euro. *The trip cost more than 5,000 euros.*
Siamo rimasti/e a casa. *We stayed at home.*
Noi invece siamo andati/e in spiaggia. *We went to the beach instead.*
A che ora siete arrivati/e? *What time did you arrive?* (**voi**)
Siete riusciti/e a convincere Matteo? *Did you manage to persuade Matteo?*

Dove sei nato/a? *Where were you born?* (**tu**)
Chiara è nata a Roma ma i suoi fratelli sono nati in Sicilia. *Chiara was born in Rome, but her brothers were born in Sicily.*
Come sono cresciuti! *Haven't they grown!*
La festa è durata fino all'alba. *The party lasted until dawn.*
La signora Galli è morta sei mesi fa. *Mrs Galli died six months ago.*
Non sono mai stato/a in Sardegna. *I've never been to Sardinia.*
Non sono mai stati/e a Venezia. *They've never been to Venice.*

Non ti sei divertito/a? *Didn't you enjoy yourself?* (**tu**)
No, mi sono stufato/a e sono tornato/a a casa. *No, I got fed up and came home.*
Non mi sono abituato/a al caldo. *I haven't got used to the heat.*
Il bambino si è addormentato in macchina. *The baby fell asleep in the car.*
Vi siete svegliati/e presto oggi? *Did you wake up early today?* (**voi**)
Quando vi siete sposati voi due? *When did you two get married?*
Dove vi siete conosciuti? *Where did you meet?*

Stare and **essere** both have the past participle **stato** *been*. Both verbs mean *to be* but **essere** is more about existing while **stare** also conveys *to stay*, as in **Stai fermo!** *Keep still!* It's translated as *be* in common expressions such as **Stai zitto!** *Be quiet!* or **Come sta?** *How are you? How are you keeping?*

word**bank**

Choose five occasions from this list and say out loud what you did at that time. Now jot the sentences down – keeping a journal in Italian is no more than doing this on a regular basis.

ieri *yesterday*
ieri mattina *yesterday morning*
ieri pomeriggio *yesterday afternoon*
ieri sera *yesterday evening*
ieri l'altro, l'altro ieri *the day before yesterday*
l'altro giorno *the other day*

il giorno prima/precedente *the day before*
il giorno prima della festa *the day before the party*
la settimana prima/precedente *the week before*
il mese prima/precedente *the month before*
l'anno prima/precedente *the year before*

lunedì, martedì … s̲abato scorso *last Monday, Tuesday … Saturday*
dom̲enica scorsa *last Sunday*
la settimana scorsa/la scorsa settimana *last week*
il mese scorso/lo scorso mese *last month*
il gennaio scorso *last January*
lo scorso maggio *last May*
l'anno scorso/lo scorso anno *last year*
l'altr'anno *the year before last*

poco fa *a short time ago*
mezz'ora fa *half an hour ago*
due giorni fa *two days ago*
qu̲indici giorni fa *a fortnight ago*
un mese fa *a month ago*
un mesetto fa *about a month ago*
due/tre/dieci anni fa *two/three/ten years ago*

Don't confuse **fa** *ago* with **fra** *in*: **fra una settimana** *in a week's time*, **fra un paio di giorni** *in a couple of days*.
Tra means the same, **tra due ore** *in two hours' time*.

sharing an experience

Not all conversations consist of short questions and answers: some questions and prompts call for more detail.

Gina, sei mai stata a Londra? *Gina, have you ever been to London?*
Siete mai stati/e a Elba? *Have you (**voi**) ever been to Elba?*
Non ci siamo mai stati/e. *We've never been there.*

>
>
> **Non ci siamo mai stati/e** shuts down the topic, but when the answer is positive, you wouldn't normally stop at a stark *yes*. The useful word **ci** *there* saves you having to repeat the name of the place.
> **Ci sono stata una volta. Quattro anni fa ci sono andata con un amico.** *I've been there once. Four years ago I went there with a friend.*
> **Ci siamo andati in vacanza molti anni fa. Così bello e tranquillo. Da ritornarci.** *We went there on holiday many years ago. So beautiful and peaceful. A place to go back to.*

There will be times when you're not simply responding, when you can't wait to share an experience.

- Grab the other person's attention:
  Adesso ti racconto ... *Just let me tell you ...*
  Che giornata! *What a day!*
  Roba da matti! *Crazy stuff!* **Roba da non credere!** *Unbelievable stuff!*
  È successo qualcosa di bello/brutto. *Something lovely/awful happened.*
  L'esperienza è stata indimenticabile. *The experience was unforgettable.*
  Non puoi immaginare cosa mi è successo! *You'll never believe what happened to me!*

- Set the scene by saying when it took place: **l'altro giorno** *the other day*, **ieri pomeriggio** *yesterday afternoon*, **due ore fa** *a couple of hours ago*, **poco fa** *a short while ago*.

- Add a sense of continuity with **poi** *then*, **dopo** *afterwards*, **dunque** *and so*. Use **e** *and*, **ma** *but*, **però** *however*, **perché** *because*.

- Create atmosphere with the occasional exclamation:
  Che perfezione! *What perfection!*
  Che casino! *What a mess!*
  Una vera catastrofe! *An absolute catastrophe!*

 Describe in about six sentences something that happened or that you did recently — it doesn't need to involve catastrophes or exotic holidays!

coping in a crisis

In an emergency situation you need to know how to get help.

Emergenza! *Emergency!*
Aiuto! *Help!*
Mi può aiutare? *Can you help me?* **Ho bisogno di aiuto.** *I need help.*
Chiamate la polizia/un'ambulanza. *Call the police/an ambulance.*

To say what's going on now you use the present tense:
C'è un incendio. *There'a a fire.*
C'è odore di gas. *There's a smell of gas.*
Sono ferito/a. *I'm hurt.* **Sono feriti.** *They're hurt.*
Non riesco a respirare. *I can't breathe.*
Sta sanguinando. *He/She's bleeding.*
È un attacco d'asma. *It's an asthma attack.*

... but to explain what's already happened, you need the perfect tense.
C'è stato un furto. *There's been a theft.*
C'è stato un incidente (stradale). *There's been a (road) accident.*
C'è stata una rapina. *There's been a theft/a robbery.*

Sono stato derubato/a. *I've been robbed.*
È stata violentata. *She's been raped.*
Siamo stati aggrediti. *We've been mugged.*

Ho perso la borsetta/il portafoglio. *I've lost my purse/wallet.*
Ha ingoiato una spina di pesce. *He/She's swallowed a fish bone.*
La macchina ha sbandato ... *The car skidded ...*
... e si è schiantata contro il paracarro. *... and crashed into the bollard.*

Sono caduto/a. *I fell. I've fallen.*
È caduto. *He fell.* **È caduta.** *She fell.*
Sono inciampato/a sul marciapiede. *I tripped on the pavement.*
È svenuta. *She's fainted.*

Mi hanno aggredito. *They attacked me.*
Mi hanno scippato la borsa. *They've snatched my bag.*
Mi hanno rubato il passaporto. *They stole my passport.*

what you had done

To change what **has** happened to what **had** happened, all you do is change
avere/essere to the imperfect (pages 80–82). It's called the pluperfect tense.

Avevo dimenticato di fare benzina. *I had forgotten to fill up with petrol.*
Avevo già chiesto perché. *I had already asked why.*
Avevi letto il libro prima di vedere il film? *Had you read the book before seeing the film?*
Non aveva dormito bene. *He hadn't slept well.*
Non ha pagato perché aveva perso il portafoglio. *He didn't pay because he had lost his wallet.*
Avevamo appena finito quando Marco è arrivato. *We had just finished when Marco arrived.*
L'avevate visto, vero? *You had seen it/him, hadn't you?*
Avevano lavorato fino a tardi il giorno prima. *They'd worked late the day before.*
Ne avevano già mangiato la metà. *They had already eaten half of it.*

Ero caduto/a due mesi prima. *I had fallen two months earlier.*
Tu eri già partito/a? *Had you already left?*
Era andata a pesca con Giulio. *She'd gone fishing with Giulio.*
Eravamo arrivati in anticipo. *We'd arrived early.*
Eravate partiti alla stessa ora? *Had you left at the same time?*
Erano appena scesi. *They had just come down.*
Entro sabato, tutto era diventato chiaro. *By Saturday, everything had become clear.*
A che ora si era svegliato/a lei? *What time had you woken up?*
Si era già addormentata. *She had already fallen asleep.*
Si erano divertiti? *Had they enjoyed themselves?*

The pluperfect is **not** the tense to use after **se** *if*.
If I had + done something is **se avessi** or **se fossi** + past participle, e.g.
    se l'avessi visto *if I had seen him*
    se fossi andato *if I had gone*

More on **avessi** and **fossi** on page 119.

talking the talk

Daniela	Hai fatto qualcosa di bello?
Renzo	Quando?
Daniela	Ieri sera.
Renzo	Ho aiutato un amico con il computer — il portatile. Abbiamo diagnosticato un problema e l'abbiamo risolto.
Daniela	Bravo!
Renzo	Dopo, siamo andati in città, abbiamo mangiato la pizza, abbiamo chiacchierato un po' e poi io sono tornato a casa.
Daniela	Beato te.
Renzo	Daniela, dove sei andata tu ieri sera? Sei andata via in fretta.
Daniela	Da Beniamino. Mi aveva telefonato.
Renzo	Beniamino? Chi è Beniamino?
Daniela	Mio cugino; l'artista. È successo qualcosa di brutto. C'è stato un furto. Hanno rubato tutta la sua roba.
Renzo	Porca miseria!
Daniela	Una vera catastrofe. Ma ... aveva lasciato la casa aperta; aveva dimenticato di chiudere la finestra. Che sbadato!

verb practice 3

1   Write these verbs in the perfect tense: all the past participles are
    regular.
    a   **guidare** to drive   **tu** ....
    b   **uscire** to go out   **voi** ....
    c   **baciare** to kiss   **lui** ....
    d   **diventare** to become   **io** ....
    e   **creare** to create   **loro** ....
    f   **essere** to be   **noi** ....
    g   **tagliare** to cut   **lei** ....
    h   **mandare** to send   **io** ....
    i   **spiegare** to explain   **tu** ....

2   Now change them to the pluperfect and say what they mean.

3   Although many **-ere** verbs have irregular past participles, there are
    clusters. See if you can work these out.
    ●   **mettere** to put **messo**: **ammettere** to admit ....; **commettere**
        to commit ....; **permettere** to allow ....
    ●   **decidere** to decide **deciso**: **ridere** to laugh ....; **sorridere** to
        smile ....; **dividere** to divide ....
    ●   **leggere** to read **letto**: **friggere** to fry ....; **correggere** to correct
        ....; **eleggere** to elect ....
    ●   **scegliere** to choose **scelto**: **cogliere** to pick ....; **accogliere** to
        welcome ....; **togliere** to remove ....
    ●   **prendere** to take **preso**: **estendere** to extend ....; **offendere** to
        offend ....; **scendere** to go down ....

4   Use these jottings as the basis of a journal entry for yesterday.
    *worked till 12; went to town after lunch; saw Paolo; did the
    shopping (la spesa); spent too much; sent an email to Salvatore
    & left a message for mum; Daniela arrived at 6*

    Add that Daniela had just left and the baby had already fallen asleep
    when your father phoned.

1 What are the past participles of **proibire** to prohibit, **tenere** to hold, **sognare** to dream, **accettare** to accept; all of them are regular.

2 Given that **Dove l'hai lasciato?** means Where did you leave it?, what's the Italian for When did you find it?

3 .... **abbiamo visitato l'isola.** What needs inserting for the sentence to say We visited the island the day before yesterday?

4 How would you tell someone you've lost your suitcase and your passport? You don't need the word for my.

5 In the perfect tense, which of these verbs use **avere** and which **essere**: **ammazzare** to murder, **esistere** to exist, **mangiare** to eat, **nascere** to be born, **morire** to die, **salire** to go up, **viaggiare** to travel.

6 How would you tell someone you (plus friends) went on a cruise last year? (**andare in crociera** to go on a cruise)

7 What do these words mean: **incendio, inciampare, incontrare, ingoiare, invece**?

8 How would you ask somebody **(lei)** what they did yesterday?

9 Given that **soddisfare** to satisfy and **stupefare** to amaze both behave like **fare** to do, what are their past participles? How would you say he satisfied and he amazed?

10 What's the difference between **quindici giorni fa** and **fra quindici giorni**?

11 **Letto, rotto, aperto, vinto, aggiunto, messo** and **speso** are the irregular past participles of which verbs? What do these verbs mean?

12 What word needs adding to **Sei stato in Grecia?** for it to mean Have you ever been to Greece?

13 If you hear **Dove vi siete conosciuti?** when you're with your partner or friend, what information are you being asked for?

14 What's the difference between **avevano immaginato** and **hanno immaginato**; and between **è uscita** and **era uscita**?

15 The Italian for misunderstanding is **un fraintendimento** and backlash is **una reazione negativa**. How would you say there's been a misunderstanding and there's been a backlash?

16 What does **prima** mean in **Giovanni era caduto una settimana prima**?

17 Where might you come across the sentence **e vissero per sempre felici e contenti**?

sei
how things were

Describing how things were, and saying what you used to do, bring yet another dimension to a conversation. Italian has a set of verb endings for this, called the imperfect tense. They're not difficult to recognise because they contain a distinctive soft **-v-** sound: **gioc**a**vo** *I was playing*, **av**e**va** *he used to have*, **and**avamo *we used to go*.

These are the endings you use to talk about what was happening, what used to happen, what happened often/regularly or carried on over a period of time. To do this, English uses, for example, *I was playing, I used to play, I would (often) play, I played* while Italian covers them all with **giocavo**.

Words such as *often, regularly, usually* are characteristic of the imperfect, but Italian doesn't always include them because using the imperfect tense is in itself enough to convey a sense of continuity.

For descriptions, you use **ero** *I was* and **era** *he/she/it was*: **ero così arrabbiato** *I was so cross*, **era stanca morta** *she was exhausted,* **era orribile** *it was horrible.* If you're keeping a journal, try to include at least one description every day.

what you used to do

Dove andavi in vacanza da bambina? *Where did you go on holiday when you were little?*

Andavi and **da bambina** show that the question isn't referring to a specific event, and so you need the imperfect to answer it.

Imperfect endings replace the **-are**, **-ere**, **-ire** of the infinitive.

lavorare *to work*	**lavor**avo *I was working*
spendere *to spend*	**spend**evo *I would spend*
fornire *to provide*	**forn**ivo *I used to provide*
	lavoravamo *we used to work*
	spendevamo *we were spending*
	fornivamo *we would provide*

Andavo spesso in Francia. *I often used to go to France.*
Giocavo sulla spiaggia ogni giorno. *I played on the beach every day.*
Alloggiavamo nello stesso hotel ogni anno. *We stayed at the same hotel every year.*
Compravamo formaggio al mercato. *We (always) used to buy cheese in the market.*
I miei genitori facevano dozzine di fotografie. *My parents would take dozens of photos.*
In quel periodo mi alzavo molto presto. *At that time I got up very early.*

---

tu	**lavor**avi	**spend**evi	**forn**ivi
lei	**lavor**ava	**spend**eva	**forn**iva
voi	**lavor**avate	**spend**evate	**forn**ivate

Lavorava per la GMC vero? *You used to work for GMC, didn't you?*
Frequentavi lo stesso bar tutti i giorni? *Did you (use to) go to the same bar every day?*
Dove andavate di sera? *Where did you go in the evenings?*
Quanto pagavate al mese? *How much were you paying per month?*

The endings for *he/she/it* are the same as for **lei** *you*, while the endings for *they* simply add **-no** to these. The stress is in the same place for them all:

| lui/lei | **lavor**ava | **spend**eva | **forn**iva |
| loro | **lavor**avano | **spend**evano | **forn**ivano |

Federica lavorava con me. *Federica used to work with me.*
Ogni anno lei riceveva un bonus. *She got/used to get a bonus every year.*
Rosa veniva da noi ogni sabato. *Rosa used to come to our house every Saturday.*
Da bambino, suo figlio soffriva di coliche. *When he was a baby, her son suffered/used to suffer from colic.*
Funziona adesso, ma non funzionava ieri. *It's working now, but it wasn't working yesterday.*
Quando Emma viveva in Australia, ci mantenevamo in contatto attraverso i social. *When Emma was living in Australia, we kept in touch via social media.*
Vivevano in modo molto semplice. *They lived a very simple life.*
Perché spendevano così tanto? *Why were they spending so much?*

feelings

English doesn't always use the words *was*, *were* or *used to* with feelings or with verbs unrelated to physical activity, such as **avere** *to have* **potere** *to be able to*, **volere** *to want* – but you still need the imperfect in Italian.

Non mi sentivo bene. *I didn't feel well.*
Avevano molti soldi. *They had a lot of money.*
Preferivo il vino rosso. *I preferred red wine.*
Pensavamo fosse amore. *We thought it was love.*
Come mai non avevi dubbi? *How come you had no doubts?*
Non osavo dire niente. *I didn't dare say anything.*
Ti piaceva il villaggio? *Did you like the village?*
Odiavano studiare ma volevano completare il corso. *They hated studying but they wanted to finish the course.*
Doveva prendere antidolorifici. *She had to/was having to take painkillers.*
Potevi ... ma non volevi. *You could ... but you didn't want to.*

how things were

To say where something was or describe how it used to be, you use the imperfect of **essere** *to be* – the only verb not to have the **-v-** sound throughout.

ero *I was*	eravamo *we were*
eri *you* (**tu**) *were*	eravate *you* (**voi**) *were*
era *you* (**lei**) *were, he/she/it was*	erano *they were*

Ero a Bologna ieri. *I was in Bologna yesterday.*
Eravamo in quattro. *There were four of us.*
Ero stanco la sera. *I was tired in the evening.*
Com'era il viaggio? *How was the journey?*
Com'era la città, prima? *How was the town before?*
Era molto elegante. *He/She/It was very elegant.*
Vent'anni fa, quest'edificio era una scuola. *Twenty years ago, this building was a school.*

dire and fare

Dire *to say, to tell* and **fare** *to make, to do* are among the very few other verbs to be irregular in the imperfect, and they both add **-c-**.

fare: facevo   facevi   faceva   facevamo   facevate   facevano
dire: dicevo   dicevi   diceva   dicevamo   dicevate   dicevano

Diceva la verità. *He/She was telling the truth.*
Non dicevano molto. *They weren't saying much.*
Che cosa faceva Zhara? *What was Zhara doing?*
Il venerdì facevano i conti. *On Fridays they used to do the accounts.*

You can use *facevo* to talk about work: *facevo l'infermiera* I was/used to be a nurse. And not only *facevo* - you can use the imperfect of any of the verbs from Chapter 3 to say what you and other people did for a living: *Lavoravo da casa* I used to work from home, *Mio fratello era insegnante* My brother was a teacher.

Have a go at saying what people you know did, e.g. *Mia zia non lavorava* My aunt didn't work, *Mio nonno era poliziotto* My grandfather used to be a policeman, *Emma si occupava della palestra* Emma looked after the gym, *Charlie lavorava in un vivaio* Charlie worked in a garden centre.

wordbank

Choose six of these expressions and use them in a sentence using the imperfect. You could add detail to say what people did for a living: *Ogni tanto Emma si occupava della palestra* Now and again Emma would look after the gym. You could recycle some of the verbs from the examples or you could use entirely different verbs – most are regular in the imperfect.

da bambino/bambina *as a child, when I was little*
da bambini/bambine *as children, when we were little*
da giovane/giovani *when I was/we were young*
da studente/studenti *when I was a student/we were students*

sempre *always*
spesso, frequentemente *often*
di solito, normalmente *usually*
abitualmente *regularly*
per un po' *for a while*
qualche volta, a volte *sometimes*
molte volte *many times*
tante volte *so many times*
parecchie volte *several times*
raramente *rarely*
mai *never*

ogni giorno *every day*
ogni settimana *every week*
ogni mese *every month*
ogni anno *every year*
ogni tanto *every now and then, now and again*
di tanto in tanto *once in a while*

tanto tempo fa *a long time ago*
a quel tempo/a quei tempi *at that time*
negli anni duemiladieci *in the 2010s*
negli anni duemila *in the noughties*
negli anni novanta *in the 1990s*
nei secoli bui *in the dark ages*
moltissimi anni fa *in the dim and distant past*
c'era una volta *once upon a time*

reminiscing

When people are getting to know each other, there's usually a mutual interest in finding out about background.

Since you are born only the once, you need the perfect tense:

Dove sei nato/nata? *Where were you born?*

Sono nato/nata nella Svizzera italiana. *I was born in Italian-speaking Switzerland.*

You also use the **perfect** for **sono cresciuto/a** *I grew up.*

Sono nato e cresciuto a Orselina. *I was born and grew up in Orselina.*

From then on, you use the imperfect.

Dove abitavi? Dove abitavate? *Where did you use to live?*

Abitavamo in un paesino. *We lived in a village.*

Era una zona abbastanza tranquilla. *It was rather a quiet area.*

Ogni inverno nevicava ... *Every winter it snowed ...*

    ... ma d'estate faceva caldo. *... but in summer it was hot.*

Avevamo uno chalet. Non era grande ... *We had a chalet. It wasn't big ...*

    ... ma ricordo che c'erano molti scalini! *... but I remember that there were lots of stairs!*

Mio padre lavorava nel settore turistico; viaggiava frequentemente. *My father worked in tourism; he used to travel frequently.*

Di tanto in tanto i nonni venivano da noi. *Now and then my grandparents would come to our house.*

Però, non succedeva molto spesso perché a quei tempi gestivano un ristorante. *But it didn't happen often because at that time they were running a restaurant.*

I miei fratelli ed io, andavamo alla scuola del paese. *My brothers and I went to the village school.*

Mi piaceva un sacco quella scuola! *I loved that school!*

La maestra si chiamava signora Benedetti. *The teacher was called Mrs Benedetti.*

A volte era un po' severa ma era bravissima. *She was a bit strict at times, but she was really good.*

Sfortunatamente, si è rotta la gamba mentre sciava. *Unfortunately she broke her leg while she was skiing.*

 Think of at least six sentences in Italian about when you were growing up. Don't forget to say them out loud.

bringing to life what you say

Adverbs, as the name suggests, add information to verbs: **succede** spesso *it happens often*, **succedeva** regolarmente *it happened regularly*, **è successo** ieri *it happened yesterday.*

They can also add information to adjectives, other adverbs and whole sentences: così **gentile** *so kind*, molto **lentamente** *very slowly*. **Purtroppo, c'è un ritardo.** *Unfortunately, there's a delay.*

Although some adverbs provide essential information, such as when or where something is done, not all adverbs saying *how* something is done are essential to basic communication — but these are the words that can bring to life what you say and make it more interesting to listen to.

---

word bank

Many Italian adverbs are formed by adding -mente to a feminine adjective, just as English adverbs can end in -*ly.*

allegramente *happily*	**orgogliosamente** *proudly*
assolutamente *absolutely*	**originalmente** *originally*
chiaramente *clearly*	**perfettamente** *perfectly*
difficilmente *with difficulty*	**profondamente** *deeply*
effettivamente *essentially*	**raramente** *rarely*
facilmente *easily*	**sbadatamente** *carelessly*
fortunatamente *luckily*	**semplicemente** *simply*
generalmente *generally*	**sicuramente** *surely*
giustamente *rightly*	**sfortunatamente** *unfortunately*
inevitabilmente *inevitably*	**sostanzialmente** *basically*
informalmente *informally*	**tranquillamente** *peacefully*
inutilmente *uselessly*	**velocemente** *quickly*
lussuosamente *luxuriously*	**veramente** *truly*

You'll also hear in modo + m adjective or in maniera + f adjective:
in modo casuale *randomly*, **in maniera innocua** *harmlessly*

... and con/senza + noun:
con entusiasmo *enthusiastically*, **con riluttanza** *reluctantly*
senza entusiasmo *unenthusiastically*, **senza pietà** *pitilessly*

chatting about what's been going on

Cos'hai fatto di bello? *What have you been up to?*
Com'è andato il weekend? *How did the weekend go?*
Com'è andata la festa? *How did the party go?*
Parlami del viaggio. *Tell me about the trip.*

In reply to questions like these, you're more than likely to be using the imperfect and the perfect tenses together, for example in a sentence where you use the imperfect to describe the circumstances in which something took place (perfect).

Il ristorante era affollatissimo quando ci siamo andati. *The restaurant was packed when we went there.*
Faceva buio quando sono arrivato/a. *It was dark when I arrived.*
Ho chiacchierato con Elsa e Carlo; parlavano con entusiasmo del soggiorno alle Maldive. *I chatted to Elsa and Carlo; they were talking enthusiastically about their trip to the Maldives.*
Mentre facevano snorkeling lei ha intravisto una tartaruga verde. *While they were snorkelling she spotted a green turtle.*
Ho visto alcune foto ma, purtroppo, la batteria dello smartphone era quasi scarica. *I saw a few photos but, unfortunately, the phone battery was almost dead.*
Quanti anni aveva Elsa quando ha conosciuto Carlo? *How old was Elsa when she met Carlo?*
Abbiamo mangiato così tanto! Gli spaghetti al nero di seppia e le capesante gratinate erano assolutamente squisiti. *We ate so much! The spaghetti and the scallops cooked au gratin were absolutely exquisite.*

Gli spaghetti al nero di seppia is spaghetti with a sauce of squid and squid ink so that the pasta ends up black in colour. Italy is famous for its pasta specialities with **frutti di mare** *seafood*. For instance, **linguine in umido di moscardini** *linguine with white octopus* and **cannelloni ripieni di nasello e gamberetti** *cannelloni filled with hake and shrimps*. The sauce for **spaghetti allo scoglio** (literally *reef spaghetti*, in reference to the crustaceans living among the rocks by the seashore) is unpredictable as it's made with the freshest shellfish/seafood available on the day.

using stare for dramatic effect

Stare *to be, to stay* has a particular use that can bring a sense of drama to what you say. To convey a sense of being right in the middle of doing something when something else happens, you use **stare** followed by a verb ending in **-ando** (**-are** verbs) or **-endo** (**-ere** and **-ire** verbs).

You can use the present tense of **stare**:
Ssh! Sto ascoltando. *Shush! I'm listening.*
Non posso chiacchierare, sto lavorando. *I can't chat, I'm busy working.*
Cosa stai facendo? *What are you doing (right now)?*
Sto seguendo le istruzioni, comunque non riesco a farlo. *I am following the instructions, but I can't manage to do it.*

... or the imperfect — but remember that the other verb saying what happened will be in the perfect tense.
Mi stavo facendo un selfie e sono caduto! *I was taking a selfie and I fell over!*
Si è bloccato il computer mentre stavo salvando il file. *The computer crashed while I was (in the process of) saving the file.*
Cosa stavi facendo quando ti ho chiamato? *What were you doing when I called you?*
È successo mentre stavano dormendo. *It happened while they were sleeping.*
Stavamo preparando i dolci quando il robot da cucina è scoppiato. *We were right in the thick of making the puddings when the food processor blew up.*

Stare followed by **per** + infinitive has a very different meaning: it means to be *just about to* do something.

Sto per finire. *I'm just about to finish.*
Stanno per partire. *They're just about to leave.*
Stavo per chiamarti quando ho ricevuto il tuo sms. *I was just about to call you when I received your text.*
Stava per rassegnare le dimissioni. *He/She was on the point of handing in his/her resignation.*
Stavano per piangere mentre ascoltavano l'inno nazionale. *They were on the verge of crying while they were listening to the national anthem.*

talking the talk

Daniela	Da bambino dove abitavi?
Renzo	Sono nato e cresciuto in una cittadina rurale. Abitavamo un po' fuori. Eravamo in quattro: io, mio fratello Angelo, mamma e papà. I nonni abitavano vicino. C'era anche la bisnonna quando io ero piccolo piccolo. Vivevamo in modo piuttosto semplice.
Daniela	La scuola ti piaceva?
Renzo	Abbastanza. Angelo e io andavamo alla scuola del paese. La maestra si chiamava signora Benedetti. A volte era un po' severa ma era bravissima. Leggere mi piaceva moltissimo ma non ero molto bravo in matematica. Non ero diligente; non ero molto sicuro di me. Preferivo stare all'aperto. Mi piaceva l'aria fresca, giocare fuori, gli amici, l'odore dell'erba, il fango.
Daniela	Avevate animali domestici?
Renzo	Sì, avevamo un cane lupo. E c'erano sempre gatti.
Renzo	Vuoi un caffè?
Daniela	Grazie.
Renzo	Beniamino abitava vicino quando eravate bambini?
Daniela	All'inizio, no. Lui è sempre vissuto in Liguria, io no.
Renzo	Dove sei nata? Dove sei cresciuta?
Daniela	Sono nata negli Stati Uniti. Mio padre lavorava a Boston; viaggiava frequentemente. Siamo tornati in Italia quando io avevo tre anni. Dopo, siamo vissuti tre anni a Torino prima di traslocare in Liguria. Vivevamo in una località di mare.
Renzo	Che lavoro faceva tuo padre?
Daniela	Lavorava – lavora – nel settore farmaceutico.

verb practice 4

1 Write these verbs in the imperfect tense.

a **volere** *to want* **tu** ....

b **avere** *to have* **noi** ....

c **conoscere** *to know* **lei** ....

d **guardare** *to watch* **loro** ....

e **prendere** *to take* **io** ....

f **discutere** *to discuss* **noi** ....

g **essere** *to be* **lui** ....

h **meritare** *to deserve* **voi** ....

2 Change the present tense verbs to the imperfect.

a Di solito prende il treno delle 11.15.

b Ogni sera vado in palestra.

c Mi alzo presto quando fa bel tempo.

d Mia figlia ha mal di gola.

e Preferisci il vino rosso?

f Gianni controlla la posta elettronica ogni cinque minuti.

g Andiamo in montagna in febbraio per sciare.

h Ogni tanto lui gioca a tennis con suo cugino.

i A che ora mangiate?

j Hanno una bellissima casa vicino a Bologna.

3 Fill the gaps with the Italian for the words in brackets, then translate the sentences. Some of them are in the perfect tense – if you need to refresh your memory, have a look at **Chapter 5**.

a .... con Riccardo; .... in città e io .... sul marciapiede.
   (*I was; we were; fell over*)

b .... nel 1984; da bambina .... in Sicilia dove i nonni .... una fattoria grande.
   (*she was born; she lived; had*)

c .... al villaggio dove tua madre .... con tuo padre?
   (*did you go; used to go*)

check point 6

1 What's the Italian for *every now and then?* What two ways can you think of to say *usually* in Italian?

2 Do you use the perfect, the pluperfect or the imperfect to talk about i) what you had done, ii) what you used to do when you were growing up?

3 Which is the only verb not to have the characteristic -**v**- sound within all its imperfect endings?

4 What's missing from **........ in spiaggia con gli amici** for it to mean *We were at the beach with friends*?

5 What would you need to change in **mangiamo bene** to say *They used to eat well*; and in **faccio tante fotografie** to say *We used to take so many photographs*?

6 Explain in Italian that your friend worked in public relations when he lived in Milan. What words change if the friend is female?

7 Rearrange the words to create a sentence: **non caldo funzionava faceva l'aria perché condizionata**. What does it mean?

8 *To daydream* is **fantasticare**: what's the difference in meaning between **sto fantasticando** and **stavo fantasticando**?

9 Fill the gap so that **A scuola .... molto brava in inglese** means *At school she was very good at English.*

10 What's the Italian for *when I was little* and *when I was a student*?

11 **Stavo per mangiare** and **Stavo mangiando** mean different things. Which means *I was (busy) eating*? What does the other mean?

12 What needs adding to **andavamo a Roma** to say *we used to go to Rome every six months*?

13 Given that the imperfect of **c'è** (which is short for **ci è**) is **c'era**, what's the imperfect of **ci sono**? How would you say *There were four tennis courts*?

14 What's the difference between **C'erano tre messaggi per Luigi** and **Ci sono stati tre messaggi per Luigi**?

15 How would you tell someone that you met Anna when you were twelve?

16 Rearrange the words to create a sentence: **è Laura stavo arrivata leggendo quando**.

17 What's the Italian for *I used to enjoy working from home?*

sette
lifestyle choices

Knowing how to say what you like and enjoy – or don't – comes in useful in all sorts of situations, whether you're referring to food or the weather, discussing work, sport, people, music, places, your interests or your pet hates.

Italian expresses liking differently from English. While English uses the verbs *to like* and *to enjoy*, Italian uses **mi piace** which literally means *pleases me, is pleasing to me*. It follows that when you like more than one thing, you need to say *are pleasing to me*: **mi piacciono**.

The equivalent of *I don't like* is **non mi piace** ... not to be confused with **mi dispiace** *I'm sorry* or **le dispiace?** *do you mind?*

Don't forget that *like* has other, quite separate meanings:
I like coffee and *I'd like a coffee* mean different things: in Italian they're **Mi piace il caffè** and **Vorrei un caffè**.

Like can mean *as*: **come nuovo** *like/as new*.
è simile a questo *it's like this one*, **così** *like this, like that*
dormire come un ghiro *to sleep like a log*, lit. *a dormouse*
cantare come una rana *to sing badly*, lit. *like a frog*

To look like is **assomigliare a**:
È tutto suo papà! Assomiglia tanto a Cesare, come due gocce d'acqua. *He's his father's boy! He looks so much like Cesare, like two peas in a pod.* lit. *like two drops of water*

what you do and don't like

what you like

Mi piace Napoli./Napoli mi piace. *Naples pleases me, i.e. I like Naples.*
Mi piace! Mi piace l'atmosfera. *I like it! I like the atmosphere.*
I tuoi colleghi mi piacciono. *I like your colleagues.*
Non mi piacciono i tatuaggi. *I don't like tattoos.*

Where English uses a verb ending in *-ing* after *like*, Italian
generally uses an infinitive.
Mi piace viaggiare. *I like travelling.*
Non mi piace perdere tempo. *I don't like wasting time.*

what other people like

To talk about what other people like, the only word that changes is **mi** (pages
182–183):
La nostra camera non ci piace. *We don't like our room lit. The room is not
pleasing to us.*
Ci piace stare all'aria aperta. *We enjoy being outdoors.*
Gli piacciono i cani. *He likes dogs.*
Non gli piacciono le vespe. *He doesn't like wasps.*
Non le piace andare dal dentista. *She doesn't like going to the dentist's.*
Gli piace Torino. A loro piace Torino. *They like Turin.*
Gli piacciono/A loro piacciono le pinete. *They like the pine forests.*

finding out what people like

Ti/le/vi piace il cibo piccante? *Do you like spicy food?*
Ti piace il tuo nuovo lavoro? *Do you like your new job?*
Cucinare le piace? *Do you enjoy cooking?*
Non vi piacciono le ostriche? *Don't you like oysters?*
Gli/Le piace fare la vela? *Does he/she like sailing?*

You need **a** when saying a particular person likes something:
La Juventus piace a Gino e a mia zia. *Gino and my aunt like
Juventus.*
For emphasis you can replace **mi** with **a me**, **ci** with **a noi**, **ti/le/vi**
with **a te/lei/voi**, **gli/le** with **a lui/lei**:
Il golf piace a me però a lei non piace. *I like golf but she doesn't
like it.*
A noi non piacciono gli addii. *We don't like goodbyes.*

what you liked or used to like

There are two ways of saying *I liked* in Italian: **mi piaceva** and **mi è piaciuto**. Both work in the same way as **mi piace** in that what you like can go before or after them; **mi** is replaced by **ti**, **le**, **ci**, etc. to say what other people liked; **non** goes beforehand to say *I didn't like*.

Mi piaceva/piacevano, the imperfect, conveys *I used to like*:
Mi piaceva l'odore dell'erba tagliata. *I liked the smell of cut grass.*
Da bambino, leggere mi piaceva moltissimo. *When I was little I loved reading.*
La scuola ti piaceva? *Did you like school? Did you use to like school?*
Prima non gli piacevano i cavolini di Bruxelles ma adesso sì. *Before, he didn't like Brussels sprouts but now he does.*

Mi è piaciuto *I liked, I enjoyed*, the perfect, is used to talk about a one-off situation:
Mi è piaciuto lo spettacolo ieri sera. *I liked the show last night.*
Il viaggio ci è piaciuto davvero. *We really enjoyed the trip.*
Ti è piaciuto il corso? *Did you enjoy the course?*
Gli è piaciuto il regalo? *Did he like the present?*
Non le è piaciuto il suo ultimo film. *She didn't enjoy his latest film.*
Non mi è piaciuto il suo atteggiamento. *I didn't like his/her attitude.*

Piaciuto changes to **piaciuta** when what you like is feminine.
L'atmosfera mi è piaciuta molto. *I really enjoyed the atmosphere.*
Vi è piaciuta la partita? *Did you enjoy the match?*

The perfect of **mi piacciono** is mi sono piaciuti (m or m/f) or mi sono piaciute (f).
Mi sono piaciuti i dettagli. *I liked the details.*
Non mi sono piaciuti i piccioni. *I didn't like the pigeons.*
Le sono piaciute le foto? *Did you like the photos?*
Ci sono piaciute le lasagne. *We enjoyed the lasagne.*

You can add sempre to mean *have always liked*:
Mi è sempre piaciuto lo sport. *I've always liked sport.*
Ci è sempre piaciuta Roma. *We've always liked Rome.*
Mi sono sempre piaciuti gli aeroporti. *I've always liked airports.*

adding nuance

Slotting words like **molto** *a lot, very much* or **tanto** *so much* into a sentence adds subtlety or depth to what you're saying. It's simple to do; because they're adverbs, there's nothing about them to change. They work in any context and are especially useful when you're talking about what you like, since *I like* and *I don't like* can sound rather stark.

Mi piace molto Luca Zingaretti. *I like Luca Zingaretti very much/a lot.*
Mi piace tantissimo sciare. *I like skiing so much.*
Le piacciono davvero le montagne. *She really likes the mountains.*
Questi ci piacciono abbastanza. *We quite like these.*
Vi piace davvero? *Do you like it really?*
La spiaggia piace un sacco ai bambini. *The little ones just love the beach.*
Il suo ragazzo le piace da morire. *She adores her boyfriend*
Gina gli piace da impazzire. *He's crazy about Gina.*

You could also use **andare pazzo per**: **Vado pazzo per la Sardegna** *I'm crazy about Sardinia. I just adore Sardinia.*

Add emphasis to the things you don't like with **non ... per niente/nulla** or **non ... affatto** *not at all.* Unlike English, Italian uses two negative words in the same sentence: **non ... mai** *never*, **non ... nessuno** *nobody.*

Non mi piace affatto la scortesia. *I can't stand rudeness.*
Non mi piacciono molto i film gialli. *I don't really like thrillers.*
Gli ospedali non mi piacciono per nulla. *I don't like hospitals at all.*
A Simone non piace per niente l'ipocrisia. *Simone hates hypocrisy.*

Mi piaceva prendere il sole ma ora non mi piace più. *I used to like sunbathing but I don't like it any more.*
Quel ristorante non piaceva a nessuno. *Nobody liked that restaurant.*
Non mi è mai piaciuto nuotare. *I've never liked swimming.*
Non mi è mai piaciuta l'arroganza. *I've never liked arrogance.*
Non mi sono mai piaciuti gli aeroporti. *I've never liked airports.*

There's also **detestare/odiare** *to hate* and **non andare pazzo per**:
Detesto/odio quel nome. *I hate that name.*
Non vado pazzo per i sottotitoli. *I'm not crazy about subtitles.*

what interests you

Mi interessa/interessano ... *I'm interested in* ... literally means ... *interest(s) me* and works in the same way as **mi piace/piacciono**.

Mi interessa la scienza. *Science interests me.*
Il suo argomento mi interessa davvero. *Your point interests me greatly.*
Le sue teorie mi interessano. *I'm interested in your/his/her theories.*
Ti interessano le barche? *Are you keen on boats?*
Le interessa l'automobilismo? *Are you/Is she interested in motor racing?*
Non gli interessa molto il fai da te. *He's not very interested in DIY.*
I cavalli gli interessano. *He's/They're interested in horses.*
Questa regione ci interessa. *We're interested in this region.*
Vi interessa vedere il duomo? *Are you interested in seeing the cathedral?*
La moda interessa a Valentina. *Valentina's interested in fashion.*

For things that don't interest you, you put **non** before **mi interessa**:
Non mi interessa il pattinaggio. *Skating doesn't interest me/doesn't appeal to me.*
Non mi interessano i cruciverba. *Crosswords don't interest me.*
La moda non interessa a Valentina. *Valentina's not interested in fashion.*
Non gli interessa quanti anni hai. *He's not interested in how old you are.*
A loro non interessa sapere. *They're not interested in knowing.*

When referring to the past you can use:
mi interessava imperfect
A scuola mi interessava la scienza. *At school I was interested in science.*
Da giovani ci interessava solo vincere. *When we were young we were only interested in winning.*
A loro non interessava lavorare. *They weren't interested in working.*

mi è interessato perfect
Mi è sempre interessato il calcio. *I've always been interested in football.*
Mi è sempre interessata la scienza. *I've always been interested in science.*
Le sue idee mi sono sempre interessate. *I've always been interested in your/his/her ideas.*
Non mi è mai interessato il gioco d'azzardo. *Gambling has never interested me.*

wordbank

gli sport *sport*

l'alpinismo/arrampicare *climbing, mountaineering*
le arti marziali *martial arts*
il calcio (a sette) *football (seven a side)*
camminare *walking*
correre, la corsa *running*, **correre la maratona** *run the marathon*
nuotare, il nuoto *swimming*
il paracadutismo *parachuting*
il parapendio *paragliding*
pattinare, il pattinaggio *skating*
sciare, lo sci *skiing*
la speleologia *potholing*
la vela *sailing*

Many sports use the English word, e.g. **il badminton, il basket, il bungee-jumping, il rugby, lo squash, il tennis, il triathlon, il windsurf.**

stare all'aperto *to be in the great outdoors*

l'aria fresca *fresh air*
l'esercizio *exercise*
la sensazione di benessere *sense of well-being*
l'essere più in forma *improved fitness*
la diminuzione della pressione *lowering of blood pressure*
la riduzione dello stress *reduced stress*
il fango *mud*
la popò di cane *dog poo*
le formiche *ants*
le mosche *flies*
le ortiche *nettles*
le vespe *wasps*
le api *bees*
le zanzare *mosquitoes*

You put *the* before a noun after **piace/piacciono** even when it isn't used in English: **Mi piace lo yoga** *I like yoga*, **Non le piacciono i ragni** *She doesn't like spiders.*

> Where English uses a verb ending in *-ing* after *like*, Italian uses either an infinitive or a noun instead: **Mi piace nuotare/il nuoto** *I like swimming*; **Gli piace leggere/la lettura** *He likes reading.*

la musica classica/pop *classical/pop music*
la musica corale/sinfonica/da camera *choral/symphonic/chamber music*
l'opera lirica (*grand*) *opera*
la musica alternativa *alternative music*
la musica contemporanea *modern music,* most of which adapts the English words, e.g. **il rock, l'hard-rock, il jazz, il punk, il blues, l'hip-hop, il rap, il tecno, l'heavy metal**

l'arte astratta/concettuale *abstract/conceptual art*
la galleria *gallery*
il museo *museum*
la mostra *exhibition*
il cinema *cinema*
il teatro *theatre*
uno spettacolo *show, performance*
uno spettacolo dal vivo *live performance*
un concerto *concert, gig*
il cast the cast; **l'attore/l'attrice** *the actor/actress*
il/la protagonista *leading actor/actress, star*
la danza moderna/il ballo da sala *modern/ballroom dance*

Sometimes Italian uses a singular word where English uses the plural, and vice versa:
Mi piace lo sport. *I enjoy sport/sports.*
Mi interessa l'atletica. *I'm interested in athletics.*
Mi piace questo binocolo. *I like these binoculars.*
Non mi piace la folla. *I don't like crowds.*
Non mi piacciono i capelli troppo corti. *I don't like hair that's too short.*
Mi piacciono molto i frutti di mare. *I like seafood.*
Mi piacciono le lasagne. *I like lasagna.*
Pasta dishes, e.g. **ravioli, tagliatelle, spaghetti** are all plural, which is why you use **piacciono**.

Use the words on this page, the previous page and the next to practise talking about what you like or don't like, what does and doesn't interest you. If your interests or pet hates aren't included, look them up in a dictionary and make a note of them. There are tips on using a dictionary coming up on page 103.

wordbank

le faccende domestiche *household jobs*
fare giardinaggio *to garden*
tagliare l'erba/la siepe *to cut the grass/the hedge*
fare il fai da te *to do DIY*
abbellire, decorare *to decorate*
tappezzare *to wallpaper*
tinteggiare *to paint*

fare la spesa *to do the food shopping*
cucinare *to cook*
dare da mangiare al *to feed the*
    bambino *baby, child,* **cane** *dog,* **gatto** *cat,* **criceto** *hamster*
occuparsi del *to look after the*
    coniglio *rabbit,* **pony** *pony,* **cavallo** *horse*
portare a passeggio il cane *to walk the dog*

mettere in ordine, ordinare *to tidy up, to clear up*
passare l'aspirapolvere *to vacuum*
spolverare *to dust*
pulire *to clean*
    i vetri *the windows*
    i bagni *the bathrooms*
    il forno *the oven*
lavare *to wash*
    i piatti *the dishes*
    il pavimento *the floors*
    la macchina *the car*
rifare il letto *to make the bed*
fare/stendere il bucato *to do/to hang out the washing*
stirare *to iron*
cucire *to sew*
caricare/svuotare *to load/unload*
    la lavatrice *the washing machine*
    la lavastoviglie *the dishwasher*
    l'asciugatrice *the dryer*
buttare la spazzatura *empty the rubbish*

expressing a preference

Preferisco non sapere. *I prefer not to know.*
Preferisco andare a piedi. *I prefer walking/to walk.*
Preferisco questa qui a quella lì. *I prefer this one to that one.*
Preferisco il mio vecchio smartphone. *I like my old smartphone better.*
Preferiamo andarci in primavera. *We prefer to go there in spring.*

Preferirei avere più opzioni. *I would prefer to have more options.*
Preferirei non andare da sola. *I'd rather not go on my own.*

Io preferisco andare in macchina: è più rapido. *I'd rather go by car: it's quicker.*
Preferiamo l'altra: è più ombreggiata. *We like the other one better: there's more shade.*
Preferisco stare a guardare perché è meno faticoso. *I prefer to watch because it's less tiring.*

Better is **migliore** when it's an adjective, i.e. when the literal meaning is *more good* and **meglio** when it's an adverb, i.e. when the literal meaning is *more well*:

Ho trovato un posto migliore. *I've found a better place.*
Questa giacca qui è migliore: è meno ingombrante. *This jacket's better: it's less bulky.*
Quella pista da sci è tra le migliori al mondo. *That ski slope is among the best in the world.*
Quale funziona meglio? *Which one works better/best?*
Sto meglio oggi – fa meno freddo. *I feel better today – it's not as cold.*
Stanno meglio anche i bambini. *The children are better, too.*

preferito *favourite*

Vivaldi è il mio compositore preferito. *Vivaldi's my favourite composer.*
Firenze è la mia città preferita. *Florence is my favourite city.*
Indovinate quali sono i miei film preferiti. *Guess which my favourite films are.*
Ecco le mie ricette preferite. *Here are my favourite recipes.*
È una delle mie attività meno preferite. *It's one of my least favourite activities.*
Il mio preferito tra i giocatori è … *The player I like best is …*

saying sorry

Mi dispiace is not the opposite of *I like* but a way of saying *Sorry*, showing regret. **Mi spiace** means the same.

Mi spiace, colpa mia. *I'm sorry, my fault.*
Mi dispiace per il disturbo. *Sorry to trouble you.*
Mi dispiace per averla turbata. *I apologise for upsetting you.*
Mi spiace molto di non aver risposto. *I'm very sorry I didn't reply.*
Mi dispiace tanto se vi ho offeso. *I'm so sorry if I've offended you.*
Scusi, davvero mi dispiace moltissimo. *I'm desperately sorry.*

Like English, Italian has various ways of apologising.

tu	Scusa.	**Scusami.**
lei	Scusi.	**Mi scusi.**
voi	Scusate.	**Scusatemi.**

Scusami, sono scivolato. *Oops sorry, I slipped.*
Scusi ... non l'ho visto. *Sorry ... I didn't see it.*
Mi scusi, ma ho fretta. *I'm sorry but I'm in a hurry.*
Come, scusi? *Excuse me? Sorry, what was that you said?*
Scusate il ritardo. *Sorry I'm late.*

Chiedo scusa, ti ho fatto male? *I beg your pardon, did I hurt you?*
Chiedo scusa per la risposta tardiva. *Please excuse the late reply.*
Chiedo scusa se vi ho ingannato. *I apologise if I misled you.*
Senti, ti chiedo scusa se ho sbagliato. *Look, I'm sorry if I made a mistake.*

Ho dimenticato il tuo compleanno. Perdonami! *I forgot your birthday. Forgive me!*
Mi perdoni. Non l'ho fatto apposta. *Do forgive me. I didn't do it on purpose.*

Mi dispiace can be used to offer sympathy but there are alternatives.
Dal profondo del cuore mi dispiace. *From the bottom of my heart I'm sorry.*
Sono davvero dispiaciuto per la sua perdita. *I'm truly sorry for your loss.*
Sentite condoglianze. *Heartfelt sympathies.*

talking the talk

Renzo	Le barche piacciono a te?
Daniela	Moltissimo. Fare la vela mi piace molto … anche il windsurf, il nuoto, lo sci nautico. Insomma, mi piacciono tutti gli sport. Tu?
Renzo	Mi piacciono gli sport, sì, però le barche non molto, soprattutto le barche a vela. E non mi piace molto il nuoto. Francamente, io preferisco il ciclismo, la corsa, l'alpinismo, camminare.
Daniela	Insomma ti piace stare all'aperto ma preferisci la terraferma all'acqua?
Renzo	Esatto! Precisamente.
Daniela	A me invece piace tantissimo il mare aperto dove faccio la vela o il windsurf. Mi dà sempre una sensazione di benessere … e riduce lo stress. E per mare non ci sono mosche o zanzare o vespe o …
Renzo	Che tipo di musica ti piace?
Daniela	Ogni tipo. Il mio compositore preferito è Puccini. Mi piace anche la musica moderna. Per esempio, mi piacciono un sacco le canzoni di Luisa Aquilani.
Renzo	Puccini piace anche a me. La musica classica mi aiuta con le faccende domestiche!
Daniela	Fai tu i lavori a casa?
Renzo	Sì. Vivo solo. Sono divorziato.
Daniela	Anch'io vivo sola. Sai, a me piace fare giardinaggio, abbellire la casa. E mi piace molto cucinare, portare a passeggio il cane.
Renzo	Tu hai un cane?
Daniela	Il mio vicino di casa ha un cane e io lo porto a passeggio.
Renzo	Di che razza è?
Daniela	È un pastore bergamasco.
Renzo	Ma che bello!

1 Which is the odd one out and why? **ape, ortica, zanzara, mosca, vespa**

2 How would you say in Italian: *We really like the room*?

3 If **Gli piacciono i videogiochi?** means *Does he like computer games?*, what's the Italian for *Does she like computer games?* and *Do they like computer games?*

4 How do you tell somebody in Italian that you don't like crowds?

5 What does **Assomigli molto a Francesca** mean?

6 Would you use **mi piaceva** or **mi è piaciuto** while commenting on a wine you've just tasted?

7 What's the Italian for *favourite* when used to talk about wines, region, museum, music, films, photos?

8 How would you apologise for being late to someone you call **tu**?

9 The three versions of *you prefer* are **preferite, preferisce** and **preferisci**. Decide which goes with **tu**, which with **lei** and which with **voi**.

10 What two ways are there of saying *They like running*?

11 How do you say *I'm very sorry, it's my fault* in Italian.

12 List three words/phrases that could go after **non mi piace** to say that you really don't like something.

13 What's the word that needs to be added to **Mi è .... piaciuto dipingere** for it to mean *I've always liked painting*?

14 Given that the Italian for *a consequence* is **una conseguenza** what's the Italian for *She's not interested in the consequences*?*

15 Is **meglio** or **migliore** the word missing from **Questa trattoria è ....?** *This restaurant is better.*

16 These are the words used with **mi piace** in a **sondaggio** *survey*. Put them in order, starting with the least favourable: **molto, abbastanza, poco, da morire, non ... per niente, moltissimo**

17 How would you tell someone that you don't much enjoy vacuuming or unloading the dishwasher, that you prefer gardening.

*If you need a reminder on plural endings for nouns, go to page 178.

how to use a dictionary

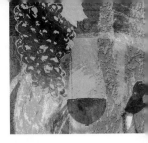

A dictionary is an essential tool for language learning, allowing you to personalise phrases and talk about exactly what you choose.

There are a number of dictionaries on the internet and available as apps. Some of them are much better presented, more detailed and more user-friendly than others, and it's a case of trying a few and seeing which suits you.

In print, dictionaries come in all sizes, from tiny pocket versions to huge tomes. It's not necessarily a case of the bigger the better: a very large dictionary can be so densely packed with information that it becomes overwhelming for someone learning a language.

grammatical terms and abbreviations

As with most tools, there's a skill to using a dictionary effectively. And, because of fundamental differences between the languages, using an Italian > English dictionary raises different issues from using the English > Italian version.

For both, you need to understand basic terms such as adjective, adverb, noun, verb (pages 175–177), because each dictionary entry is defined by its grammatical category. This is abbreviated, and the abbreviations are very similar in both languages, with *noun* a notable exception: its translation can be **nome** or **sostantivo** and some Italian dictionaries abbreviate it to **s**.

art **articolo** *article*	*agg* **aggettivo** *adj adjective*
avv **avverbio** *adv adverb*	*fam* **familiare** *familiar/colloquial*
f **femminile** *feminine*	*inv* **invariabile** *invariable*
irreg **irregolare** *irregular*	*m* **maschile** *masculine*
n **nome** *noun*	*pl* **plurale** *plural*
prep **preposizione** *preposition*	*pp* **participio passato** *past participle*
pers **persona** *person*	*sing* **singolare** *singular*
pron **pronome** *pronoun*	*v* **verbo** *verb*
s **sostantivo** *noun*	*volg* **volgare** *vulg vulgar*
vi/vtr **verbo intransitivo/transitivo** *intransitive/transitive verb*	

Most dictionaries include a comprehensive list of the abbreviations used.

italiano → inglese

Some words belong in more than one grammatical category, and a few nouns look identical but have a different gender and meaning.

capitale *n* capital: 1 *nm* money; 2 *nf* principal town/city.

lavoro I *nm* work, job, employment, labour: **cena di** ~ business dinner; **contratto di** ~ employment contract; **datore di** ~ employer, boss; ~ **domestico** housework; **forza** ~ workforce; ~ **nero** black market; ~ **di squadra** team work. **II** *v* *1ᵃ pers sing* **lavorare** to work.

personale I *nm* personnel, staff. **II** *agg* personal: **identità** ~ ID.

piano I *nm* **1** floor, storey; **2** design, plan, blueprint; **3** project; **4** flat surface; **5** (*mus*) piano; **6** (*geog/geol*) plain; **7** ~ **cottura** hob. **II** *agg* even, level. **III** *avv* **1** slow, slowly; **pian** ~ gradually, little by little; **2** quietly, softly.

ricco *agg* rich, wealthy, prosperous, lavish; ~ **sfondato**, **stra**~ hugely rich.

secondo I *nm* (*time*) second, meat/fish course, runner-up. **II** *agg* second, secondary. **III** *prep* according to; **IV** *v* *1ᵃ pers sing* **secondare** to second, to support.

Many online dictionaries allow you to search for a word exactly as you come across it. But a traditional Italian > English dictionary lists nouns in the singular, adjectives with the masculine singular ending and verbs in the infinitive. This means that a word you're looking for may not appear exactly as you came across it. For example:

- **Regole** and **dettagli** are the plurals of **regola** *rule* and **dettaglio** *detail*, which are what you'll find listed. Irregular plurals such as **mano/mani** *hand/hands* tend to be flagged up.
- Other than **pari** *equal, even* and **impari/dispari** *unequal, odd*, any adjective ending in -**i** is plural.
- To find the meaning of **scegliamo**, you need to work out that -**iamo** is a **noi** verb ending and that the infinitive is **scegliere** *to choose*.
- If ever you struggle with a verb, think of irregulars, e.g. **vado** *I go* bears little resemblance to **andare** *to go*. However, a good dictionary will include common irregularities.
- Look out for words containing **c** or **g** that have added **h** before **e** or **i** to preserve their hard sound. **Droghe** is the plural of **droga** *drug*; **ricche** is the feminine plural of **ricco** *rich*; **sprechi** and **paghi** are the **tu** forms of **sprecare** *to waste* and **pagare** *to pay*.

English → Italian

Many English words belong in a single grammatical category, e.g. *terrain* is a noun, *write* can only be a verb, *genuine* can only be an adjective. But there are also many that belong in two or more categories, e.g. *sock* can be something you wear on your foot (noun) or to hit somebody (verb); *snipe* can be a bird (noun), to shoot or to jeer (verbs); *back* can be the rear part (noun), to support (verb) or the opposite of front (adjective).

content **I** *n* **1** contenuto *m*; **2** book ~s indice *m*. **II** *adj* contento, soddisfatto.

lock **I** *n* **1** serratura *f*: combination ~ serratura a combinazione; **2** (*hair*) ricciolo *m*; **3** (*wrestling*) presa *f*; **4** (*rugby*) terza linea centro *m*; **5** (*canal*) chiusa *f*. **II** *v* chiudere a chiave.

pitch **I** *n* **1** (*music*) tono *m*; **2** (*sales*) parlantina *f*; **3** (*sports*) campo *m*; **4** (*tar*) catrame *m*, bitume *m*; **5** ~ and putt minigolf *m*. **II** *adj* ~ dark buio pesto. **III** *v* **1** (*throw*) lanciare; **2** ~ tent piantare.

table **I** *n* **1** (*furniture*) tavola *f*, tavolo *m*, tavolino *m*; bedside ~ comodino *m*; dressing ~ toletta *f*; **2** (*chart*) tabella *f*; **3** (*chem*) periodic ~ tavola periodica *f*; **4** (*math*) ~s tabelline *f pl*; **5** (sport) ~ tennis ping pong *m*; **II** *adj* da tavola. **III** *v* ~ a motion presentare una proposta.

Spelling is, of course, critical. While *hangar* and *hanger* might sound very similar in English, they have no connection whatsoever in Italian: *a hangar* is **un capannone** while *a hanger* is **un attaccapanni** or **una gruccia**.

Armed with a dictionary, it can be easy to get carried away and start translating word for word from English. One of the many reasons why this is a recipe for disaster lies in English phrasal verbs, which are made up of two parts: a verb followed by a preposition or adverb, e.g.

ask in, ask out, ask around
break down, break in, break out, break up
get about, get away, get by, get in, get off, get on, get over
give away, give back, give in, give up
hang around, hang on, hang out, hang up
throw away, throw up

Each has a specific meaning and so has to be treated as an individual item, not as two words. More often than not, the Italian equivalent is a single word.

look v 1 **guardare**; 2 ~ at **guardare, osservare**; 3 ~ after **badare, occuparsi di**; 4 ~ into **investigare**; 5 ~ for **cercare**; 6 ~ out **fare attenzione**; 7 ~ over (*inspect*) **ispezionare**, (*overlook*) **dare su**; 8 ~ up (*seek info*) **cercare**.

put l v 1 **mettere**; 2 ~ away **mettere a posto**; 3 ~ down (*disparage*) **denigrare**, (*kill*) **sopprimere**; 4 ~ off (*deter*) **dissuadere, scoraggiare**; (*postpone*) **rimandare**; 5 ~ out **estinguere, spegnere**; 6 ~ up (*accommodate*) **ospitare**, (*raise*) **alzare, sollevare**; 7 ~ up with **sopportare, tollerare**. ll **messo** *irreg pp* **mettere**.

take v 1 **prendere**; 2 ~ after **rassomigliare a**; 3 ~ apart **smontare**; 4 ~ away, (*math*) **sottrarre**, (*food*) **portare via**; 5 ~ off **togliere**, (*imitate*) **imitare**, (*aero*) **decollare**; 5 ~ out **estrarre, portare fuori**.

If ever you're not sure which option to use, look it up in the other direction.

Above all, never attempt a literal translation of idiomatic phrases such as *the elephant in the room, the dog's dinner, I could eat a horse, to go cold turkey, he's my rock, to spit with rain* or *to spit feathers*, which don't have the idiomatic meaning in Italian.

1   Which of these fit into more than one grammatical category?
    clear, drive, duck, jam, moral, online, permit, port, present, press, rock, sand, sardine, square, squash, state

2   Work out what you'd need to look up to find the meaning of these words, then look them up in a dictionary.

nouns:	**amiche, barche, laghi, pizzichi, profughi**
adjectives:	**stanche, bianchi, larghe, greci**
verbs:	**va, preghiamo, scarichi, neghi, paghiamo**

3   Although rarely an issue – because context makes it clear – a few words can have more than one derivation: **giochi** and **elenchi** could be nouns or parts of verbs. Identify both as you'd find them in a dictionary.

    (See page 201 for answers.)

otto
making plans

Una festa, originally *a feast day,* is now used for any celebration, festival, party or day off. **Le feste** are celebrated in style, with family, food and drink playing a central role. If you're lucky enough to be invited along, it's worth making sure you know how to accept or to decline graciously. It's also pretty crucial to get the date and the time right.

Italians embrace their celebrations with enthusiasm, starting in early January with **la festa della Befana** *the festival of Befana*, an old woman who brings gifts to Italian children on the eve of Epiphany. The **Carnevale** season follows in February, a time of partying until **Martedì Grasso** *Shrove Tuesday* heralds **la Quaresima** *Lent*, lasting until **Pasqua** *Easter* which is the culmination of **la Settimana Santa** *Holy Week*. In addition to **la Festa del Lavoro** *Labour day* on 1 May, **la Festa della Repubblica** *Republic Day* on 2 June and **Ferragosto** in mid-August, there are numerous **feste** and saints' days before **Natale** *Christmas* and **Capodanno** when the new year is celebrated.

When a public holiday falls on a Tuesday or a Thursday, many people make a long weekend of it by taking the Monday or Friday off as well. This is called **fare il ponte** *making the bridge.*

when?

lunedì m	*Monday*
martedì m	*Tuesday*
mercoledì m	*Wednesday*
giovedì m	*Thursday*
venerdì m	*Friday*
sabato m	*Saturday*
domenica f	*Sunday*

Non posso venire giovedì: aiuto Franca nella galleria il giovedì/ogni giovedì. *I can't come on Thursday: I help Franca in the gallery on Thursdays/ every Thursday.*
Ci vediamo domenica. *See you on Sunday.*
La domenica non c'è nessuno. *There's nobody there on Sundays.*

gennaio *January*	**luglio** *July*
febbraio *February*	**agosto** *August*
marzo *March*	**settembre** *September*
aprile *April*	**ottobre** *October*
maggio *May*	**novembre** *November*
giugno *June*	**dicembre** *December*

Vado in Galles in/ogni agosto. *I go to Wales in/every August.*
Sono nato, È nato/a ... *I was born, He/she was born ...*
    ... in gennaio. *... in January.*
    ... il dodici ottobre. *... on the 12th of October.*
    ... nel millenovecentonovantatré. *... in 1993.*
    ... nel duemilaquindici. *... in 2015.*

There are several ways of arranging to meet someone.

A domani allora! *Till tomorrow then!*
Ci vediamo venerdì? *Shall we meet up on Friday?*
Facciamo domenica da Paolo? *Shall we make it Sunday at Paolo's?*
Vediamoci sabato per fare due chiacchiere. *Let's get together on Saturday for a chat.*
Magari possiamo fissare un incontro per martedì/per il ventidue? *Maybe we can arrange a meeting for Tuesday/for the 22nd?*

what time?

Quando? A che ora? *When? At what time?*

a **mezzogiorno/mezzanotte**	*at midday/midnight*
all'**una**	*at one o'clock*
alle **due**, alle **tre, ecc.**	*at two o'clock, at three o'clock, etc.*
alle **otto e un quarto**	*at a quarter past eight*
alle **dieci e mezzo**	*at half past ten*
alle **tre meno un quarto**	*at a quarter to three*
alle **(ore) ventitré**	*at 23.00, at 11 p.m.*
alle **nove e trenta**	*at 09.30*
alle **quattro e quaranta**	*at 04.40*

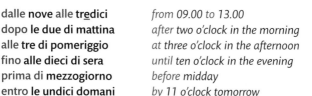

The little word **alle** *at* makes all the difference.
Time: **Ci vediamo alle diciannove.** *See you at seven o'clock in the evening.*
Date: **Ci vediamo il diciannove.** *See you on the 19th.*

dalle **nove alle tredici**	*from 09.00 to 13.00*
dopo **le due di mattina**	*after two o'clock in the morning*
alle **tre di pomeriggio**	*at three o'clock in the afternoon*
fino **alle dieci di sera**	*until ten o'clock in the evening*
prima di **mezzogiorno**	*before midday*
entro **le undici domani**	*by 11 o'clock tomorrow*

You confirm a time in much the same way as the date:
Ci vediamo all'ora dell'aperitivo. *See you at cocktail time.*
Ci vediamo alle tre in punto. *See you at three o'clock on the dot.*
Ti/Le va bene domani mattina? *Is tomorrow morning OK for you?*
Facciamo le dieci? *How about ten o'clock?*
Ci sarò alle dieci precise. *I'll be there at ten o'clock sharp.*

Listen out for interesting expressions involving time of day:

al **crepuscolo**	*at twilight*
al **tramonto**	*at sunset*
all'**ora di punta**	*at rush hour*
all'**ultimo momento**	*at the 11th hour/last minute*
alle **ore piccole**	*in the small hours*
alle **prime luci dell'alba**	*at the crack of dawn*

suggesting things to do

The simplest way of suggesting things to do is to use a verb ending in **-iamo**, which is the Italian equivalent of *let's*. The same ending can be used after **perché non** *why not*.

Andiamo in spiaggia. *Let's go to the beach.*

Facciamo un picnic. *Let's have a picnic.*

Non restiamo qui. *Let's not stay here.*

Perché non andiamo in una tattoria sul lungomare per una cena anticipata. *Why don't we go to a restaurant on the seafront for an early dinner.*

There are also phrases you can use, some of them followed by an infinitive.

Ti va di andare alla festa del vino domenica? *Do you fancy going to the wine festival on Sunday?*

Le va di passeggiare un po' e magari prendere un gelato o una granita al limone? *Would you like to go for a little walk and maybe have an ice cream or a lemon granita?*

Sabato andiamo in montagna. Vi va di venire anche voi due? *On Saturday we're going to the mountains. Do you two fancy coming as well?*

Hai voglia di andare in palestra stasera? *Do you feel like going to the gym this evening?*

Avete voglia di venire a fare colazione da noi? Comprerò dei cornetti. *Do you fancy coming for breakfast at our place? I'll buy some croissants.*

Others can be followed by a noun or an infinitive.

Che ne dici di una birra artigianale? *How about a craft beer?* (**tu**)

Che ne dice di una partita a tennis domani? *How about a game of tennis tomorrow?* (**lei**)

Che ne dite di andare al bar per scambiare delle opinioni? *How about we go to the bar to share ideas?* (**voi**)

A suggestion can take the form of an invitation.

Sei invitato/a da Piero stasera. *You're invited to Piero's this evening.*

Siete tutti invitati a una festa: venerdì mia mamma compirà sessant'anni. *You're all invited to a party: on Friday my mother will be 60.*

wordbank

Structures like **ti va di** and **ha voglia di** are easy to use – you can follow them with any phrase starting with an infinitive, such as discovering a town, exploring further afield or trying out something new.

andare in città *go into town*
fare il giro del centro storico *wander round the old town*
vedere l'anfiteatro/il duomo *see the amphitheatre/cathedral*
visitare il museo/i negozi/il casinò *visit the museum/shops/casino*
andare all'opera/a un concerto *go to the opera/to a concert*
fare un salto da Francesca; le facciamo una sorpresa *drop in on Francesca; let's surprise her*
mangiare la pizza *go for a pizza*

noleggiare un motorino *rent a scooter*
prendere il treno locale fino a ... *take the local train as far as ...*
esplorare la zona circostante *explore the surrounding area*
andare alla sagra del tartufo/del cinghiale *go to the truffle/wild boar fair*
gironzolare per il mercato agricolo *wander round the farmers' market*
passeggiare tra i vigneti *stroll round the vineyards*
degustare vini/prodotti locali *taste local wines/products*
andare a cavallo; ci sono scuderie qui vicino *go riding; there are stables nearby*
salire sulla collina/sulle scogliere *climb the hill/the cliffs*
attraversare l'isola a piedi *walk across the island*
fare una passeggiata lungo la spiaggia *go for a walk along the beach*
camminare nella neve *walk in the snow*

fare arrampicata *go rock climbing*
giocare a bocce/a pallavolo *have a game of boules/volleyball*
fare il bagno *go swimming*
fare un giro in barca *go on a boat trip*
andare a pesca in alto mare *go deep-sea fishing*
provare a fare lo sci nautico *have a go at waterskiing*
prendere una lezione di tuffi *have a diving lesson*

 Practise using some of these with, e.g. ti va di ... , che ne dite di ... Out loud, of course. Then practise changing verbs to the noi form so that they mean let's ... e.g. Attraversiamo l'isola a piedi. **Let's walk across the island.**

accepting and declining graciously

Molto gentile. *How kind of you.*
Grazie dell'invito. *Thank you for the invitation.*
Grazie mille per avermi invitato/averci invitati. *Many thanks for inviting me/ us.*

yes please

Accetto ... *I accept ...*
    ... senza esitazione. *... without hesitation.*
    ... con piacere/gioia. *... with pleasure/delight.*
Volentieri. *With pleasure.*
Di buon grado/buona voglia. *Gladly, willingly*
Mi/Ci piacerebbe molto. *I/We'd love to.*
Certamente, senz'altro. *Certainly, definitely.*
Che buona/bella idea! *What a good/lovely idea!*
Ci sarò! *I'll be there!*
Non vedo l'ora. *I can't wait.*
Magari! *Yes please!*

no thank you

Magari! *If only! I wish!*
Mi dispiace ma ... *I'm sorry but ...*
Non mi sarà possibile. *It won't be possible.*
Non potrò ... *I won't be able to ...*
Temo di non poter ... *I'm afraid I can't ...*
Non posso/possiamo. *I/We can't.*
Non so se posso ... *I don't know if I can ...*
Non sono sicuro di poter ... *I'm not sure if I can ...*
    ... per impegni di lavoro. *... for work reasons.*
    ... perché ho già un impegno. *... because I'm already committed.*
Purtroppo ... *Unfortunately ...*
È un vero peccato ma ... *It's a real shame but ...*
Spero di esserci ma ... *I hope to be there but ...*
Farò il possibile ma ... *I'll do my best but ...*
    ... sarò fuori città. *... I'll be out of town.*
    ... siamo impegnati. *... we're already committed.*
Grazie comunque. *Thank you anyway.*
Magari un'altra volta. *Maybe another time.*

magari

Magari is one of those versatile words that you hear often, and its meaning is affected by context.

If only! I wish! You wish!
Vieni anche tu? *Are you coming too?* **Magari!** *If only! I should be so lucky.*
Hanno vinto ieri sera? *Did they win last night?* **Magari!** *If only! You wish!*
Sei arrivato in tempo? *Did you get there on time?* **Magari!** *I wish!*

If only ...
Magari fosse vero! *If only it were true!*
Magari giocassi come Federer. *If only I played like Federer.*
Magari avessimo più tempo. *If only we had more time.*
Magari potessimo stare qui per sempre. *If only we could stay here forever.*
Magari fosse tutto così facile. *If only everything were this easy.*
Magari fossi venuto anche tu. *If only you had come too.*

perhaps, maybe, I guess
Magari sì, magari no. Chissà? *Maybe yes, maybe no. Who knows?*
Magari domani vengo anch'io. *Perhaps tomorrow I'll come too.*
Magari è necessario. *I guess we ought to.*
Magari non lo sapevano. *Maybe they didn't know.*
Non l'ho visto: magari è ammalato? *I haven't seen him: perhaps he's ill?*
Ci vediamo stasera? *See you this evening?* **Magari sì.** *Yes, hopefully.*

definitely
Ti accompagno? *Shall I come with you?* **Magari.** *Yes please.*
Vi piacerebbe vivere a Roma? *Would you like to live in Rome?* **Magari!** *We'd love to!*
Vuoi che l'organizzo io? *Shall I organise it?* **Magari!** *Brilliant!*
Ti va una birra? *Fancy a beer?* **Magari! ... cin cin.** *And how! ... cheers.*
Dovrei proprio scusarmi. *I really ought to apologise.* **Be', magari!** *Well you can say that again!*

even if
Tanto vale andarci, magari anche a piedi! *Might as well go there, even if I/we have to walk!*

good wishes

Auguri *all the best, best wishes* is an all-purpose way of offering your good wishes: **auguri a tutti** *best wishes to everyone.* **Auguroni!** *Great big wishes!*

Every celebration and milestone has a tailor-made greeting:
Buon Anno. *Happy New Year.*
Buon Carnevale. *Enjoy Carnevale.*
Buon Natale. *Happy Christmas.* **Buona Pasqua.** *Happy Easter.*
Buona festa della mamma. *Happy Mother's Day.*
Buon anniversario. *Happy Anniversary.*
Buon compleanno. *Happy Birthday.*
Buon onomastico. *Happy Name Day. Happy Saint's Day.*

The custom of offering good wishes isn't confined to big occasions; in Italy there's a phrase for any and every situation:
Buon divertimento. *Have a good time. Enjoy yourself/yourselves.*
Buona festa. *Have a happy feast day/holiday.*
Buon fine settimana/buon weekend. *Have a good weekend.*
Buon lavoro. *Enjoy your work. Have a good day at work.*
Buon viaggio. *Safe journey.*
Buon volo. *Have a good flight.*
Buona fortuna. *Good luck.*
Buona giornata. *Have a good day.*
Buona guarigione. *Get well soon.*
Buona permanenza. *Have a pleasant stay.*
Buona serata. *Enjoy your evening.*
Buone vacanze. *Enjoy your holiday. Have a good holiday.*

You can make it more formal by starting with **ti/le/vi auguro** *I wish you*:
Ti auguro un buon volo. *I hope you have a safe flight.*
Le auguro (una) buona permanenza. *I wish you an enjoyable stay.*
Vi auguriamo buon Natale. *Our best wishes for Christmas.*
Grazie. Ricambio/Ricambiamo gli auguri. *Thank you. And the same to you too.*

... or you can be less formal:
Un bacione per il tuo compleanno! *A big kiss for your birthday!*

talking about the future

Italian verbs have a set of endings for talking about the future. They replace the final -**e** of the infinitive of -**ere** and -**ire** verbs:

io	-ò	noi	-emo
tu	-ai	voi	-ete
lei/lui	-à	loro	-anno

rispondere *to reply*: **risponderò** *I will reply*; **risponderanno** *they will reply*

fornire *to provide*: **fornirai** *you will provide*; **forniremo** *we will provide*

-**are** verbs have the same endings as -**ere** verbs:
comprare *to buy*: **comprerò** *I will buy*; **compreremo** *we will buy*

The future of **essere** is different: **sarò** *I will be*, **sarai** *you will be* etc.
Sarà pronto entro la fine del 2019. *It will be ready by the end of 2019.*
Many other verbs don't quite follow the regular pattern but are still recognisable: **andare**: **andrò** *I will go*; **avere**: **avrò** *I will have*; **fare**: **farò** *I will do*; **potere**: **potrò** *I will be able to.*

Talking about what hasn't yet happened doesn't necessarily use the word *will* in English or the future tense in Italian.
A che ora arriva il volo? *What time does the flight arrive?*
Tornano a scuola tra una settimana. *They go back to school in a week.*
A settembre Luca andrà a scuola. *In September Luca will go to school.*
C'è una riunione alle undici. *There's a meeting at 11 o'clock.*
Ci sarà una riunione alle ore undici. *There will be a meeting at 11 o'clock.*
Comincerà alle undici precise. *It will start at 11 o'clock on the dot.*
Arriverà in anticipo. Ci aspetterà. *She'll arrive early. She'll wait for us.*
Se c'è un ritardo ti chiamerò. *If there's a delay I'll call you.*
Farò del mio meglio. *I will do my best.*
Sopravviverò! *I will survive!*

In English you can say you're ***going to*** do something, but in Italian you use the future tense — you only use **andare** *to go* when it actually involves going somewhere.

Non perderanno. Vedrai! *They're not going to lose. You'll see!*
Ti aiuterà Nico; io non ci sarò. *Nico's going to help you; I won't be there/I'm not going to be there.*

weather permitting

Outdoor activities such as sailing, flying, mountaineering or skiing require thinking ahead and understanding **il meteo/le previsioni meteo/le previsioni del tempo** *the weather forecast.*

Che tempo farà domani? *What's the weather going to be like tomorrow?*
Quali sono le previsioni (meteo) per i prossimi giorni? *What's the weather forecast for the next few days?*

Il meteo dà sole per domenica. *The forecast is for* (lit. *gives*) *sun on Sunday.*
Le previsioni danno venti forti. *The forecast is for strong winds.*
Danno pioggia e venti forti. *Rain and strong winds are forecast.*
Se fa bello facciamo una grigliata? *If it's fine shall we have a barbecue?*
Anche se c'è poco vento vorrei fare windsurf. *Even if there isn't much wind, I'd like to go windsurfing.*
Se c'è abbastanza neve si può fare snowboard. *If there's enough snow we can go snowboarding.*
Se le previsioni sono favorevoli andiamo in montagna. *If the forecast is good we'll go into the mountains.*
Dicono che ci sarà un'ondata di caldo. *They're saying that there's going to be a heatwave.*

For those who prefer a less scientific prognosis: **Rosso di sera: bel tempo si spera. Rosso di mattina: maltempo s'avvicina.** *Red (sky) at night, good weather we hope. Red in the morning, bad weather's on its way.*
Cielo a pecorelle, acqua a catinelle. *Fluffy clouds (little sheep) in the sky, heavy rain coming.*

More often than not, the weather tends to be either commented on or described.
Che bel tempo! *What good weather!*
Che tempo splendido! *What glorious weather!*
Brutto tempo, vero? *Miserable weather, isn't it?*
Ma che caldo/freddo oggi! *It's so hot/cold today!*
Che vento, una vera burrasca. *So windy, a real gale!*
Che bel venticello. *What a beautiful breeze.*
Davvero umido oggi, no? *Really humid today, isn't it?*
Questa pioggia continua mi dà sui nervi. *This non-stop rain is getting on my nerves.*
Non mi piace per niente questa nebbia. *I hate this fog.*
C'è un'afa che si muore! *This muggy heat is killing!*

the weather now

Che tempo fa da voi? *What's the weather like where you are?*

Several expressions use **fa** or **è** for talking about the weather:
Fa bello/brutto. *It's a lovely/horrible day.*
Fa così caldo: fa un caldo da morire! *It's so hot: it's way too hot!*
Fa quaranta gradi all'ombra. *It's 40 degrees in the shade.*
Fa un po' freschino. *It's a bit chilly.*
Fa freddo qui: fa un freddo polare. *It's cold here: it's arctic.*

È un po' nuvoloso. *It's a bit cloudy.*
È mite. *It's mild.* **È molto umido.** *It's very humid.*
È ventoso. Tira vento. *It's windy.*
Piove: piove a dirotto. *It's raining: it's pouring down.*
C'è una pioggerella fine. *There's a fine drizzle.*
Si vede la neve sui monti. *You can see snow on the mountains.*
Quest'anno c'è poca neve. *There's not much snow this year.*

... and what it was like

Che tempo faceva? Che tempo ha fatto? *What was the weather like?*

The reply can use the imperfect (pages 80–82) or the perfect (page 68–70) depending on whether you're describing continuing or one-off weather.
Piove. *It's raining.*
Pioveva ieri. *It was raining yesterday.*
È piovuto durante la notte. *It (has) rained during the night.*

Italian also uses both tenses for expressions with **fa** and **è**, even though English tends to stick to *was*:
Fa caldo. *It's hot.*
  Faceva caldo. Ha fatto caldo. *It was hot.*
È afoso. *It's close, muggy.*
  Era afoso. È stato afoso. *It was muggy.*
C'è vento. *It's windy.*
  C'era vento. C'è stato vento. *It was windy.*

Faceva freddo nella camera. *It was cold in the room.*
C'è stato un rovescio a mezzogiorno. *There was a downpour at lunchtime.*
C'è stata una bella nevicata durante la notte. *A nice lot of snow fell during the night.*

what you would do

Just as the future verb endings convey *will do*, there are conditional endings that convey *would do*. The conditional is often followed by *if* ... or *but* ..., indicating that there are conditions attached, hence the name.

> The conditional has nothing whatsoever to do with the other English meaning of *would* that refers to the past and means *used to*, as in *She would sit and stare for hours*.

These conditional endings simply take the place of future endings:

io	-ei	noi	-emmo
tu	-esti	voi	-este
lei/lui	-ebbe	loro	-ebbero

rispondere *to reply*: **risponderei** *I would reply*
fornire *to provide*: **fornirebbero** *they would provide*
comprare *to buy*: **comprerei** *I would buy*; **compreresti** *you would buy*
arrivare *to arrive*: **arriverebbe** *he/she/it would arrive*

The same verbs are irregular in the future and the conditional, e.g.
andrei *I would go*   **avrei** *I would have*   **dovrei** *I should*
sarei *I would be*   **farei** *I would do*   **potrei** *I'd be able to*
vorrei *I'd want, I'd like*

Non oserei! *I wouldn't dare!*
Preferiresti l'altro? *Would you prefer the other one?*
Sarei molto grato. *I would be very grateful.*
Inviterebbero Maria ma è a Torino. *They would invite Maria but she's in Turin.*
Mangerei una pizza ma sono a dieta. *I'd eat a pizza but I'm on a diet.*
Direi di sì. *I'd say yes.*
Sarebbe troppo caro. *It would be too expensive.*
Non vorreste rimanere qui? *Wouldn't you like to stay here?*

> When a conditional is linked to *if* + another verb, this other verb will have **-ss** in its ending (see next page).
> **Sarebbe bellissimo se fosse vero.** *It would be wonderful if it were true.*
> **Ci andrei io, se avessi i soldi.** *I would go myself if I had the money.*

if ...

If shows there's a condition attached to the main part of the sentence, and conditional sentences in Italian come in three types:

I do .../I will do ... if the condition is met.
I would do ... if the condition were met.
I would have done ... if the condition had been met.

In the second and third types, you'll hear verb endings containing a very distinctive **-ss**: these are the imperfect subjunctive.

Puoi se vuoi. *You can if you want.*
Potresti se volessi. *You could if you wanted.*
Avresti potuto se avessi voluto. *You could have if you'd wanted.*

Ti aspetto se fai presto. *I'll wait for you if you hurry.*
Ti aspetterei se facessi presto. *I would wait for you if you hurried.*
Ti avrei aspettato se solo avessi fatto presto. *I would have waited for you if only you'd hurried.*

Mi chiama se vuole sapere. *He calls me if he wants to know.*
Mi chiamerebbe se volesse sapere. *He'd call me if he wanted to know.*
Mi avrebbe chiamato se avesse voluto sapere. *He would have called me if he'd wanted to know.*

Lo farò se posso. *I'll do it if I can.*
Lo farei se potessi. *I'd do it if I could.*
L'avrei fatto se avessi potuto. *I would have done it if I could have.*

The subjunctive endings are included in the verbs in the **Grammar Summary**. Two that you'll come across regularly are **avere** and **essere**.
avere: avessi avessi avesse avessimo aveste avessero
essere: fossi fossi fosse fossimo foste fossero

se avessi i soldi *if I had the money*
se solo avessi più tempo *if only I had more time*
se fossi più ricco/giovane/in forma *if I were richer/younger/fitter*
se io fossi in te *if I were you*

se avessi capito/pensato/visto *if I'd understood/thought/seen*
se solo avessimo saputo/chiesto/avuto *if only we'd known/asked/had*
se fossero andati/venuti/rimasti *if they'd gone/come/stayed*
se non fosse stata così stanca *if she hadn't been so tired*

talking the talk

Renzo	Vai in città a mezzogiorno?
Daniela	Forse. Perché?
Renzo	Hai voglia di fare il giro del centro storico?
Daniela	Buona idea. Facciamo un salto da Francesca: le facciamo una sorpresa. Poi andiamo tutti e tre a mangiare la pizza.
Renzo	Perché no?
Daniela	Che peccato che Francesca non c'era.
Renzo	Infatti. Sai, il meteo dà bel tempo. Ti va di andare a una festa del vino?
Daniela	Che bella idea! Dove e quando?
Renzo	Ad Alba, nella provincia di Cuneo. C'è una festa questo fine settimana, domenica, nel centro storico della città. Magari dopo si può fare una passeggiata in collina.
Daniela	Mi piacerebbe molto.
Renzo	... e potremmo andare in una trattoria per una cena anticipata.
Daniela	Non vedo l'ora.
Renzo	Allora, ci vediamo qui domenica, alle nove di mattina. Partiremo subito – magari dopo un caffè. Va bene?
Daniela	Ci sarò. Alle nove in punto.
Renzo	Ti è piaciuta Alba?
Daniela	Moltissimo. La festa del vino anche.
Renzo	Fra una settimana mia mamma compirà sessant'anni. Senti, sabato andiamo tutti in montagna. Ti va di venire anche te?
Daniela	Che gentile. Ma purtroppo non mi sarà possibile siccome ho già un impegno.
Renzo	Peccato! Allora ti piacerebbe venire a pranzo da me domani? Ci saranno la mamma e altri.
Daniela	Con piacere. A che ora?
Renzo	Verso mezzogiorno.
Daniela	A domani allora.

verb practice 5

1   Write the future forms of these verbs and say what they mean.

a   rispondere   tu ....
b   andare   loro ....
c   prendere   voi ....
d   durare   .... (it)
e   mettere   noi ....
f   dimenticare   lei ....
g   riuscire   io ....
h   fare   lui ....
i   arrivare   noi ....
j   succedere   .... (it)
k   essere   io ....
l   avere   tu ....

2   Now change them all to the conditional and say what they mean.

3   Identify these as present, past, future or conditional and say what they mean. If you need to refresh your memory of the tenses, see pages 185–188.

a   dipenderà   b   organizzate
c   ha telefonato   d   studiano
e   decideranno   f   trasformerebbero
g   preferiremo   h   preferiremmo
i   hanno accusato   j   continuerò

4   Match the two halves to make sentences:

a   se avessi più soldi   i   non sarei stato in ritardo
b   se avessi avuto più soldi   ii   avrebbero capito perché
c   se potessi trovare il suo   iii   comprerei una macchina
      indirizzo
d   se il volo fosse arrivato   iv   sarei andato in palestra
      in orario
e   se mangiassimo meno   v   ti avrei invitato
f   se avessi avuto tempo   vi   avrei comprato una macchina
g   se mi avessi dato il tuo   vii   dimagriremmo
      numero
h   se mi avessero ascoltato   viii   inviterei Barbara

checkpoint 8

1 Which are the two days on either side of **venerdì**, and the three months before **agosto**?

2 What's the difference in meaning between **ci vediamo il tredici** and **ci vediamo alle tredici**?

3 What do you add to **buon** on someone's birthday, at Christmas, to wish them well in their work, on a journey, on a flight and at the weekend?

4 Based on meaning, put into two groups of three **burrasca, pioggia, venticello, rovescio, pioggerella** and **vento**.

5 Using **avere voglia di**, how would you invite two friends to go for a walk on the cliffs?

6 Which of these are you unlikely to use when accepting an invitation? **non vedo l'ora, purtroppo, volentieri.**

7 What are **le ore piccole**? And what can you add to **alle quattro** to emphasise punctuality?

8 In reply to good wishes, how do you say *the same to you*?

9 What are **sagra, scuderia, salire** and **scogliera**?

10 **Forse potrei andare a pesca.** Which word has to change for this to say *Perhaps we could go fishing*?

11 Say the Italian for *Let's* with **noleggiare, esplorare, visitare, organizzare** and **celebrare**? What do they all mean?

12 **Se non .... così indaffarato** busy, **farei il giro del centro storico oggi.** Is the missing word **fossi** or **avessi**?

13 How do **fa freddo** and **è mite** change when referring to last week?

14 Complete the sentence **Il giorno di Natale è il ....**

15 Talking to a couple and therefore using **voi**, how would you say *I'd wait for you if I could*?

16 What does **Chissà?** mean?

17 How do you thank someone for an invitation and say that unfortunately you're already committed?

18 **Che ne dici di giocare a squash domenica alle dieci (il trenta aprile)?** Text a reply saying *I wish! but I can't*, then suggesting midday on the following day.

nove
needs must

Some verbs are more essential than others. If you were to analyse what you say in English over a day or two, you'd probably be amazed at how often the words *must, want, can, may, need, have to, should, could, might, ought* crop up. These are not words you can easily look up in a dictionary: in Italian they're expressed by the three key verbs **volere** *to want*, **dovere** *to have to* and **potere** *to be able to*.

You will probably have come across aspects of them already, associated with practical situations such as:
Vorrei vedere la camera. *I'd like to see the room.*
Devo cambiare treno? *Do I have to change train?*
Posso parcheggiare qui? *Can I park here?*

Too often they stay associated in the mind with these situations and their contribution to everyday conversation gets overlooked — when in reality these verbs are indispensable. They will allow you to voice your wildest desires and your most mundane obligations.
They're easy to use and all three verbs work in the same way. The verb following them is in the infinitive. Information can simply be tacked on to this minus its final **-e**: **vorrei ved**ere *I'd like to see*, **vorrei veder**la *I'd like to see it/ her*. The way the past tenses are used is similar for all three verbs.

Volere è potere *To want is to be able to: Where there's a will there's a way.*

what you want to do

Volere is the verb you use to say what you want to do. It's also how you find out what other people want and is the basis of invitations.

It's irregular in the present tense:

voglio, vuoi, vuole, vogliamo, volete, vogliono

Voglio tornare indietro. *I want to go back.*
Voglio solo aggiungere che ... *I just want to add that ...*
Non vogliamo mai partire. *We don't ever want to leave.*
Se vuole, andiamo stasera. *If you want to, we'll go tonight.*
Vuoi venire anche tu? *Do you want to come as well?*
Volete riposarvi un po'? *Do you want to rest for a while?*

You can use it in the future too:

vorrò, vorrai, vorrà, vorremo, vorrete, vorranno

Vorrò fare una foto di gruppo. *I shall want to take a group photo.*
Tu non vorrai sistemarti mai! *You'll never want to settle down!*
Non so che cosa vorrà fare Lucia. *I don't know what Lucia will want to do.*
Non vorremo mai ritornare. *We will never want to go back.*

I want can sound a bit blunt or demanding. While English uses *would like* instead, Italian softens it by using the conditional of **volere**.

vorrei, vorresti, vorrebbe, vorremmo, vorreste, vorrebbero

Vorrei proporre un brindisi. *I'd like to propose a toast.*
Vorrei correre una maratona. *I'd like to run a marathon.*
Non vorresti sapere di più? *Wouldn't you like to know/to find out more?*
Vorremmo evitare i soliti luoghi. *We'd like to avoid the usual places.*
Vorreste fare due passi? *Would you like to go for a little walk?*
Vorrebbero venire anche loro? *Would they like to come as well?*

Adding **bene** to **volere** alters its meaning: **ti voglio bene** *I love you.* The shortcut **tvtb** stands for **ti voglio tanto bene** *I love you so much.* **Amare**, which also means *to love*, is more intense: **ti amo** *I love you*; **amo i miei** *I love my family*, **amo questo paese** *I love this country.*

When talking about the past, English uses *wanted*, while Italian uses both the imperfect **volevo** and the perfect **ho voluto** according to circumstances.

The imperfect, which is regular, is probably the tense you'll use more often. It's about wanting to do something over an indeterminate period of time.

Volevo mostrarti questo. *I wanted to show this to you.*
Da bambino volevo **fare il calciatore.** *When I was a kid I wanted to be a footballer.*
Non vol**e**vano v**i**vere all'**e**stero. *They didn't want to live abroad.*
Mia figlia non voleva **mai andare a scuola.** *My daughter never wanted/used to want to go to school.*

The perfect tense expresses *have wanted to*, and is also how to express a one-off desire or urge which took place at a specific moment in time; the outcome is usually known. The past participle of **volere** is **voluto**.

Stamattina, alle nove, ho voluto **telefonarle ma lei non c'era.** *This morning, at 9 o'clock, I wanted to phone you, but you weren't there.*
Ho voluto **controllare s**u**bito.** *I wanted to check straightaway (and I did).*
Abbiamo voluto **scoprire di più.** *We wanted to find out more (and we did).*
Non l'abbiamo voluto **svegliare.** *We didn't want to wake him up (and we didn't).*
Ho **sempre** voluto **vedere l'aurora boreale.** *I have always wanted to see the northern lights.*
Abbiamo **sempre** voluto **viaggiare.** *We've always wanted to travel.*

avere or essere in the perfect tense?
I wanted to can be **ho voluto** or **sono voluto/a**. But **sono voluto** is only used if the following verb normally takes **essere**, and even then you'll often hear **ho voluto** used instead.
Lucia ha voluto/è voluta **partire da sola.** *Lucia wanted to leave by herself.*
Hanno voluto/Sono voluti **rimanere dai nonni.** *They wanted to stay at their grandparents'.*

This applies also to **potere** and **dovere** and to other past tenses such as the pluperfect and past conditional, e.g. **Avrei voluto sapere** *I would have liked to know*, **Sarei potuto andare** *I could have gone.*

what you have to do

It sounds surprising, but *must, have to, ought, should, need to, had to, be supposed to, be obliged to, be required to, be meant to* can all be conveyed by the various tenses of **dovere**, with some overlap between them.

The present tense is irregular:

devo, devi, deve, dobbiamo, dovete, devono

Devo controllare. *I must check.*
Devo ammettere che rimango stupito. *I have to admit I'm amazed.*
Non devi ricordarmelo! *You don't need to remind me (of it)!*
Lei deve confermare la data. *You must confirm the date.*
Deve sapere se sono arrivati. *She has to know if they're arrived.*
Dobbiamo essere in aeroporto due ore prima del volo. *We need to be at the airport two hours before the flight.*
A che ora dovete partire voi? *What time do you have to leave?*

In the future, it can mean *will have to* or *be going to have to*:

dovrò, dovrai, dovrà, dovremo, dovrete, dovranno

Dovrò controllare. *I will have to check.*
Dovrai assolutamente smettere di fumare. *You really are going to have to quit smoking.*
Dovremo stare attenti. *We'll have to/we're going to have to be careful.*
Dovrai/Dovrà/Dovrete scegliere i migliori. *You'll have to choose the best.*

Using the conditional changes the meaning to *ought to, should, be supposed to* or *be meant to*:

dovrei, dovresti, dovrebbe, dovremmo, dovreste, dovrebbero

You'll often hear **proprio** *really* used with this.
Dovrei proprio controllare. *I really ought to check.*
Dovrei proprio sbrigarmi. *I really should hurry.*
Non so cosa dovrei fare. *I don't know what I'm supposed to do.*
Forse dovresti scusarti. *Maybe you ought to apologise.*
Lei non dovrebbe esitare. *You shouldn't hesitate.*
Dovremmo chiedere perché no. *We should ask why not.*
Credo che dovreste chiamare Gianni. *I think you're meant to call Gianni.*
Dovrebbero richiedere un rimborso. *They ought to ask for a refund.*

When talking about the past, Italian uses the imperfect **dovevo** (regular) and the perfect **ho dovuto**. The rationale is similar to **volere** (page 125), with the imperfect used most of the time but the perfect needed for a one-off event.

The imperfect translates *had to, used to have to, should have* and *was meant/supposed to*:
Ogni giorno dovevo aspettare a lungo. *I had to wait ages every day.*
Dovevamo andare in vacanza l'anno scorso ma ... *We were meant to be going/We should have gone on holiday last year but ...*
Non dovevi arrivare oggi. *You weren't supposed to arrive today.*
Doveva andare spesso a Cuba? *Did you have to go to Cuba often?*
Dovevate chiamarmi ieri. *You were supposed/meant to call me yesterday.*

... while the perfect translates *had to* and *have had to*. In the perfect, you'll come across **ho dovuto** and **sono dovuto** for *I had to*, but **ho dovuto** is the more common.
Cos'hai dovuto fare? *What did you have to do?*
Ho dovuto controllare l'orario. *I had to check the timetable.*
Sono dovuto/a partire subito. *I had to leave straightaway.*
Siamo dovuti andare a piedi. *We had to/were obliged to walk.*
Ha dovuto ricominciare? *Have you had to start again?*
Quanto avete dovuto pagare? *How much did you have to pay?*

It's very common to want to say *I should have, I ought to have*. In Italian, you use the infinitive of what you ought to have done after:

avrei, avresti, avrebbe, avremmo, avreste, avrebbero dovuto

Avrei dovuto controllare. *I should have checked.*
Non avremmo dovuto chiedere. *We ought not to have asked.*
Avresti dovuto lasciare un messaggio. *You ought to have left a message.*
Avrebbero dovuto sospettare. *They should have suspected.*

Listen out for **bisogna/bisognava** *it is/was necessary*. It can often be used in similar circumstances to **dovere** for *I, we, you, they* or *one*.
Bisogna stare attenti. *One needs to be careful.*
Bisogna arrivarci presto. *We should get there early.*
Bisogna riflettere un po'. *I need to think about it.*
Bisognava leggere le istruzioni. *They should have read the instructions.*

wish lists

What you want to do and what you have to do are often very different things. **Volere** is the verb for wishes and dreams, whether the decisive **voglio** *I want to* or the more aspirational **vorrei** *I'd like to.*

There may be things that you want to do in the short to medium term.
cambiare lavoro *change job*
perdere dieci chili *lose ten kilos*
mettermi in forma *get fit*
prendere la patente di guida *get a driving licence*
correre la maratona in quattro ore *run a marathon in four hours*
visitare Berlino *visit Berlin*
andare negli Stati Uniti *go to the States*

List five things you want to do in the next 12 months. If they involve going to places, **to** is *in* with continents, most countries, regions and large islands: *in Australia, in Italia, in Abruzzo, in Cornovaglia* Cornwall, *in Sardegna.*

But it's *in + the* for the UK: *nel Regno Unito,* and for countries with a plural name: *negli Stati Uniti ...* and *a* with cities, towns, and anything smaller: *a Roma, a Bergamo, a Notting Hill, a Capri.*

Think long term. Are any of the following on your *bucket list* **lista di cose da fare prima di morire** lit. *list of things to do before you die?*

nuotare coi delfini *swim with dolphins*
visitare Angkor Wat in Cambogia *visit Angkor Wat in Cambodia*
circumnavigare capo Horn in barca a vela *sail round Cape Horn*
vedere il sole di mezzanotte in Antartide *see the midnight sun in Antarctica*
osservare il sorgere del sole all'equatore *watch the sun rise at the equator*
scalare il Kilimangiaro *climb Kilimanjaro*
fare un safari nel Masai Mara *go on safari in the Masai Mara*
fare trekking in Mongolia *go trekking in Mongolia*
fare immersioni nella Grande Barriera Corallina *dive in the Great Barrier Reef*

Create your bucket list in Italian, looking up any words you need, and say out loud what's on it.

... and to-do lists

Dovere brings you back down to earth. Use **devo** *I must, I need to* for the things you really have to get on with, such as:

trovare le scarpe da ginnastica *find my trainers*
comprare del latte *buy some milk*
fare benzina *put petrol in the car*
ricaricare il telefonino *charge my mobile*
ritirare dei soldi al bancomat *get some money from the cash machine*
portare a passeggio il cane *take the dog for a walk*
pagare le bollette *pay the bills*
rinnovare l'assicurazione dell'auto *renew the car insurance*
mandare un biglietto di auguri a Mamma *send Mum a birthday card*
telefonare a Tommasina *phone Tommasina*
dire a Davide che domani c'è l'allenamento *tell Davide there's training tomorrow*

In Italian you send *to* someone, phone *to* someone and tell *to* someone.

Use **dovrei** for the things you ought to do. You can add **proprio** *really* for the items that rank somewhere in between **devo** and **dovrei**.

iscrivermi in palestra *join a gym*
finire il modulo/il compito *finish the module/the assignment*
sistemare il capanno *sort out the shed*
contattare Luca *get in touch with Luca*
scongelare il congelatore *defrost the freezer*
prendere un appuntamento dal dentista *make a dental appointment*
mangiare di meno *eat less*
andare a trovare mia zia *go and see my aunt*
essere più severo coi miei figli *be stricter with my children*
fregarmene del giudizio degli altri *not care what other people think*

 Most of us conduct a running commentary in our heads, reminding ourselves of what we need to do, who we need to get in touch with, what we might like to do at the weekend and so on. If you regularly use Italian for this inner monologue, you'll find that it becomes a habit, one which results in a step-change in your progress. Try adding simple comments and questions: How interesting, When's Will's birthday?, What a good idea. It goes without saying that, when you're on your own, you can do this out loud.

what you can do

You use **potere** to say what you can do. It also translates *may* in a question.

Like **volere** and **dovere**, it's irregular in the present tense.

posso, puoi, può, possiamo, potete, possono

Posso offrire una prospettiva alternativa. *I can offer a different perspective.*
Posso vedere? *Can I see? May I see?*
Posso proporre un brindisi? *May I propose a toast?*
Puoi darmi un passaggio? *Can you give me a lift?*
Lei mi può spiegare come funziona? *Can you explain to me how it works?*
Si può sempre dire no. *You/One can always say no.*
Non si può sempre vincere. *We/One can't always win.*
Possiamo offrirvi un bicchiere di vino? *Might we offer you a glass of wine?*
Potete aiutarmi a tradurre questo? *Can you help me translate this?*

You'll often hear **ti dispiace se?** *do you mind if?* used instead of *can/may?* For **lei** and **voi** you replace **ti** with **le** or **vi**.
Ti dispiace se chiudo la porta? *May I/Do you mind if I close the door?*
Le dispiace se ci sediamo qui? *May we/Do you mind if we sit here?*
Vi dispiace se metto qui la valigia? *Can I/Do you mind if I put my bag here?*

The future of **potere** can mean *will be able to, be going to be able to* or *will be allowed to*:

potrò, potrai, potrà, potremo, potrete, potranno

Non potrò aspettare a lungo. *I'm not going to be able to wait for long.*
Chissà quando potrò riprovarci. *Who knows when I'll be able to try again.*
Magari potrai dormire in aereo. *Perhaps you will be able to sleep on the plane.*
Potrà parcheggiare qui di fronte? *Will you/he/she be able to park opposite?*
Solo così potremo scoprire la verità. *Only in this way will we be able to discover the truth.*

Could is a word to look out for because it has several meanings.

It can mean **would be able to**: the conditional, which is also translated *might*.

potrei, potresti, potrebbe, potremmo, potreste, potrebbero

Non potrei essere più felice. *I couldn't be happier.*
Potrei parlarti? *Could/Might I speak to you?*
Forse potreste aiutarci? *Maybe you could help us?*
Potremmo invitare gli altri. *We would/might be able to invite the others.*
Potremmo cenare un po' prima. *We could/might have dinner a bit earlier.*

When *could* means **was able to/used to be** able to, you use the imperfect:

potevo, potevi, poteva, potevamo, potevate, potevano

Potevo vedere il mare dal terrazzo. *I could see the sea from the terrace.*
Potevi sentire tutto? *Were you able to hear everything?*
Ho chiesto se potevo fare una foto. *I asked if I might take a photo.*
Potevamo fare festa tutta la notte. *We used to be able to party all night.*
Non potevamo aspettarci di più. *We couldn't have expected more.*

The perfect tense **avere + potuto; essere + potuto/a, potuti/e**, is also translated *could* or *was able to* in English.

Ho potuto solo sognare. *I could only dream.*
Non ho potuto farne a meno. *I couldn't help it.*
Io non sono potuto/a entrare. *I couldn't get in.*
Io non sono potuto entrare. *I couldn't get in.*

Look out for the following, where *can/could* are **not** translated by **potere**.
When *can* means *manage to*, **riuscire a** is often used.
Non riesco ad aprirlo. *I can't open it.*
Non riesce a dormire. *He/She can't sleep.*
Non riuscivano a nascondere la delusione. *They couldn't/weren't able to hide their disappointment.*

When *can* means *know how to*, **sapere** is used:
Sanno nuotare? *Can they swim?*
Non importa se non sai giocare. *It doesn't matter if you can't play.*
Non sapeva né leggere né scrivere. *She couldn't read or write.*

(More on **sapere** on the next page.)

knowing someone or something

Sapere and **conoscere** both mean *to know* but they're not interchangeable. **Sapere** means *to know how to do something* or *to know a fact*; **conoscere** *to know* or *get to know a person, to be familiar with a place or a concept*.

present

sapere: so, sai, sa, sappiamo, sapete, sanno
conoscere: conosco, conosci, conosce, conosciamo, conoscete, conoscono

Sa cucinare? *Can he cook? Does he know how to cook?*
So che vivono qui vicino. Lo so. *I know that they live round here. I just know (it).*
Come lo sai? *How do you know?*
Sai dove? Sai l'indirizzo? *Do you know where? Do you know the address?*

Non conosce i miei colleghi. *He/She doesn't know my colleagues.*
Vorrei conoscere Elena. *I'd like to meet/get to know Elena.*
Conosco bene Londra. *I know London well.*

imperfect

Ieri sapevo dove trovarli. *Yesterday I knew where to find them.*
Non sapevo se ridere o piangere. *I didn't know whether to laugh or cry.*
Lo sapevi già? *You already knew?*

Conoscevo tutte le scorciatoie. *I knew/used to know all the shortcuts.*
Da studente conoscevo bene Londra. *When I was a student I knew London well.*

perfect

Sapere translates *learnt/heard/found out* while **conoscere** translates *met*:
Ho saputo la verità ieri. *I learnt/found out the truth yesterday.*
Come hai saputo dove trovarmi? *How did you find out where to find me?*
Abbiamo sempre saputo perché. *We've always known why.*

Come hai conosciuto l'amore della tua vita? *How did you meet the love of your life?*
Ho conosciuto Stefano tre anni fa; io avevo vent'anni. *I met Stefano three years ago; I was twenty.*
Non conoscevo l'hotel: l'ho conosciuto tramite internet. *I didn't know the hotel: I found (out about) it on the internet.*

other uses of volere, dovere and potere

Volere and **dovere** aren't always followed by an infinitive: they can both be followed by a noun.

Voglio un caffè. *I want a coffee.*
Vogliamo qualcosa di abbordabile. *We want something affordable.*
Vorrei un boccone. *I fancy a bite to eat.*
Vorremmo il risotto con salsiccia. *We'd like the risotto with sausage.*
Da bambina volevo un cane. *When I was little I wanted a dog.*
Ho sempre voluto una macchina sportiva. *I've always wanted a sports car.*

Dovere means *to owe* as well as *to have to*.
Ti devo una birra. *I owe you a beer.*
Quanto le devo? *How much do I owe you?*
Mario mi doveva cento euro. *Mario owed me 100 euros.*
Gli dobbiamo un grosso favore. *We owe him a big favour.*

Il volere, il dovere and il potere are all nouns, meaning *will/wish/ wishes*; *duty/obligation*; *power*.
Si è sposata contro il volere della famiglia. *She married against the wishes of her family.*
Il volere dei cittadini sarà rispettato. *The will of the people will be respected.*
Hanno ignorato il volere dei figli. *They ignored the wishes of their children.*

Fai il tuo dovere. *Do your duty. Do what you have to do.*
Lidia non ha un grande senso del dovere. *Lidia doesn't have a strong sense of duty.*
Abbiamo tutti i diritti e i doveri. *All of us have rights and obligations.*

Lo sport ha il potere di unire la gente. *Sport has the power to unite people.*
Mia madre deve avere poteri soprannaturali! *My mother must have supernatural powers!*
Cerca il potere assoluto ad ogni costo. *He's looking for absolute power at any price.*

talking the talk

Renzo	Cos'hai fatto ieri sera?
Daniela	Niente di interessante. Sono rimasta a casa. Ho dovuto pagare le bollette. Dovrei anche rinnovare l'assicurazione dell'auto. Tu?
Renzo	Sono rimasto a casa anch'io – non volevo uscire. Ho aggiunto due cose alla mia lista.
Daniela	Quale lista?
Renzo	La lista di cose da fare prima di morire. Cosa c'è sulla tua?
Daniela	Io non ho una lista. Però mi interessa l'Antartide. Vorrei andarci. Voglio vedere il sole di mezzanotte ... e i pinguini.
Renzo	Bello! Luisa – la sorella di Virginia – è stata in Antartide.
Daniela	Dove ha conosciuto Piero Santorio?
Renzo	Mah! Non lo so. Aspetta ... si sono conosciuti a Milano credo.
Daniela	Tu lo conosci?
Renzo	Santorio? L'ho conosciuto al matrimonio di Angelo e Virginia. ... Ma perché ti interessa tanto?
Daniela	Boh .... per curiosità. Dove hai conosciuto tua moglie ... la tua ex-moglie?
Renzo	Ci siamo conosciuti all'università. Eravamo molto giovani. Il matrimonio è durato solo due anni. E tu, come hai conosciuto l'amore della tua vita?
Daniela	Non l'ho ancora conosciuto ... comunque ...
Daniela	Allora, andiamo?
Renzo	Posso proporre una cosa?
Daniela	Dimmi.
Renzo	Ho voglia di fare due passi; voglio vedere il porto. Vuoi venire anche tu?
Daniela	Non posso. Devo andare in città. Magari un altro giorno.
Renzo	Non potresti andarci un po' più tardi?
Daniela	Magari fosse così facile.
Renzo	Vuoi un caffè prima di andare via? Potrei offrirti un bicchiere di vino al bar?
Daniela	Grazie ma dovrei sbrigarmi. Ciao ciao. A domani.
Renzo	A domani. Beh ... tanto vale tornare a casa.

verb practice 6

1   Sort these into three groups under the headings **volere**, **potere**, **dovere**:
    ought, could, was supposed to, wanted to, may, must, should have, would like to, can, had to, used to have to, used to be able to

> For the following activities you need to be familiar with the various endings of **volere**, **potere**, **dovere**.

2   Many of the examples have focused on *I*, *we* and *you*. Now it's time to practise talking about other people.

   • Convert at least 12 of the *I/we* … examples to mean *he/she* …
     by changing the verb ending, e.g. **dovrei controllare** *I ought to check* → **dovrebbe controllare** *he/she ought to check*. This will help you to remember the words as well as to learn the verb endings.

   • Choose at least six random examples from each of **volere**, **potere**, **dovere** and convert *I/we/you* … to *they* … by changing the verb ending.

3   Fill the gaps with the present tense of **dovere**, **potere** and **volere**. Time yourself — then do this again in a couple of hours' time, again in a day, and again in two days. Come back to it yet again after a week.

a	dovere	lei ………………	voi ………………
b	volere	noi ……………	tu ………………
c	dovere	loro …………	io ………………
d	potere	lui ………………	io ………………
e	volere	tu ………………	loro …………
f	potere	io ………………	noi ……………
g	dovere	tu ………………	noi ……………
h	potere	lei ………………	lui ………………
i	volere	io ………………	voi ………………

4   Have a go at putting the above list in the future, the conditional and the imperfect. Now use a dozen or so to create sentences, and say them out loud.
    The vocabulary in this and previous chapters might come in useful, but you might also like to personalise what you say by looking up some new words.

1 What's the difference between **devo cominciare subito** and **dovrei cominciare subito**?

2 How would you explain that Giorgio has to leave and that he wants to take a group photo?

3 A social media site has a **persone che potresti conoscere** feature. What do you think it's about?

4 What's the Italian for *I've always wanted to travel*?

5 Which of these are not in the conditional: **potrei, dovrebbero, potremo, vorrebbe, dovresti, dovrete, vorremmo, potranno, vorreste, vorrei.**

6 **Imparare** means *to learn*: what's the Italian for *I'd like to learn, I ought to learn, I must learn, I want to learn, I had to learn, I can learn, I could learn*?

7 What two ways are there of saying in Italian *We wanted to explore the surrounding area*?

8 How would you ask someone **(lei)** if they mind if you open the window?

9 Fill the gaps with **so** or **conosco**: non .... l'indirizzo, ... dove lavorano, ... sua sorella, ... perché è qui, ... Luca da tre anni.

10 What English saying expresses **volere è potere**?

11 If you hear **Potrei darti un passaggio alla stazione**, what are you being offered?

12 What does **Rossi non è riuscito a segnare** mean?

13 The verbs *to choose, to explain, to discover, to quit/give up* and *to dream* are all in this chapter and they all begin with the letter **s**. What are they in Italian?

14 How does adding **bene** to **volere** change the meaning, and what does **tvtb** stand for?

15 Identify four pairs of opposites from **sapere, perdere, trascurare, vietare, fingere, vincere, permettere, indovinare** and **curare**. What's the meaning of the one that's left over?

16 What needs to change in **Dovresti assolutamente scusarti** for it to mean *You really will have to apologise*?

17 How would you explain in Italian that you were meant to go on a cruise **(in crociera)** last year but that you had to cancel the booking **(disdire la prenotazione)**? Use *we* in your answer.

dieci
sharing opinions

Whether you're chatting to a neighbour or someone you've met on holiday, socialising with Italian business contacts, taking part in a cultural exchange or meeting your child's new Italian mother-in-law, it's very satisfying to be able to exchange views on anything and everything.

Regardless of whether the subject under discussion is a mutual acquaintance, a local **trattoria**, the state of the beach, international sport or major issues such as climate change or migration, the basic language structures you need are the same. They will allow you to air your views without sounding blunt or over-assertive, and, of course, to invite other people's views.

A point of view becomes much more convincing when it's supported. There are words that make an opinion sound persuasive and self-evident, such as **chiaramente** *clearly* and **ovviamente** *obviously*, but what usually clinches an argument is a solid rationale and/or an impressive statistic or two.

Be prepared: it's useful to recognise the Italian words for major issues. And as a foreign visitor you may well be asked **Cosa pensa della situazione politica da voi?** *What do you think about the political situation in your country?* or, at least as likely, **Per che squadra tifi?** *Which team do you support?*

asking someone's opinion

When you're listening to someone and they look at you and say **non ti pare?**/ **non le pare?**, they're asking for your opinion on the matter.

È splendido, non ti pare? Che voce! *He's amazing, don't you think? What a voice!*
È complicato, non le pare? *It's complicated, don't you think?*
Hanno giocato bene, non vi pare? *They played well, don't you think?*

Another way of asking for someone's view is **Qual è la tua/sua opinione?** Or you can use **secondo** *according to.*
Secondo te, è una buona idea? *Do you think it's a good idea?*
È possibile, secondo lei? *Is it possible, in your opinion?*
Secondo voi due, qual è la migliore soluzione? *According to you two, which is the best solution?*

Alternatives to **secondo** include:
Cosa ne pensi tu? Cosa ne pensa lei? *What do you think about it?*
A tuo/suo avviso ...? A tuo/suo parere ...? *In your opinion ...?*
A tuo parere, è abbastanza piccante? Cosa ne pensi? *Do you think it's hot enough? What do you reckon?*
La situazione è insopportabile; cosa ne pensa lei? *The situation's intolerable; what do you think about it?*
Vorrei sapere se, a tuo avviso, è accettabile riciclare i regali di Natale. *I'd like to know if you think it's OK to recycle Christmas presents.*

In a discussion you're likely to hear unexpected verb endings because a verb following **credere che** *to believe that* is in the subjunctive (page 140).
Subjunctive endings aren't difficult to remember since the present tense **io**, **tu** and **lei** endings are all the same, while the **loro** ending simply adds **-no**, e.g. **finire** *to finish*: **io/tu/lei finisca, loro finiscano.**

Credi che la dieta includa tutti i nutrienti fondamentali? *Do you believe the diet includes all the essential nutrients?*
Crede che esista vita altrove? *Do you believe that life exists elsewhere?*
Credete che capiscano tutto? *Do you believe they understand everything?*

When **credere** comes last, without **che**, this is not an issue:
È pronto questo, non credi? *This is ready, don't you think?*

saying what you think

The most straightforward way of offering your opinion is to use **a mio parere/secondo me** *in my view*, **direi** *I'd say*, or to put **credo** *I believe*/**penso** *I think* at the end of what you're saying.

Non è adatto, credo. *I don't think it's suitable.*
Sono così pratici, secondo me. *I think they're so handy.*
Secondo la mia modesta opinione, sono tutti pazzi. *In my humble opinion they're all mad.*
È grave, direi. *It's serious, I'd say.*
Non c'è dubbio secondo me. *There's no doubt in my mind.*
A mio parere, è un'opportunità da non perdere. *It's an opportunity not to be missed, if you ask me.*
Inoltre, questa è, secondo me, una partita decisiva. *What's more, this is, in my view, a crucial match.*

Credere in means *to believe in something*:
Credi in te stesso. *Believe in yourself.*
Credo nella libertà di parola. *I believe in free speech.*
Crede fortemente nel karma. *He/She believes strongly in karma.*
Credono negli extraterrestri. *They believe in extraterrestrials.*

As well as **credere che**, phrases such as **ritengo che** *I'm of the opinion that* and **sospetto che** *I suspect that* are followed by the subjunctive (see next page).

Several common verbs have distinctive irregular subjunctive forms:

andare *to go*	vada	**potere** *to be able to*	possa
avere *to have*	abbia	**sapere** *to know*	sappia
dovere *to have to*	debba	**volere** *to want*	voglia
essere *to be*	sia	**fare** *to make, do*	faccia

Credo/Penso che l'idea sia pazzesca. *I believe/think the idea's crazy.*
Ritengo che sia tempo sprecato. *I maintain that it's a waste of time.*
Sono convinto che Paolo possa vincere. *I'm convinced Paolo can win.*
Mio figlio sospetta che abbiano mentito. *My son suspects that they lied.*
Io ritengo che lui sappia già. *I reckon he already knows.*
Non credo che vogliano venire. *I don't think they want to come.*

the subjunctive

Although the subjunctive exists in English: *if I were in charge; she's insisting you be there,* it's no longer heard widely. Italian uses its subjunctive more routinely, not only after words like **credere che** *to believe that* but after most verbs that involve personal attitudes, sentiments, tastes, wishes or opinions, i.e. expressing anything that isn't solid fact.

 Subjunctive verb endings are easy to recognise, especially in the past tenses. If you forget to use them yourself, don't worry: you will still be understood.

recognising the subjunctive

- The **present subjunctive** endings are similar to the present tense. They're included for regular and irregular verbs in the Grammar summary.
- The **imperfect subjunctive** endings (pages 185–192) include a distinctive **-ss-** e.g. **lavorare** → **lavorassi**.
- The **perfect subjunctive** uses the present subjunctive tense of **avere** or **essere** + past participle:
  avere: abbia, abbia, abbia, abbiamo, abbiate, abbiano
  essere: sia, sia, sia, siamo, siate, siano
- The **pluperfect subjunctive** uses the imperfect subjunctive tense of **avere** or **essere** + past participle.
  avere: avessi, avessi, avesse, avessimo, aveste, avessero
  essere: fossi, fossi, fosse, fossimo, foste, fossero

The subjunctive is usually introduced by **che**, which means *that.* Even though *that* is often left out in English, **che** is always needed in Italian.

When the verb before **che** is in the present tense, you use the present or the perfect subjunctive:
Credo che Marco parta oggi. *I believe Marco's leaving today.*
Spero che non piova. *I hope it doesn't rain/it's not raining.*
Suppongo che arrivino in ritardo. *I suppose they'll arrive late.*
Immagino che tutto sia pronto. *I imagine everything's ready.*
È preferibile che vada io. *It's better that I should go.*
È importante che ci sia Salvatore. *It's important that Salvatore be there.*

Penso che Marco sia già partito. *I think Marco's already left.*
Dubito che Luisa l'abbia visto. *I doubt whether Luisa has seen him.*
Può darsi che abbia perso l'altro. *It may be that he's lost the other one.*

When the verb before **che** is in the conditional or a past tense, you use the imperfect or the pluperfect subjunctive:
Vorrei che tu fossi qui con noi. *I wish you were here with us.*
Vorrei che tornasse. *I'd like him to come back.*
Pensavo che fosse gratuito. *I thought it was free.*

Era probabile che Marco fosse già partito. *Marco had probably left already.*
Dubitavo che Luisa l'avesse visto. *I doubted that Luisa had seen him.*
Pensavo che avessero capito. *I thought they had understood.*

The pluperfect subjunctive is used after **se** to say *if I had*:
se avessi voluto *if I'd wanted*
se l'avessi visto *if I'd seen him*
se solo avessi saputo *if only I'd known*
se fossi andato **io** *if I'd gone*
se non fossi stato **convinto** *if I hadn't been convinced*

The subjunctive is triggered not only by **che** but by words like:
benché *although* and **purché** *provided that*, **affinché** *so that*, **a meno che non** *unless*.
Vengo anch'io a meno che non piova. *I'll come too unless it's raining.*
È molto bravo benché non lo sappia. *He's very good even though he doesn't know it.*
Le dico questo affinché capisca il contesto. *I'm telling you this so that you understand the background.*

It's also used with superlatives:
Davvero uno dei migliori gelati che abbia mai mangiato. *Truly one of the best ice creams I've ever eaten!*
Il letto era il più grande che avessimo mai visto. *The bed was the largest we'd ever seen.*
Sono i peggiori che abbia mai provato. *They're the worst I've ever tried.*

agreeing and disagreeing

How you agree and disagree with someone has all to do with the context of the discussion. There's a world of difference between a dialogue on quality issues in the boardroom, an exchange of views on immigration at a reception and friendly banter about football in the bar.

agreeing

Bravo! *Well said! Hear, hear!*
Esatto. Infatti. Addirittura. *Indeed.*
È vero. Così vero! *It's true. So true!*
Precisamente. *Precisely.* **Assolutamente sì!** *Absolutely so!*
Hai/Ha/Avete ragione. *You're right*
Sono d'accordo con te/lei/voi. *I agree with you.*
Siamo perfettamente d'accordo. *We're completely agreed.*
Siamo in sintonia. *We're on the same wavelength.*
Indubbiamente. *Undoubtedly.*
Senza ombra di dubbio. *Without a shadow of a doubt.*
Sei un genio! *You're a genius!*
Ci hai azzeccato! *You've got it! You've nailed it!*

disagreeing

No, mi dispiace ma non sono d'accordo. *No, I'm sorry but I don't agree.*
Abbiamo una divergenza di opinione. *We have conflicting views.*
C'è stato un (grosso) fraintendimento, pare. *There's been a (huge) misunderstanding, it seems.*
Mi scusi ma lei si è sbagliato a mio parere. *Excuse me but you're mistaken in my view.*
È forse questione di punti di vista. *It's perhaps a matter of opinion.*
Manco per niente! *Nothing of the sort!*
Ma per carità! Stai scherzando? *For goodness' sake! Are you kidding?*
Ma dai ... che sciocchezze! *Oh, come on ... what nonsense!*
Stupidaggini! *Rubbish!*

Anch'io *so do I, me too* and neanch'io *neither do I* are indispensable little phrases. You can use them on their own or within a sentence.
Anch'io penso che Marco abbia ragione. *I too think Marco's right.*
L'avrei detto anch'io. *I would have said it too.*
Non lo so neanch'io. *I don't know either.*

making a case

Phrases such as **per esempio** *for example*, **in primo luogo** *first of all*, **in secondo luogo** *secondly*, **in conclusione** *to conclude* help to structure a discussion.

You'll also need words like **perché** *because*, and **dato che, siccome, dal momento che, visto che** *given that, since, as*.

A mio parere, guadagnano un sacco perché sono davvero bravi. *In my view, they earn loads because they're really talented.*
Dal momento che sono così bravi, meritano i soldi che guadagnano. *Since they're so talented they deserve the money they earn.*
Non credo che sia giusto perché non pagano le tasse. *I don't think it's right because they don't pay taxes.*
Siccome non abbiamo cifre precise, è difficile sapere. *As we don't have precise figures, it's hard to know.*
È accettabile, credo, visto che ci sono vantaggi ambientali. *I believe it's acceptable as there are environmental advantages.*
Rimango zitto perché la questione è complessa. *I'm keeping quiet because the issue is a complex one.*
Lo posso confermare dato che ho esperienza personale del settore. *I can confirm this given that I have personal experience of the sector.*

Perché, dato che, etc. aren't restricted to discussing major issues:
Voglio andarci perché ho letto che è proprio una meraviglia. *I want to go there because I've read that it's really wonderful.*
Dobbiamo andare a piedi perché non ho fatto benzina. *We'll have to walk because I haven't put petrol in the car.*
Preferisco stare a casa oggi perché Livia non sta bene. *I'd rather stay at home today because Livia's not feeling well.*
Siccome Livia non sta bene, preferisco stare a casa con lei. *Since Livia's not feeling well, I'd rather stay at home with her.*
È curioso, secondo me, dato che lui non conosce Salvatore. *It's odd, in my opinion, bearing in mind that he doesn't know Salvatore.*
Visto che fa così caldo, occorre un posto all'ombra. *As it's so hot, we need a place in the shade.*
Dal momento che non ho ancora visto il menù, non ho scelto. *Given that I haven't seen the menu yet, I haven't chosen.*
Dato che ho dimenticato la password, non posso trovare l'indirizzo. *Since I've forgotten the password, I can't find the address.*

what do *you* think?

Secondo me ... *In my opinion ...*
    il governo dovrebbe ... *the government ought to ...*
    ogni individuo potrebbe ... *every individual could ...*
    le comunità devono ... *communities must ...*

 Give your opinion (out loud) on some major issues, mixing and matching the above cues with some of the verbs and topics below. Vary what you say by using *a mio parere* **in my view**, or include *credo* I **believe**/*penso* I **think** at the end of the sentence. Try alternatives for *governo, individuo* and *comunità*, and look up any words that aren't included but that you feel strongly about.

word bank

affrontare *to tackle*
aiutare *to help*
aumentare *to increase*
concentrarsi su *to focus on*
contribuire a *to contribute to*
dare un giro di vite su *to clamp down on*
denunciare *to report*
eradicare *to eradicate*
ignorare *to ignore*
imporre *to impose*
legittimare *to legalise*
migliorare *to improve*
proibire *to ban*
promuovere *to boost*
proteggere *to protect*
riciclare *to recycle*
ridurre *to reduce*
sconfiggere *to defeat*
sostenere *to support*
sviluppare *to develop*

la lotta per/contro *the fight for/against*
la sicurezza *security*
l'ordine pubblico *law and order*
l'estremismo *extremism*
il crimine informatico *cybercrime*
il furto d'identità *identity theft*
il traffico di droga *drug trafficking*
la tossicodipendenza *drug addiction*
il tossico *drug addict*
l'ambiente (m) *environment*
le energie rinnovabili *renewable energies*
il riscaldamento globale *global warming*
l'esplorazione spaziale *space exploration*
l'economia *economy*
le imposte *taxes*
l'elusione (f) **fiscale** *tax avoidance*
lo stipendio minimo *minimum wage*
il sussidio (statale) *(state) benefits*
i diritti umani *human rights*
i diritti degli animali *animal rights*
le pari opportunità *equal opportunities*
la migrazione *migration*
legale *legal*, **abusivo/clandestino** *illegal*

numbers and statistics in conversation

Statistics create the impression that you really know what you're talking about. If you need a reminder of Italian numbers, go to page 194.

You can introduce your figures with:

Secondo i dati più recenti ... *According to the latest figures ...*
I dati/I fatti dimostrano che ... *The data/facts show that ...*
Le cifre rivelano che ... *The figures reveal that ...*
Il fatto è che ... *The fact is that ...*
È un dato di fatto che ... *It's a fact/a given that ...*

È un dato di fatto che costa più di cinquecento mila euro. *It's a fact that it's costing more than 500,000 euros.*
Il fatto è che lo stipendio minimo è di quindici euro all'ora. *The fact is that the minimum wage is 15 euros an hour.*
Lo Stadio Olimpico di Roma può ospitare più di ottantamila spettatori. *The Olympic Stadium in Rome can hold more than 80,000 spectators.*
Secondo il verbale, c'erano ventun persone alla riunione di giovedì. *According to the minutes, there were 21 people at Thursday's meeting.*
Le cifre dimostrano che meno di cinquanta persone sono scappate. *The figures show that fewer than 50 people escaped.*
Secondo Giampaolo, hanno vinto ventisei milioni di sterline. *According to Giampaolo, they won 26 million pounds.*

% is **per cento** and percentages start with **il**: **il venticinque per cento** *25%*, **il cinquanta per cento** *50%*:
Contiene meno del dieci per cento **di grassi.** *It contains less that 10% fat.*
Offre uno sconto fino al venti per cento. *He's offering up to 20% discount.*
I dati dimostrano un aumento del cinque per cento **rispetto al 2016.** *The figures show an increase of 5% compared to 2016.*
I dati più recenti dimostrano che l'inflazione annuale è dello zero virgola tre per cento. *The latest data show that annual inflation is 0.3%.*
La banca prevede una crescita tra il due virgola cinque **e il tre per cento.** *The bank is predicting growth of between 2.5% and 3.0%.*
Questo è al cento per cento **biologico.** *This is 100% organic.*

Alongside absolute numbers, Italian has words for approximate numbers.

È andato a Roma per un paio di mesi. *He's gone to Rome for a couple of months.*
Sono qui per una decina di giorni. *I'm here for ten days or so.*
Ci sono stata parecchie volte: una dozzina di volte forse. *I've been there several times: maybe a dozen times.*
Ci vediamo fra una ventina di minuti. *See you in about twenty minutes.*
Dimostra una trentina di anni ... invece ne ha 56! *She looks about 30 but she's 56!*
Abbiamo visto una cinquantina di elefanti. *We saw about 50 elephants.*
Ho letto un'ottantina di pagine, credo. *I think I've read 80 pages or so.*
Sono arrivati un centinaio di profughi. *About 100 refugees have arrived.*
C'erano centinaia di tifosi in città. *There were hundreds of fans in town.*
Ieri c'era/c'erano un migliaio di turisti in centro città. *There were about a thousand tourists in the town centre yesterday.*
Vedi gli storni, ce ne sono tantissimi − migliaia direi. *Look at the starlings, there are so many of them − thousands I'd say.*
Che schifo ... milioni di mosche. *How disgusting ... millions of flies.*

Quarantina is the origin of the English *quarantine*. During the Black Death, ships arriving in Venice had to lie at anchor for 40 days to ensure they didn't bring the plague into the city.

Ordinals, i.e. *first, second, third*, etc. (page 195) are adjectives so when they're used with a noun, the endings have to agree.

Durante la seconda guerra mondiale ... *During the second world war ...*
È la sua terza moglie. *She's his third wife.*
Il Leone è il quinto segno zodiacale. *Leo is the fifth sign of the zodiac.*
Rosina è arrivata all'ottavo mese di gravidanza. *Rosina's reached the eighth month of her pregnancy.*
Oggi celebra il suo ottantesimo compleanno. *It's his 80th birthday today.*
Ci sono riusciti al decimo tentativo. *They were successful at the tenth attempt.*
Questa serie è la quindicesima e l'ultima. *This series is the 15th and the last.*
È arrivato ventisettesimo alla maratona di Londra. *He came 27th in the London marathon.*
Ha smarrito gli occhiali per l'ennesima volta. *She's lost her glasses for the umpteenth time.*

more or less

There's no Italian equivalent of *-er* in words like *higher, easier, richer* — you use **più** *more* + the adjective.

Questo puzzle è più facile. *This puzzle is easier.*
Laura è più giovane e più snella. *Laura's younger and slimmer.*
I rischi sono più alti. *The risks are higher.*
Sei più paziente di me. *You're more patient than me.*

There's no equivalent of *-est* either:
È il centro commerciale più grande d'Europa. *It's the biggest shopping mall in Europe.*
L'allerta terrorismo è al livello più alto. *The terror alert is at the highest level.*
Lei è, senza ombra di dubbio, la più brava. *She is, without a shadow of a doubt, the most able.*

Meno *less* works in the same way.
Sei meno paziente di me. *You're less patient than me.*
È meno ricco di suo padre. *He's not as rich as his father.*
Questo corso di golf è meno stimolante. *This golf course is less challenging.*
È il meno carismatico di tutti. *He's the least charismatic of all.*
Gli hotel sono i meno cari. *The hotels are the least expensive.*
È la persona meno critica che conosca. *He/She's the least judgemental person I know.*

> **Più** and **meno** aren't necessarily followed by an adjective: they can be followed by a number, a noun or an adverb.
> **Hanno pagato più di un milione.** *They paid more than a million.*
> **È morto più di sei mesi fa** *He died over six months ago.*
> **Bastano meno di cinquanta euro.** *Less than 50 euros will do/is enough.*
> **C'è meno rumore qui.** *There's less noise here.*
> **Ci sono meno zanzare qui.** *There are fewer mosquitoes here.*
> **Corre meno rischi adesso.** *He takes fewer risks now.*
> **Bene, lo dico più chiaramente.** *OK, I'll say it more clearly.*
> **Ci vengono meno spesso.** *They come here less often.*

The Italian for *better/best* and *worse/worst* don't use **più** and **meno**.

Questo sito è migliore; anzi è il migliore. *This site is better; in fact it's the best.*

È la migliore cucina del mondo. *It's the best food in the world.*

Questo qui spiega meglio cosa fare. *This one explains better what to do.*

La previsione è peggiore. *The forecast is worse.*

Questa crisi è la peggiore di sempre. *This crisis is the worst ever.*

Sta peggio stamattina. *He's feeling worse this morning.*

Sempre and possibile add weight to comparisons:

La situazione diventa sempre più complicata. *The situation's becoming more and more complicated.*

L'attrazione tra di loro diventa sempre più forte. *The attraction between them is getting stronger and stronger.*

Passo sempre meno tempo in palestra. *I spend less and less time in the gym.*

Ci vado il meno spesso possibile. *I go there as little as possible* (lit. *the least often*).

Ieri il traffico era il peggiore possibile. *Yesterday the traffic was the worst possible/as bad as it could be.*

Many everyday sayings include **più** and **meno**:

Mai più! *Never again!*

Venite al più presto. *Come as soon as you can.*

Ci sarò alle sei al più tardi. *I'll be there at six at the latest.*

Possiamo chiacchierare del più e del meno. *We can chat about this and that.*

Per di più *And what's more* ... **ha più soldi che cervello.** ... *he's got more money than sense* (lit. *brain*).

Meno male! *Just as well!/Thank goodness!*

Practise *più* and *meno* with the adjectives from page 33 and page 36 to describe and compare a few people and places. **Than** is *di* when you're comparing one person or thing with another, as in *Mia madre è più tollerante di mio padre* **My mother is more tolerant than my father.** But when you're comparing words in the same grammatical category, e.g. two adjectives or two verbs, **than** is *che*: *Mio padre è più cinico che tollerante* **My father is more cynical than tolerant;** *Preferirei aspettare che tornare più tardi* **I'd prefer to wait than to come back later.**

talking the talk

Daniela	Vieni?
Renzo	Dove?
Daniela	Al castello. Voglio andarci perché ho letto che è proprio una meraviglia.
Renzo	Va bene ... ma dobbiamo andare a piedi dal momento che non ho fatto benzina.
Daniela	D'accordo. Comunque, non è molto lontano, vero?

Daniela	Bel posto no? Così tranquillo.
Renzo	Davvero. E che panorama!
Daniela	Vuoi un gelato?
Renzo	Preferirei un bicchiere di vino. Conosci il Bar Saverio?
Daniela	Sì, so dove si trova.
Renzo	Andiamoci. Possiamo chiacchierare del più e del meno.

Daniela	Renzo ... voglio spiegarti dove sono andata ieri sera.
Renzo	Non è necessario.
Daniela	A mio parere, ti devo una spiegazione dato che sono andata via così in fretta.
Renzo	Dove sei andata?
Daniela	Da mio cugino ...
Renzo	Beniamino?
Daniela	Sì. Aveva paura.
Renzo	Paura? Perché?
Daniela	Crede che Arturo, un suo vicino di casa, possa essere un tossico. Beniamino l'ha visto con una siringa.
Renzo	Sul serio? Accidenti! Secondo me, la tossicodipendenza è una tragedia
Daniela	Non so che fare ...

1   What word is missing from **senza** .... **di dubbio** for it to mean *without a shadow of a doubt.*

2   If you hear **secondo lei** directed at you, what are you being asked for? What other phrases can you think of with the same meaning?

3   Having started an explanation with **in primo luogo,** how would you introduce your next point?

4   Write in UK figures **sette virgola cinque per cento** and **zero virgola quattro per cento**.

5   How would you express *Hear, hear* in Italian and say you couldn't agree more?

6   What do **fraintendimento, in sintonia, stupidaggini, dimostrare** and **chiacchierare** all mean?

7   Name two ways in addition to **perché** of introducing an explanation to support your opinion.

8   What does **sia** mean in **Lei crede che sia una buona idea?**

9   **Alla gara partecipano una settantina di ragazzi, tra i dodici e i quindici anni di età.** How many youngsters are taking part in the **gara** *race* and how old are they?

10 What's missing from this sequence?

    quarto .... **dodicesimo** .... **ventesimo** ....

11 **Stefano è più giovane di Alessandro e ha due anni più di Orlando.** Who's the youngest of the three boys? What's *youngest* in Italian?

12 What does someone want to know if they ask **Per che squadra tifi?**

13 What fits in the gap to say *hundreds of birds*: .... **di uccelli?**

14 Given that the plural of **un fantasma** *a ghost* is **fantasmi**, how would you ask somebody **(tu)** if they believe in ghosts?

15 How can you exit a discussion tactfully in Italian by saying *We have conflicting views?*

16 What do you think is the difference between **l'evasione fiscale** and **l'elusione fiscale?**

17 Fill the gap in **i nostri progetti stanno diventando** .... **più fattibili** for it to mean *our plans are becoming more and more feasible.*

undici
inside information

There's no better way of finding out about a place than by talking to the locals. They're the ones with inside information about what's available, how to do something, where to buy the best olive oil or a replacement charger for your phone, where to go for healthcare, who's who. And they always know the best places to eat.

Tapping into this local knowledge involves asking questions and explaining why you want the information. The language structures you need work in any context: you simply slot in the relevant vocabulary. Don't forget the strategies on pages 54–55 for making sure that people understand you and that you understand their replies.

An unusual verb ending is likely to be an imperative, which is the structure used to tell someone to do something, to give advice and instructions. If you've come across basic directions such as **Prendi la prima a sinistra** *Take the first on the left* or **Vada sempre dritto** *Go straight on*, then you already have experience of the imperative.

In Italy they say **Chi mangia bene vive bene** *He who eats well lives well*. Food is central to Italian life, and it's much talked about, whether it's sourcing the best items, finding out about what's on offer in a **gastronomia** *deli*, asking how to make something, or just chatting about the food on your plate or on the menu.

what's available

C'è *there is* and ci sono *there are*, are the most basic Italian phrases yet among the most versatile.

You can use them with a noun:
C'è Anna? *Is Anna here?* **C'è il medico?** *Is the doctor there?*
C'è tempo? *Is there time?* **C'è vento?** *Is there wind? Is it windy?*
C'è pane integrale? *Is there wholemeal bread?*
Ci sono altri tipi di farmaci? *Are there other types of medication?*
Non ci sono più amaretti? *Are there no amaretti left?*

... or with da + infinitive:
C'è da mangiare al bar? *Is there food in the bar?*
C'è un mondo/un sacco di cose da fare. *There are loads of things to do.*

They're equally useful in other tenses.

future

Ci sarà **Anna?** *Will Anna be there?*
Ci sarà **da bere per tutti.** *There will be enough to drink for everyone.*
Ci saranno **molti problemi.** *There will be many problems.*
Non ci saranno **Sara e Gianluca.** *Sara and Gianluca won't be there.*

conditional

Ci sarebbe **un rischio?** *Would there be a risk?*
Ci sarebbero **effetti collaterali?** *Would there be side effects?*
Non ci sarebbe **abbastanza spazio.** *There wouldn't be enough room.*

imperfect

Perché c'era **Anna?** *Why was Anna there?*
Non c'era **niente da vedere.** *There was nothing to see.*
C'era **molta gente.** *There were a lot of people there.*
C'erano **molti tifosi inglesi.** *There were many England/English fans.*

perfect

C'è stato **un terremoto.** *There's been an earthquake.*
C'è stata **molta confusione.** *There's been a lot of confusion.*
Ci sono stati **cambiamenti?** *Have there been (any) changes?*
Ci sono state **tantissime discussioni.** *There have been so many discussions.*

someone or something's missing

There isn't and *there aren't* are **non c'è** and **non ci sono**.

Non c'è posto/tempo/traffico. *There's no room/time/traffic.*

Giorgio non c'è. *Giorgio isn't here/there.*

Non ci sono asciugamani. *There aren't any towels.*

Non ci sono i ragazzi? *Aren't the children here?*

Non ce n'è. *There isn't any (of it)/there isn't one (of them).*

Non ce ne sono. *There aren't any (of them).*

There is another common way of expressing a lack of something, using **mancare** *to be missing/lacking*.

Manca qualcosa/qualcuno. *Something/Someone's missing.*

Manca Giorgio. *Giorgio's not here.*

Manca soltanto la torta. *The only thing missing is the cake.*

È perfetto: non manca niente. *It's perfect: there's nothing missing.*

Mancano due bicchieri. *We're two glasses short.*

Mancava atmosfera. *It lacked character.*

Mancava il wifi/l'aria condizionata. *There was no Wi-Fi/air conditioning.*

Mancavano i ragazzi. *The children weren't there.*

Mi manca, which works in a similar way to **mi piace/mi piacciono** page 92, conveys *I'm missing ...* in both a physical and emotional sense:

Mi manca una scarpa. *I'm missing one shoe.*

Gianmarco mi manca molto. *I really miss Gianmarco.*

Ti manca l'Italia? *Do you miss Italy?*

Gli manca la voce. *He's lost his voice.*

Ha nostalgia di casa: la famiglia le manca. *She's homesick: she misses her family.*

Mi mancano il cibo, il clima, gli amici. *I miss the food, the climate, my friends.*

Ci mancano i soldi per andarci. *We don't have the money to go there.*

Vi mancano i figli? *Are you missing the children?*

You use **mancare** to tell someone you're missing them:

Mi manchi. *I miss you.* lit. *You are missing to me.*

Mi manchi tanto. *I miss you so much.*

Mi manchi anche tu. *I miss you too.*

Mi mancate entrambi. *I miss you both.*

finding out how to do something

You can ask how to do just about anything with **Come faccio a ...?** or **Come si fa a ...?** *How do I/you/one go about ...?* Both are followed by an infinitive.

Come faccio a prenotare online? *How do I go about booking online?*
Come faccio ad aggiungere una foto? *How do I add a photo?*
Come faccio a spegnere la luce? *How do I turn the light off?*
Come si fa a connettersi al wifi? *How does one connect to the Wi-Fi?*
Come si fa ad archiviare dati su internet? *How do you store data online?*
Come si fa a noleggiare una bici? *How do you go about renting a bike?*

Come si + third person of a verb, i.e. the one used with **lei**, corresponds to *How does one ... ?* or *How is ... done?*
Come si chiama questo? *What's this called?*
Come si dice ... in italiano? *How do you say ... in Italian?*
Come si esce da qui? *How do you get out of here?*
Come si gioca a bocce? *How do you play boules?*
Come si prepara la pasta fresca? *How do you prepare fresh pasta?*
Come si cambia la batteria? *How does one change the battery?*

When the verb refers directly to something plural, it has a plural ending:
Come si apre questo coso? *How do you open this contraption?*
Come si aprono le ostriche? *How do you open oysters?*
Come si mangia il mango? *How do you eat mango?*
Come si mangiano i litchi? *How do you eat lychees?*

 See how many similar questions you can come up with in just ten minutes. Use a mix of the words in the examples, some of the following words and any other words you know. Don't forget to say the questions out loud.

accendere to switch on, caricare to charge, curare to cure, evitare to avoid, garantire to guarantee, nascondere to hide, noleggiare to hire, recuperare to retrieve, scoprire to find (out), usare to use

il caricabatterie charger, la ciambella doughnut, il guadagno profit, la luce light, la macchinetta coffee maker, il numero number, i postumi della sbornia hangover, gli scacchi chess, il singhiozzo hiccups, il successo success, la tivù televison, la verità truth

asking for advice and information

A simple open question uses a question word (page 27).
Chi devo chiamare? *Who do I need to call?*
Dove si trova l'uscita? *Where's the exit?*
Qual è la data di scadenza? *What's the expiry date?*

When you want your question to sound less abrupt, you can start with:
Mi sai/sa dire ... *Can you tell me; do you know ...*
Qualcuno mi sa dire ... *Can anyone tell me ...*
... without changing anything else.

Mi sa dire cosa è successo? *Can you tell me what (has) happened?*
... qual è la migliore gelateria? *... which is the best ice cream shop?*
... dove trovo un hotspot wifi? *... where I can find a Wi-Fi hotspot?*
... dove possiamo acquistare il formaggio locale? *... where we can get local cheese?*
... quanta gente c'era? *... how many people there were?*
... perché fa questo strano rumore? *... why it's making this funny noise?*

Qualcuno mi sa dire come si arriva allo stadio? *Can anyone tell me how you get to the stadium?*
... qual è il punteggio? *... what the score is?*
... chi ha segnato? *... who scored?*
... perché mancava Giorgio? *... why Giorgio wasn't there?*
... dove trovo il gasolio meno caro? *... where I find the cheapest diesel?*
... a che ora apre la farmacia? *... what time the chemist's opens?*

You need **se** *if* in questions without a question word:
Mi sa dire se c'è qualche novità? *Can you tell me if/whether there's any news?*
Mi sai dire se il Conad vende le maschere da snorkeling? *Can you tell me if/whether Conad* (the supermarket) *sells snorkelling masks?*

Qualcuno mi sa dire se ci sono asciugamani? *Can anyone tell me whether there are any towels?*
Qualcuno mi sa dire se hanno chiamato il medico? *Can anyone tell me if they've called the doctor?*

giving advice and instructions

Official signs telling you to do or not do something use the infinitive:
SPINGERE *PUSH*
TIRARE *PULL*
PERICOLO! NON ENTRARE *DANGER! DO NOT ENTER*
SPEGNERE LE LUCI *SWITCH OFF LIGHTS*
RITIRARE LO SCONTRINO ALLA CASSA *GET YOUR RECEIPT AT THE PAY POINT*

When you're talking to someone, you use a more polite way of giving them advice or instructions and making suggestions: this is called the imperative.

Noi: identical to the present tense unless it's a reflexive verb, which adds **ci**:
Andiamo. *Let's go.* **Restiamo qui.** *Let's stay here.*
Facciamoci un selfie. *Let's take a selfie.*

Voi: identical to the present tense unless it's a reflexive verb, which adds **vi**:
Provate questo dolce: l'ho fatto io. *Try this dessert: I made it myself.*
Chiamate la guardia medica! *Call the emergency services!*
Prendete il farmaco a stomaco pieno. *Take the medicine on a full stomach.*
Divertitevi! *Enjoy yourselves!*
Sbrigatevi! *Hurry up!*
Ricordatevi questo numero. *Remember this number.*
Assicuratevi di avere tempo a disposizione. *Make sure you allow plenty of time.*
Non preoccupatevi. *Don't worry.*

Tu has imperative verb endings, and adds **ti** to a reflexive verb.

-are	-ere	-ire	-ire (-isc verbs)
-a	-i	-i	-isci

Aspetta! *Wait!*
Lascia che ti aiuti. *Let me help you.*
Unisci le due parti. *Join the two parts.*
Calmati! *Calm down!*
Riposati un po'. *Have a little rest.*

But when telling someone you call **tu** *not* to do something, you put **non** in front of the infinitive, not the imperative:
Non dire niente. *Don't say anything.*
Non alzarti troppo presto. *Don't get up too early.*
Non preoccuparti. *Don't worry.*

Lei has imperative verb endings, and adds **si** in front of a reflexive verb:

-are	-ere	-ire	-ire (-isc verbs)
-i	-a	-a	-isca

Cerchi nella borsa. *Have a look in the bag.*
Segua attentamente le istruzioni. *Please follow the instructions carefully.*
Unisca i pezzi. *Join the pieces together.*
Si diverta. *Enjoy yourself.*
Non si aspetti un miracolo! *Don't expect a miracle!*
Non si preoccupi. *Don't worry.*

Predictably, the most commonly used verbs have irregular imperatives, e.g.

	tu	lei	voi	
andare	vai/va'	vada	andate	*go*
avere	abbi	abbia	abbiate	*have*
dare	dai/da'	dia	date	*give*
dire	di'	dica	dite	*tell*
essere	sii	sia	siate	*be*
fare	fai/fa'	faccia	fate	*do*
stare	stai/sta'	stia	state	*stay/be*
tenere	tieni	tenga	tenete	*hold*
uscire	esci	esca	uscite	*go out*
venire	vieni	venga	venite	*come*

Mi raccomando is used often to add weight or urgency to an imperative:
Sbrigati! Mi raccomando! *Do get a move on. Please!*
State attenti, mi raccomando. *For heaven's sake, please take care.*
Chiamami domani, mi raccomando. *Call me tomorrow. OK?*
Non dimentichi il documento d'identità. Mi raccomando. *Don't forget your ID whatever you do.*
Mi raccomando, quando esci chiudi la porta! *Close the door when you go out for pity's sake!*

everyday instructions

You'll come across the imperative in many everyday phrases:

Colga l'attimo! *Seize the moment! Carpe diem.*
Abbia coraggio. *Have courage. Be strong.*
Faccia pure. *Please do. Go ahead. By all means.*
Fai del tuo meglio. *Do your best.*
Fatti gli affari tuoi. *Mind your own business.*
Forza! Fatti animo! *Come on! Cheer up!*
Non farci caso./Non ci faccia caso. *Take no notice. Forget it.*
Metticela tutta! *Give it everything!*
Nessuno si muova! *Nobody move!*
Sta' zitto. *Be quiet.*
Stai lì! *Stay there!*
Tenga il resto. *Keep the change.*
Sii serio! *Be serious!*
Stringi i denti! *Come on! Be strong! Grit your teeth!*
Tenga gli occhi spalancati. *Keep your eyes peeled.*
Mangia bene, ridi spesso, ama molto. *Eat well, laugh often, love a lot.*

... on a computer, which uses **tu**:

Apri *Open*	**Chiudi** *Close*
Clicca su *Click on*	**Condividi** *Share*
Salva *Save*	**Stampa** *Print*

... and in recipes, some of which use **voi**, some **tu** and some the infinitive.

Insaporite con una buona presa di sale, un pizzico di pepe e un pochino di noce moscata grattugiata. *Season with a good pinch of salt, a pinch of pepper and a touch of grated nutmeg.*

Togliete dal forno, fate raffreddare e spolverate di zucchero a velo. *Remove from the oven, cool and dust with icing sugar.*

Imburra e infarina uno stampo da 24 cm. *Butter and flour a 24 cm mould.*
Separa i tuorli dagli albumi. *Separate the egg yolks from the whites.*

Asciugare e adagiare sui piatti la rucola e i pomodorini. *Dry the rocket and the tomatoes and arrange on the plates.*

Inserire in una terrina l'olio, la scorza di limone e la senape. *Put in a mixing bowl the oil, lemon zest and mustard.*

food talk

Food and drink play such a central role in Italian life that it's well worth
having a stock of expressions relating to them.

Ha fame? *Are you hungry?*
Ho fame/sete. *I'm hungry/thirsty.*
Ho una fame da lupi. *I'm famished.*
È ora di pranzo però non ho appetito. *It's lunchtime but I'm not hungry.*
Mi mangerei un cavallo. *I could eat a horse.*
Muoio di sete. *I'm dying of thirst.*
Lei mangia come un uccellino e lui come un lupo *She eats like a little bird
and he eats like a wolf.*
Mi fa venire l'acquolina in bocca. *It's making my mouth water.*

È buono? *Is it good?*
È buonissimo/squisito. *It's very good/superb.*
È gustoso/saporito. *It's tasty/full of flavour.*
Sono ottimi/deliziosi. *They're excellent/delicious.*
È il/la migliore che abbia mai mangiato/bevuto. *It's the best I've ever eaten/
drunk.*
Sono pieno come un uovo. *I'm absolutely full.* lit. *I'm as full as an egg.*
È un po' troppo forte/piccante per me. *It's a bit too strong/spicy for me.*
Non sono abbastanza dolci/salati. *They're not sweet/salty enough.*

Il conto per favore. *The bill please.*
Offro io. *My treat.*
Offriamo noi. *Our treat.*
Questo giro lo pago io. *I'm paying for this round.*
Tocca a me/a noi pagare. *It's my/our turn to pay.*
Facciamo alla romana. *Let's go Dutch. Let's share the cost.*

Some food expressions are not to be taken literally:
Non fare il salame. *Don't be an idiot.* lit. *Don't act like a salami.*
Tutto finisce a tarallucci e vino. *It will all turn out just fine.* lit. *It
all ends with tarallucci biscuits and wine.*
Siamo alla frutta. *All done, we've hit rock bottom, party's over.* lit.
We're at the fruit course.
A tavola non si invecchia. *Time spent eating is time well spent.* lit.
At the table you don't grow old.

health matters

Talking about how you're feeling physically isn't confined to A&E: there are times when it's tactful to explain, for example, why you can't eat something.

Mangia pure! Non ti piace? *Do eat! Don't you like it?*
Sono ... *I'm ...*
>... **diabetico.** ... *diabetic.*
>... **celiaco.** ... *coeliac.*
>... **vegetariano/vegano.** ... *vegetarian/vegan.*
>... **allergico al glutine/al frumento/a ogni tipo di noci.** ... *allergic to gluten/to wheat/to every kind of nut.*
>... **intollerante ai latticini.** ... *intolerant to dairy produce.*

Devo stare attento a quello che mangio. *I have to watch what I eat.*
Contiene arachidi? *Does it contain peanuts?*

Camilla non ha mangiato niente. Non sta bene? *Camilla hasn't eaten a thing. Isn't she well?*
Si sente malissimo. *She feels dreadful.*
Le fa male il dente. *Her tooth hurts.*
Ha la febbre. *She has a temperature.* (more on page 31)
Ha avuto un attacco di emicrania. *She's had a migraine.*
Ha un'intossicazione alimentare. *She has food poisoning.*

Vuoi assaggiare questo vino? *Do you want to try this wine?*
Solo un goccio/un dito/un bicchierino. *Just a drop/a tiny glass.*
Non bevo alcolici. *I don't drink alcohol.*
Prendo farmaci per ... *I take medication for ...*
>... **la pressione alta.** ... *high blood pressure.*
>... **il diabete.** ... *diabetes.*
>... **mal di cuore/disturbi cardiaci.** ... *a heart condition.*

Sono incinta (di cinque mesi). *I'm (five months) pregnant.*

Non ti piacciono le patatine? *Don't you like chips?*
Mi piacciono moltissimo ma sono a dieta. *I love them but I'm on a diet.*
Non mangio quasi niente. *I'm hardly eating anything at all.*
Devo perdere cinque chili entro ottobre. *I need to lose five kilos by October.*

Similarly, you might need to explain why you aren't keen or able to join in. Or why someone else isn't.

Che ne dice di salire al castello? *How about going up to the castle?*
Soffro di artrite. *I suffer from arthritis.*
Mi fanno male le ginocchia quando salgo/scendo le scale. *My knees hurt when I go up/go down steps.*
Mia moglie ha un tendine infiammato. *My wife has an inflamed tendon.*
Abbiamo camminato troppo ieri. *We walked too far yesterday.*
Sono disidratato, credo. *I think I'm dehydrated.*

Non vieni in palestra? Che hai? *Aren't you coming to the gym? What's up?*
Mi sono stirato un muscolo ... *I've pulled a muscle ...*
        ... del polpaccio, dell'inguine. *... in my calf, in my groin.*
Non riesco a piegare il ginocchio. *I can't bend my knee.*
Ho esagerato con l'allenamento ieri. *I overdid the training yesterday.*
Sono stanco morto! *I'm dead tired!*
Sono distrutto! *I'm shattered!*

Manca Pierino. Dov'è? *Pierino's not here. Where is he?*
È stato ricoverato all'ospedale. *He's been taken to hospital.*
Ha avuto un collasso stamattina. *He collapsed this morning.*
Aveva un forte dolore ... *He had a sharp pain ...*
        ... al torace/allo stomaco. *... in his chest/in his stomach.*
C'è stato un incidente. *There was/There has been an accident.*

Andiamo in spiaggia? *Shall we go to the beach?*
Mi fa male la testa. *My head hurts.*
Mi gira un po' la testa. *I feel a bit dizzy.*
Magari ho preso troppo sole ieri. *Maybe I had (lit. took) too much sun yesterday.*
Ho preso una bella scottatura. Guarda! *I'm really sunburnt. Look!*

You don't need the words *my, your, his, her* when you're talking about your body. The structures you use make it clear who it belongs to:
Mi fa male la schiena. *My back hurts.*
Ti fa male la schiena? *Does your back hurt? Is your back hurting?*
Gli/Le fa male la schiena. *His/Her back's hurting.*

wordbank

il cibo *food*

il pasto *meal*
> **un pasto bilanciato/equilibrato** *a balanced meal*
> **un pasto di prima scelta** *a gourmet meal*
> **saltare un pasto** *to skip a meal*
> **gli antipasti** *appetisers, hors d'œuvres* lit. *before meals*
un vino a tutto pasto *a wine that can be drunk throughout the meal*

una dieta ... *a* ... *diet*
> ... **rigida** *strict* ...
> ... **iperproteica** *high-protein* ...
> ... **ricca di grassi** *high-fat* ...
> ... **a basso contenuto di carboidrati** *low-carb* ...

> *la dieta mediterranea*
>
> *Gli elementi principali della dieta mediterranea sono la verdura, la frutta, l'olio di oliva, i cereali poco raffinati, il pane, il pesce e il vino. Si mangia più pesce che carne, e la dieta è povera di grassi saturi, ricca di vitamine e minerali.*

il linguaggio del cibo

Mangiare is by no means the only way to say *to eat* in Italian. **Mangiucchiare** means to eat something half-heartedly, to play with one's food. It can also mean *to eat little and often, to graze*.

Piluccare and **spilluzzicare** mean *to nibble* or *pick at food*, and **uno schizzinoso** is *a fussy eater*: **Mio nipote è così schizzinoso** *My nephew is such a picky eater.*

At the other end of the scale are **divorare** and **trangugiare** *to wolf down*. **Un'abbuffata** is *a feast, a slap-up meal*, while **abbuffarsi di** and **ingozzarsi di** mean *to binge on food*: **A Pasqua mi ingozzo di cioccolata** *At Easter I binge on chocolate.*

To over-indulge on drink is **sbronzarsi** and *a heavy drinking session* is **una sbronza** or **una sbornia**.

Un buongustaio is *a gourmet, a foodie*; **un mangione** is *someone who eats a lot* while **ingordo** and **goloso** mean *greedy*. *A food critic* is **un critico gastronomico**.

talking the talk

Renzo	Ciao Daniela. Ma dove sei? Perché non sei qui?
Daniela	C'è stata un'emergenza. Una crisi.
Renzo	Accidenti! Cosa è successo? Dove sei?
Daniela	Calmati. Sono all'ospedale ... al Policlinico ...
Renzo	Oddio. Che cos'hai?
Daniela	Calmati. Non hai capito. Sto benissimo io, ma Beniamino mi ha chiamato. Arturo è stato ricoverato all'ospedale. Ha avuto un collasso. Sta male.
Renzo	Arturo? Il tossico?
Daniela	Macché tossico! Aveva la siringa perché è diabetico. Beniamino è così scemo.
Renzo	È un vero cretino, secondo me.
Daniela	Stiamo aspettando il medico. Ti chiamerò quando c'è qualche novità. Ciao. A più tardi.
Renzo	Ciao. Coraggio.
Renzo	Daniela! Come stai?
Daniela	Stanca morta. Distrutta!
Renzo	Arturo sta meglio?
Daniela	Deve restare in ospedale per dei test. Non riesce a mangiare o a bere.
Renzo	Tu hai fame? Vuoi mangiare qualcosa? Io mi mangerei un cavallo.
Daniela	Grazie, no, ma mi piacerebbe bere qualcosa. Magari sono disidratata – mi gira un po' la testa. Mi sai dire se c'è una farmacia qui vicino?
Renzo	Vieni.

checkpoint 11

1   Identify six pairs of opposites from **chiudere, entrare, spingere, spegnere, trovare, dimenticare, uscire, perdere, accendere, aprire tirare.** What does the one that's left over mean?

2   Referring to a meal, how would you say *It's the best I've ever eaten*?

3   Adapt **Che ne dici di visitare Roma?** to ask a couple of friends if they fancy visiting Venice? Remind them that Alessandro's there.

4   How do you find out if there will be enough room and if there will be something to eat?

5   What phrase can you add to an imperative to show you really mean it?

6   Which of the symptoms listed is unlikely to be caused by **la febbre da fieno**? **difficoltà respiratoria, mal di gola, naso chiuso, occhi rossi, mal d'orecchio, dolore al polpaccio**

7   In a restaurant or a bar, how would you offer to pay and how would you suggest you share the bill?

8   What do **riposati** and **sbrigati** mean? How do they change when used with someone you call **lei** and with two people?

9   Starting with **come**, what ways can you think of to ask how you'd go about changing the password?

10 What other way can you think of to say **I miei genitori non ci sono** and **Sergio non c'è**?

11 At the end of a meal, how might you say that you're full?

12 What do you change in **Mi fa male il torace** to say *His chest is hurting*? And how do you say *He takes medication for high blood pressure*?

13 **Cuoce** and **cuociono** come from **cuocere** *to cook*. Decide which you need in the gaps. **Come si .... la quinoa? Come si fa a .... le castagne** *chestnuts*? **Come si .... il riso? Come si .... le castagne?**

14 What does **Esca!** mean? What's the infinitive of the verb?

15 How do you ask if something contains wheat?

16 How do you start a question with *Can you tell me*? Using this, ask what's happened, how to get to the old town, if there's any news.

17 If someone says **Siamo alla frutta**, what do they mean?

dodici
keeping in touch

Whether you're keeping in touch with people or with what's going on in the world, the chances are that you'll be doing it via the internet. To access it on your tablet or smartphone in Italy, you might need **Avete il wifi libero?** *Do you have Wi-Fi?* and **Qual è la password?** *What's the password?* Italian **wifi** is usually pronounced as in English but you might also hear *wee fee*.

Even if you're no technophile, the influence of technology on everyday life is such that it's worth understanding key terminology in Italian. This isn't a major hurdle, as English words are widely used. That said, you may not instantly recognise some of them as the way they're pronounced can be Italian through and through.

What's interesting for someone learning Italian is the way the adopted words are used. Their origin might be English but they're governed by the rules of Italian grammar, making them the perfect illustration of those rules.

As in other languages, shortcuts are increasingly prevalent on the internet, particularly on social networking sites. It can be a bit disconcerting when you first come across **3mendo** or **xfetto**, which mean **tremendo** and **perfetto**, because **3** is **tre** and the mathematical symbol **x** is said **per**.

l'itanglese

The number of English words used in Italian has grown hugely in recent years. The phenomenon is called **l'itanglese** or sometimes **l'anglitaliano**.

It's very noticeable in the world of **il business**:
Penso di organizzare un meeting per discutere lo slogan. *I'm thinking of organising a meeting to discuss the slogan.*
Magari un workshop? *Perhaps a workshop?*
Per tutto il team? *For the whole team?*
Io preferirei una conference call. *I'd prefer a conference call.*

Lo sport regularly involves English words:
Sai giocare a ping pong? *Can you play ping pong?*
Che ne dici di una partita di badminton? *How about a game of badminton?*
Hai visto il derby sabato? *Did you watch the derby on Saturday?*

La musica classica in English relies almost exclusively on Italian words while in Italy **la musica contemporanea** adopts many English words.
Va pazzo per il rap. *He's crazy about rap music.*
Suona la chitarra in una band. *He plays the guitar in a band.*

Some words are surprising, such as **il baby parking** *crèche, childcare centre*, **il box** *small garage*, **il mobbing** *workplace bullying*, **lo smoking** *dinner jacket*.

Where food and Italian are concerned, English probably imports more words than it exports, although not necessarily as they originated. **Un panino** literally means *little bread* or *bread roll*; **panini** is the plural. An ordinary sandwich in Italy is **un panino** or **un tramezzino** – not the heated/grilled kind sold in the UK as 'a panini'.

Prosciutto is the generic word for *ham*. For thinly sliced cured ham such as Parma ham, you need to specify **prosciutto crudo**, as opposed to **prosciutto cotto** *cooked ham*.

Latte is *milk* and if you ask for **un latte** in an Italian bar, milk is what you may well be given, not milky coffee, which is **caffè latte**.

Vorremmo mangiare fuori/all'aperto means *We'd like to eat outside*. Don't use **al fresco**: it means *in the cool* and is slang for *in jail*.

L'itanglese is most in evidence in the world of IT. English words predominate on the internet, particularly among the computer savvy and on social media. Like other borrowed words, they're used according to the rules of Italian grammar.

Nouns have a **gender**, and **articles** generally respect normal spelling conventions: **il chat, il cloud, il blogger, l'app, l'hotspot, lo streaming, la homepage, le emoticon, un nickname, un forum, un vlog, uno slideshow, uno smiley, una mail.**

Plurals don't add *s*.
I suoi blog sono incredibili. *His/Her/Your blogs are incredible.*
Hai letto i tweet di Orlando? *Did you read Orlando's tweets?*
Ho ricevuto quattro mail da mia mamma oggi. *I've received four emails from my mother today.*

-are is added to **verbs** — and nouns — to create **infinitives**, e.g. **crashare, draggare e droppare, goog(o)lare, messaggiare, twittare, zoomare.**
The newly minted verbs use the **endings** of regular **-are** verbs and have a **past participle** ending in **-ato**.

Non riesco a loggare/loggarmi. *I can't log in.*
Mentre stavo surfando su YouTube. *While I was surfing on YouTube.*
Clicca sull'icona. *Click on the icon.*
Ieri mia figlia ha chattato con un'amica per due ore. *Yesterday my daughter chatted (online) to a friend for two hours.*
Ha twittato la sua decisione ieri. *He tweeted his verdict yesterday.*
Non ti ha messaggiato? *Hasn't she messaged you?*
Il gioco è crashato tre volte. *The game (has) crashed three times.*
Tu e Noè siete stati taggati nella foto. *You and Noè have been tagged in the photo.*

Don't assume that every English term can be italianised.

To scan is **fare scansione** or **scannerizzare** because **scannare** means *to slaughter* and is also used colloquially to mean *to rip off, to fleece.*

A mobile phone is **un cellulare, uno smartphone** or **un telefonino. Un mobile** is *a piece of furniture.*

Chattare has the specific meaning of *to chat online*; *to have a chat* is **chiacchierare** or **fare due chiacchiere.**

saying thank you

At the end of a visit come the goodbyes and the thanks. **Arrivederci** is positive and cheerful as it means *until we see each other again*, whereas **addio** *farewell* (literally *to God*) is more solemn.

A simple *thank you* is **grazie** but you can add to it when you want your thanks to be more enthusiastic.
Grazie molte/tante/infinite. *Thank you very/so much/a million.*
Grazie mille. Mille grazie. *Thank you so much.*
Grazie di nuovo. *Thanks again.*
Grazie a te/lei/voi. *Thank you.*

Thank you for can either be **grazie per:**
Grazie per la vostra accoglienza. *Thank you for your hospitality.*
Grazie per tutto quello che hai fatto. *Thanks for everything you've done.*

... or **grazie di** (or **del, della,** etc.)
Grazie di tutto. *Thanks for everything.*
Molte grazie del passaggio. *Thank you very much for the lift.*
Grazie mille dell'aiuto. *Thanks for your help.*
Grazie della collaborazione. *Thank you for the work we've done together.*

There are other ways of expressing your appreciation:
Non so come ringraziarti/la/vi. *I don't know how to thank you.*
Sei un angelo/un santo! *You're an angel/a saint!*
Sei/È molto gentile. Troppo gentile. *You're very kind. Too kind.*
Siete davvero generosi. *You're really generous.*
Ti devo un grosso favore. *I owe you big time.*

Mi sono divertito un sacco. *I've had a great time/a ball.*
Ci siamo divertiti un mondo. *We've had a wonderful time.*

Grazie rarely passes without a response:
    Prego. *You're welcome.*
    Di niente. Non c'è di che. *Think nothing of it.*
    Figurati. Si figuri. *Not at all. My pleasure.*
    È stato un piacere. *It's been a pleasure.*

keeping in touch

After the goodbyes and thanks, talk usually turns to staying in touch.

Arrivederci. *Goodbye.*
È stato un piacere conoscerti/la/vi. *It's been a pleasure meeting you.*
Speriamo di tornare l'anno prossimo. *We hope to come back next year.*
Mi mancherai. *I'll miss you.* **Mi mancherete tutti.** *I'll miss you all.*
Ci sentiamo presto. *We'll be in touch soon.*

You've already come across the language structures you need.

asking questions: chapters 2 and 11

Qual è il tuo indirizzo email? *What's your email address?*
Qual è il suo numero di telefono? *What's your phone number?*
Tu sei su WhatsApp? *Are you on WhatsApp?*
Come faccio ad installare WhatsApp? *How do I install WhatsApp?*
Come fai tu a condividere le foto? *How do you share your photos?*

dovere, potere: chapter 9

Dovremmo tenerci in contatto. *We ought to keep in touch.*
Possiamo scambiarci gli indirizzi? *Can we exchange addresses?*
Potremmo creare un gruppo su Skype. *We could set up a Skype group.*
Gino potrebbe pubblicare le migliori foto. *Gino could post the best photos.*

future: chapter 8

Ti telefonerò domenica. *I'll call you on Sunday.*
Vi troverò su Facebook. *I'll find you on Facebook.*
Ti darò tutti i dettagli tramite sms. *I'll text you all the details.*
Caricheremo il video sul cloud. *We'll upload the video to the cloud.*

imperative: chapter 11

Mandami un sms o una mail. *Send me a text or an email.*
Contattatemi su FaceTime, va bene? *FaceTime me, OK?*
Non dimenticare di ... *Don't forget to ...*
  ... condividere le foto su icloud. *... share the photos on iCloud.*
  ... scrivermi una mail. ... *write me an email.*

phone calls and emails

If you're planning to phone someone, it's worth knowing the following:

Pronto. *Hello.*
Chi parla? *Who's calling?* **Con chi parlo?** *Who am I speaking to?*
Parlo con Bruno? *Is that Bruno? Am I speaking to Bruno?*
Hai/Ha il numero di Bruno? *Do you have Bruno's number?*
Scusi, ho sbagliato numero. *Sorry, I've got the wrong number.*

Sono Josh. *Josh speaking/This is Josh.*
Non ti/la sento bene. *I can't hear you very well.*
La linea è disturbata. *It's a bad line.*
Il segnale è debole. *The signal's weak.*
Ho una sola tacca del segnale. *I've only got one bar.*
Ho la batteria quasi scarica. *I haven't got much battery left.*
Lasciate un messaggio dopo il segnale acustico. *Please leave a message after the tone.*

Il mio indirizzo email è ... La password è ... Il sito è ...

For these, you need to know how to spell out words (page 19) and you need punctuation marks.

*	**asterisco**	-	**trattino**	
@	**chiocciola**	_	**trattino basso**	
/	**barra**	,	**virgola**	
\	**barra inversa**	#	**cancelletto, hashtag**	
&	**e commerciale**	ABC	*upper case* **maiuscola**	
.	**punto**	abc	*lower case* **minuscola**	
!	**punto esclamativo**		*(in brackets)* **tra/fra parentesi**	
?	**punto interrogativo**		*space* **spazio**	

The way to say **www.** is *voo·voo·voo poon·toh*.

In Italian a personal email usually starts with **Caro/Cara**, unless you're on closer terms, in which case use **Carissimo/Carissima**. You can finish with:

> **tanti cari saluti** *best wishes*
> **tante belle cose** *all the very best*
> **un abbraccio** *love* lit. *a hug*
> **bacioni** *much love* lit. *big kisses*

shortcuts

Shortcuts are as much an online phenomenon in Italian as they are in English, especially on social media sites and in chatrooms. New shortcuts are coined regularly.

The aim is to be as brief as possible, while still comprehensible:
che and **chi** become ke and ki
ho, hai, ha are written o, ai, a
ba&ab **baci e abbracci** *kisses and hugs*
cmq **comunque** *however*
cpt **capito** *understood*
dom **domani** *tomorrow*
midi **mi dispiace** *sorry*
qls **qualcosa** *something*
qlc **qualcuno** *somebody*
risp **rispondimi** *get back to me*

> x on its own means **per** and as a result you have:
> xme **per me** *for me*
> xfv **per favore** *please*
> xdere **perdere** *to lose*
> xò **però** *but, however*
> xke **perché** *why, because*

They follow the same principles in Italian as in English. For example, English transcribes the sound *ate/eight* as 8: *great > gr8, wait > w8*, but in Italian 8 is **otto**, so r8 is **rotto** *broken*.
Three is **tre**, so 3no is **treno** *train*.
Six is **sei**, the same word as *you are*: **tu sei** tu6, **Ci sei?** c6? *Are you there?*,
Dove sei? dv6 *Where are you?*
Sette *seven* gives 7mbre *September*.

> Acronyms abound, including:
> ap **a presto** *see you soon*
> cvd **ci vediamo dopo** *see you after/later*
> fdv **felice di vederti** *happy to see you*
> tat **ti amo tanto** *love you loads*
> ttp **torno tra poco** *back soon*
> tvtb **ti voglio tanto bene** *love you to bits*

word bank

computer talk

IT is **l'informatica** and *computer* is **un computer**, pronounced *com-poo-terr*.

il computer fisso *desktop*
il tablet *tablet*
il portatile *laptop*
lo schermo *screen*
il salvaschermo *screensaver*
il cursore/la freccia *cursor/arrow*

la tastiera *keyboard*
il tasto *key*
il mouse *mouse*
la barra degli strumenti *toolbar*
la stampante *printer*
la chiavetta USB *memory stick*

il documento *document*
il file *file*
la cartella *folder*
la banca dati *database*

l'allegato *attachment*
il nome utente *user name*
la password *password*
l'icona icon

il sito internet, il sito web *website*
la pagina web *web page*
il navigatore *browser*
il collegamento/il link *link*

l'URL (*oo·erreh·elleh*) *URL*
il segnalibro *bookmark*
preferito *favourite*
bloccato *frozen, crashed*

accendere *to switch on*
aggiornare *to update*
allegare *to attach*
annullare *to undo*
avviare *to boot up*
cancellare *to delete*
cercare *to search (for)*
connettersi *to connect*

digitare *to key in*
fare il backup di *to back up*
mandare una mail *send an email*
modificare *to edit*
navigare, surfare *to browse/surf*
riavviare *to re-start, re-boot*
scaricare *to download*
spegnere *to shut down*

Create ten sentences in Italian, combining structures such as come faccio a ... or come si ... with these verbs and nouns: e.g. How do I turn the printer on? How do I go about uploading this photo? How does this document open? Or use other verbs you know to say you'd like to check your email, you want/need/ought to send an email, attach/update/edit a file or photo, find a link. Try asking if there's a password and what it is.

talking the talk

Renzo	Cosa prendi?
Daniela	Un caffè e un panino al prosciutto ... prosciutto e formaggio.
Renzo	Mangiamo dentro o fuori?
Daniela	All'aperto. Fa così bello oggi. E mi piace il giardino.
Renzo	Hai letto il blog di Orlando ieri?
Daniela	No.
Renzo	Dovresti leggerlo. È incredibile.
Renzo	Dunque, abbiamo quasi finito. Cosa fai la settimana prossima?
Daniela	Penso di andare in Liguria a trovare i miei genitori. Ho ricevuto quattro mail da mia mamma oggi ... e tre ieri.
Renzo	Beh. Grazie per la collaborazione.
Daniela	Figurati. Grazie a te. È stato un piacere. Mi mancherai.
Renzo	Allora. Abbiamo finito. Siamo alla frutta.
Daniela	Sì. Purtroppo. Dove vai adesso?
Renzo	Non lo so. Tu?
Daniela	Non lo so neanch'io. Tu hai il mio numero di telefono, vero?
Renzo	Sì. Dovremmo anche scambiarci gli indirizzi email, non ti pare?
Daniela	Assolutamente. Il mio è ...
Renzo	Che ne dici di un aperitivo da Saverio?
Daniela	Andiamo.

checkpoint 12

Most of the vocabulary is from this chapter but some of the language structures assume knowledge from the rest of the book.

1   What's the Italian for *We'll be in touch soon*?

2   Why would you not put **un mobile** in your pocket?

3   Guess which, if any, of these are used in Italian: **il backup, il benchmark, il corner, lo shopping, matchare, fotoscioppare, linkare, followare, downlodare**

4   Why wouldn't you say that you'd like to eat **al fresco**?

5   What are **cancelletto, chiocciola, virgola, punto** and **parentesi**?

6   If you're told **Ha sbagliato numero**, what have you done?

7   What single word is missing from **Grazie .... bellissima giornata** for it to mean *Thank you for the wonderful day*?

8   A word is added to **un computer** to specify that it's *a desktop*. What is it and what's the Italian for *a keyboard*?

9   How do you ask if there's Wi-Fi available?

10 What are **ki, ke** and **dv6** short for? What do you think **xdonami** means?

11 Given that **scaricare** means *to download*, how do you say in Italian *I need to/We ought to/We could download the photos*, *Gianni will download the file* and *They have downloaded the files*?

12 How do you tell someone not to forget to do something **(tu, lei** and **voi)**?

13 Using knowledge from this and previous chapters, how would you say *I have lost my memory stick* and *we need to buy a charger*?

14 Add endings to these verb stems so that they mean i) *I will* **scriv_, googl_**; ii) *we will* **torn_, condivid_**; iii) *they will* **mand_, scambi_** What do they mean?

15 *It's been a pleasure meeting you* — how do you say it in Italian?

grammar terminology

Adjectives are words that describe nouns and pronouns: *good idea*, *strong red wine*, *my fault*, *She's tall*, *It was weird*. In Italian, unlike English, they change their final vowel according to what they're describing.

Adverbs add information to verbs, adjectives, other adverbs and whole sentences: *a very good idea*, *He's acting weirdly*, *Luckily he's not here*.

Agreement: An Italian article or adjective has to agree with, i.e. match, the noun or pronoun it relates to, in terms of gender (masculine or feminine) and number (singular or plural).

Articles are **definite**: *the house, the houses*, or **indefinite**: *a house, an area*.

The **conditional** is the verb form used to say what would or could happen.

Consonants and vowels make up the alphabet: the vowels are a, e, i, o, u; the rest are consonants.

The **endings** of words are the final letter(s). In English, a verb ending in *-ed* tells you it happened in the past. In Italian, endings are much more widespread, with nouns, adjectives and verbs relying on them to convey essential information.

Feminine: See Gender.

Gender: In Italian, every noun is either masculine (m) or feminine (f). This is its gender, and you need to know a noun's gender because words used with it, such as articles and adjectives, have corresponding masculine and feminine forms in Italian.

The **imperative** is the verb form used to give instructions or commands: *Wait for me*, *Don't say that*, *Take the first left*.

The **imperfect tense** of a verb is used to describe how things were and to talk about things that happened over a period of time or repeatedly.

Infinitive: Italian verbs are listed in a dictionary in their infinitive form, ending in **-are**, **-ere** or **-ire**. The English equivalent uses *to*: **mangiare** *to eat*, **avere** *to have*, **capire** *to understand*.

An **intransitive** verb is one that does not have a direct object, e.g. *to arrive, to laugh, to die*.

Irregular nouns, verbs or adjectives don't behave in a predictable way like regular ones and have to be learnt separately.

Masculine: See Gender.

Negatives are words like *not, never, nothing, nobody* and *not ... ever, not ... anybody, not ... anything.*

Nouns are the words for living beings, things, places and abstract concepts: *father, analyst, Siân, giraffe, chair, village, Rome, time, courage.*

Number refers to the difference between **singular** (one) and **plural** (more than one).

The **object** of a verb is at the receiving end. An object can be direct: *He made a joke*; or **indirect**, in which case it is often preceded by *to* or *at: He laughed at the joke.*

Ordinal numbers are *first, second, third, fourth,* etc.

The **past participle** of a verb is used with *have* when talking about the past: *I have finished, He has eaten, They had gone.*

The **perfect tense** of a verb is used in Italian to talk about the past; it is equivalent to the English *I worked* and *I have worked.*

The **person** of a verb indicates who or what is doing something:

1st person = the speaker: *I* (singular), *we* (plural)

2nd person = the person(s) being addressed: *you*

3rd person = who/what is being talked about: *he/she/it/they*

Personal pronouns are words like *I, you, we, she, her, them.*

The **pluperfect** tense translates *had done something.*

Plural means more than one.

Prepositions are words like *by, in, on, with, for, through, next to.*

The **present tense** of a verb is used to talk about things being done now: *I work, I'm working.*

Reflexive pronouns are mi, ti, si, ci, vi, used as an integral part of reflexive verbs.

Reflexive verbs in Italian have -si at the end of the infinitive: **alzar**si *to get up.*

Regular nouns, adjectives, verbs, etc. conform to a pattern and are entirely predictable.

Relative pronouns are words like *which, who, that,* used to join together parts of a sentence without repeating the noun.

Singular means one, while **plural** means more than one.

The **stem** of an Italian verb is what's left when you remove the **-are, -ere** or **-ire** ending of the infinitive.

The **subject** of a sentence is whoever or whatever is carrying out the verb: *They have two children*, *Anna reads the paper*, *This house cost a lot of money*, *Peace is possible*.

Subject pronouns are *I, we, you, he, she, they*.

The **subjunctive** is a form of a verb that's rarely used in English, other than in phrases like if *I were you*, but is widely used in Italian in defined grammatical circumstances.

Superlative is *the most* ... when comparing several things.

A **syllable** is a unit that contains a vowel and consists of a single sound: *can* has one syllable, *can-ter* has two, while *Can-ter-bu-ry* has four.

Tense refers to when the verb is happening: in the past, present or future. Tenses have names, e.g. present, perfect, imperfect.

A **transitive** verb has a direct object, e.g. *to catch ...*, *to make ...*, *to open ...*, whereas an **intransitive** verb does not, e.g. *to arrive, to laugh, to die*.

Verbs relate to doing and being and are identifiable in English because you can put *to* in front of them: *to live, to be, to speak, to play, to think, to have, to need*.

Vowels and consonants make up the alphabet: the vowels are a, e, i, o, u; the rest are consonants.

grammar summary

nouns

Every Italian noun is either masculine (m) or feminine (f); this is its gender. Nearly all nouns end in **-o**, **-a** or **-e** in the singular. In the plural, you don't add **-s** as in English: you change the final vowel instead.

singular nouns ending in	in the **plural**
-o : nearly always m	-o → -i
-a : generally f	-a → -e
-e : some m, some f	-e → -i

- Nouns ending in **-ista** can be masculine or feminine: **il/la giornalista**; similarly, many professions ending in **-e**: **il/la dirigente** *executive*, **il/la cliente** *client*;
- Most nouns ending in **-ma** are masculine: **il problema, il clima**;
- Adopted foreign nouns and nouns ending in an accented vowel don't change in the plural: **i computer, gli chef, le specialità**;
- Most nouns ending in **ga/go/ca/co** add **h** in the plural: **amica →amiche, luogo → luoghi**. But when **co** follows a vowel, **-h** is not normally added: **amico → amici**;
- Many occupations and professions have masculine and feminine forms: **impiegato/impiegata** *office worker*, **ragioniere/ragioniera** *accountant*, **investigatore/investigatrice** *detective*. However, the way professions are referred to is changing (page 15).

articles

There are several Italian words for *the* and *a*, depending on whether the following word is masculine or feminine, singular or plural, starts with a vowel or a consonant.

	a/an	*the* singular	*the* plural	before ...
m	un **giorno** uno **sconto** un **anno**	il **giorno** lo **sconto** l'**anno**	i **giorni** gli **sconti** gli **anni**	consonant z, s + consonant vowel
f	una **strada** un'**idea**	la **strada** l'**idea**	le **strade** le **idee**	consonant vowel

Since it's the initial letter that decides the article, it can be different when the article and the noun are separated:

il giorno *the day but* **lo stesso giorno** *the same day*
una strada *a road but* **un'altra strada** *another road*

Un/una is not inserted between essere and nouns of nationality or religion:
È canadese *He's a Canadian;* **È musulmana** *She's a Muslim.* Traditionally, the rule applied also to occupations: **Sono scienziato** *I'm a scientist* but **un/uno/una** is increasingly used: **Sono uno scienziato/una scienziata**.

Italian uses the definite article more than English does – most noticeably in sentences like **non mangio la carne** *I don't eat meat*, **Non mi interessano i social** *I'm not interested in social media* – and also before:

- countries: **l'Italia, gli Stati Uniti** *USA*
- abstract nouns: **abbandonare la speranza** *to give up hope*
- illnesses: **ha la bronchite** *she has bronchitis.*

The combines with: **a** *at/to*; **da** *from*; **di** *of*; **in** *in*; **su** *on.*

	il	lo	l'	la	i	gli	le
a	al	allo	all'	alla	ai	agli	alle
da	dal	dallo	dall'	dalla	dai	dagli	dalle
di	del*	dello*	dell'*	della*	dei*	degli*	delle*
in	nel	nello	nell'	nella	nei	negli	nelle
su	sul	sullo	sull'	sulla	sui	sugli	sulle

*del, dello, etc. can mean *some* as well as *of the*

adjectives

In Italian, an adjective agrees with what it describes according to whether that is masculine or feminine, singular or plural. This does not mean that they always end in the same vowel.

Adjectives ending in **-o** in the dictionary have four possible endings:

	singular	plural
m	**vino italiano** **motore italiano**	**vini italiani** **motori italiani**
f	**birra italiana** **stazione italiana**	**birre italiane** **stazioni italiane**

Adjectives ending in **-e** have only two possible endings:

m	vino francese	vini francesi
	motore francese	motori francesi
f	birra francese	birre francesi
	stazione francese	stazioni francesi

When adjectives and nouns are next to each other:

- most adjectives generally go after the noun: **un posto speciale** *a special place*, **una considerazione importante** *an important consideration*;
- colour and nationality always go after the noun: **il vino bianco** *white wine*, **la bandiera italiana** *the Italian flag*;
- **primo, secondo, terzo,** etc. go before the noun: **primo soccorso** *first aid*, **seconda classe** *second class*;
- ... as do common adjectives like **bello** *beautiful*, **brutto** *ugly*, **buono** *good*, **cattivo** *bad*, **grande** *big*, **piccolo** *small*, **breve** *short*, **lungo** *long*, **nuovo** *new*, **vecchio** *old*, **stesso** *same*, **vero** *real*: **una brutta parola** *an ugly word*, **un piccolo aperitivo** *a small aperitif*;
- changing the position of the adjective adds emphasis to it: **una parola brutta**; **un'importante considerazione**.

Before a noun:

- **buono/a** and **grande** often shorten to **buon** and **gran**: **un buon vino, una buon'idea, un gran piacere, la Gran Bretagna.**
- **bello** has endings similar to the definite article and **quello** *that*: **un bel sole, un bell'albergo.** However, it's regular when on its own or after a noun: **bello, bella, belli, belle.**

il	bel	quel
lo	bello	quello
l'	bell'	quell'
la	bella	quella
i	bei	quei
gli	begli	quegli
le	belle	quelle

possession

The definite article is used with possessive adjectives, which agree with the gender of what's owned not the owner. *My car* is always **la mia macchina**, regardless of who's talking.

	m	f	m pl	f pl
my	il mio	la mia	i miei	le mie
your **tu**	il tuo	la tua	i tuoi	le tue
your **lei**, *his/her*	il suo	la sua	i suoi	le sue
our	il nostro	la nostra	i nostri	le nostre
your **voi**	il vostro	la vostra	i vostri	le vostre
their	il loro	la loro	i loro	le loro

- **Suo** can mean *your* (**lei**), *his, her* or *its*: **la sua macchina** can mean *your car, his car, her car.* **L'Italia e la sua storia** *Italy and its history.*
- When talking about just one member of the family, with no adjective or other information added, the definite article is used only with **loro**: **mia madre** *my mother*, **suo fratello** *his/her/your brother*, **vostro padre** *your father* ... but **la loro nonna** *their grandmother*, **la mia sorella maggiore** *my big sister*, **il suo fratellastro** *his/her stepbrother*, **la mia sorellina** *my little sister*, **il suo ex marito** *her ex-husband.*
- While **il mio** + noun means *my*, **il mio** on its own means *mine*. The same goes for all the others, e.g. **le tue** *yours*, **la nostra** *ours.*

this, that

Questo *this* and **quello** *that*:
- go before the noun, where **quello** has endings similar to the definite article and **bello** (page 180);
- mean *this one/that one* or *these/those* without a noun: **Mi piace questa ma non mi piacciono quelle** *I like this one but I don't like those*;
- often have **qui** *here* and **lì** *there* added in comparisons: **Questa qui o quella lì?** *This one here or that one?*

adverbs

Adverbs of manner can be formed by:
- adding **-mente** to a feminine singular adjective:
  chiaro → **chiaramente**; **semplice** → **semplicemente**;
- using **in modo** + masculine adjective: **in modo intelligente**;
- using **in maniera** + feminine adjective: **in maniera garbata** *politely.*

Other common adverbs include **molto** *very*, **un po'** *a bit*, **troppo** *too*, **così** *so*, **piuttosto** *rather.*

The ending of an adverb never changes: **una notizia molto brutta** *very bad news*, **questi casi sono veramente rari** *these cases are really rare.*

comparisons

Adjectives and adverbs are compared with **più** *more* and **meno** *less*:
più elegante *more stylish*, **più chiaramente** *more clearly*,
meno caro *less expensive*, meno **rapidamente** *less quickly*

- *Than* is **di** (or **del**, **della**, etc, when followed by *the*) before a noun, pronoun or number:
  Qui, la carne è più caro del pesce. *Here, meat is dearer than fish.*
  Sei più bravo di me. *You're better than me.*
  Ho pagato meno di 50 euro. *I paid less than 50 euros.*
- *Than* is **che** when comparing words in the same grammatical category:
  Ho più sete che fame. *I'm more thirsty than hungry.*
  Fa meno caldo qui che sul terrazzo. *It's less hot here than on the terrace.*
- *The* + **più/meno** means *the most/least*: **la più elegante** *the most stylish*, **i più veloci** *the fastest*, **il meno caro** *the least expensive*.

prepositions

Some prepositions correspond to more than one English usage.

a	*at* **a casa, a mezzogiorno**; *in* **abito a Londra**
	to (a city or smaller) **vado a Roma**
	with cities, town, villages and small islands
in	*in* **abito in Inghilterra**; *to* (a region or larger) **vado in Inghilterra**
	by **vado in aereo/in macchina**
	with countries, regions, continents and most big islands
da	*from* **a due chilometri da Roma**
	since/for **lavoro qui da aprile/da cinque anni**
	for (purpose) **occhiali da sole, campo da golf**
di	*of* **una bottiglia di vino; una borsa di pelle**
	than **questa è più cara di quella**
per	*for* **una lettera per me**; *in order to* **per comunicare con Anna**

object pronouns

Object pronouns (*me, us, you, him, her, it, them*) can be the direct object of a verb: *Guy saw her*; or the indirect object: *Guy listened to her*. In Italian, *him, her, it* and *them* are different words when direct and when indirect.

mi *me, to me*	**ci** *us, to us*
ti *you, to you* tu	**vi** *you, to you* voi
la *you*; **le** *to you* lei	
lo *him*; **gli** *to him*	**li/le** *them* m/f
la *her*; **le** *to her*	**gli/loro** *to them* m and f

Indirect object pronouns are used with structures like **mi piace** *I like* and **mi interessa** *I'm interested in*. Generally the pronouns go before a verb, e.g.
Mi capisce? *Do you understand me?*
Gli ho scritto. *I've written to him.*

But they follow an infinitive, attaching themselves to it without its final **e**:
È impossibile trovarla. *It's impossible to find her.*
Bisogna scrivergli. *You have to write to him.*

With **dovere** *to have to*, **potere** *to be able to* and **volere** *to want to* + infinitive, pronouns can go first or be attached to the infinitive:
Mi puoi spiegare le regole? *Can you explain the rules to me?*
Puoi spiegarmi le regole?

A past participle has to agree with *him*, *her*, *it* and *them*.
Anna? La macchina? Non l'ho vista. *Anna? The car? I haven't seen her/it.*
I ragazzi? Non li ho visti. *The boys? I haven't seen them.*

ne

Ne *some, any, of it, of them* is used with quantities and numbers even though it's often not needed in English: **non ne vuole** *he doesn't want any (of it)*, **ne ho tre** *I have three (of them)*, **ne ho mangiato poco** *I ate very little of it*.

Ne can also mean *of/with/about it* or *them* with adjectives and verbs that are associated with **di**: **ne sono ben conscio** *I'm well aware of it*, **ne siamo soddisfatti** *we're satisfied with it*, **Maria ne parla/sogna molto** *Maria talks/dreams a lot about it*.

combining pronouns

Indirect object pronouns change when used together with direct object pronouns or **ne**. **Mi, ti, ci, vi** change to **me, te, ce, ve** and **gli** and **le** change to **glie-**. They go before the direct object pronoun/**ne**. **Glie** combines with **lo, la, li, le, ne**:

	lo	la	li	le	ne
mi	me lo	me la	me li	me le	me ne
ti	te lo	te la	te li	te le	te ne
gli/le	glielo	gliela	glieli	gliele	gliene
ci	ce lo	ce la	ce li	ce le	ce ne
vi	ve lo	ve la	ve li	ve le	ve ne
gli	glielo	gliela	glieli	gliele	gliene

Me lo spedirà? *Will you send it to me?*
Gliene ho comprato uno. *I've bought one (of them) for him.*

subject pronouns

singular	1	**io** *I*
	2	**tu** *you*: someone you call by their first name
	3	**lei** *you*: someone you don't know well
		lei/lui *she/he*

plural	1	**noi** *we*
	2	**voi** *you*: more than one person
	3	**loro** *they*

Because the ending of the verb is generally enough to show who is doing something, these are used much less than in English, usually only for emphasis, contrast or clarification of *you/he/she*.

verbs

English verbs rely on subject pronouns to show who's carrying out a verb, as well as words like *does, was, were, will* to show when it's being carried out. Italian verbs carry all this information in the ending of the verb itself.

There are three groups of Italian verbs, their infinitives ending in **-are**, **-ere** and **-ire**, e.g. **abitare** *to live*, **v̲endere** *to sell*, **partire** *to leave*.
Removing the infinitive ending leaves the verb stem: **abit-**, **vend-**, **part-**.
Other endings can be added to the stem to convey specific information:

a̲bito *I live*   **vend**eva *s/he used to sell*   **part**irà *he will leave*

There are sets of endings for each of the following:
present tense: *happens, is happening*. After **da**: *has been happening* since a particular time or for a period of time.
future tense: *will happen, is going to happen*
conditional: *would happen (if)*
imperfect tense: *was happening, used to happen, happened repeatedly or regularly*
perfect tense: *happened, has happened, did happen*
pluperfect tense: *had happened*
subjunctive: *happens, happened* based on the speaker's feelings, opinions, tastes rather than solid fact
past participle: *happened* after *had, have, will have, would have* in past tenses
gerund: used after **stare** to indicate happening at the very time of speaking
imperative: commands and instructions for **tu, lei, noi, voi**

The next four pages set out these various endings for **regular** verbs in each of the three groups, i.e. those that follow the standard pattern. Pages 190–193 show how many widely used verbs deviate from these patterns: these are classed as **irregular.**

pattern for regular verb ending in -**are**

infinitive   aspett**are** *to wait*
stem: aspett-

	present	future	conditional
io	aspett**o**	aspett**erò**	aspett**erei**
tu	aspett**i**	aspett**erai**	aspett**eresti**
lui/lei	aspett**a**	aspett**erà**	aspett**erebbe**
noi	aspett**iamo**	aspett**eremo**	aspett**eremmo**
voi	aspett**ate**	aspett**erete**	aspett**ereste**
loro	asp**e**tt**ano**	aspett**eranno**	aspett**er**e**bbero**

	imperfect	perfect
io	aspett**avo**	ho aspett**ato**
tu	aspett**avi**	hai aspett**ato**
lui/lei	aspett**ava**	ha aspett**ato**
noi	aspett**avamo**	abbiamo aspett**ato**
voi	aspett**avate**	avete aspett**ato**
loro	aspett**a**v**ano**	hanno aspett**ato**

	present subjunctive	imperfect subjunctive
io	aspett**i**	aspett**assi**
tu	aspett**i**	aspett**assi**
lui/lei	aspett**i**	aspett**asse**
noi	aspett**iamo**	aspett**assimo**
voi	aspett**iate**	aspett**aste**
loro	asp**e**tt**ino**	aspett**a**ss**ero**

past participle   aspett**ato**

gerund   aspett**ando**
imperative   aspett**a**, aspett**i**, aspett**iamo**, aspett**ate**

pattern for regular verb ending in -ere

infinitive   **vendere** to sell
stem: vend-

	present	future	conditional
io	vendo	venderò	venderei
tu	vendi	venderai	venderesti
lui/lei	vende	venderà	venderebbe
noi	vendiamo	venderemo	venderemmo
voi	vendete	venderete	vendereste
loro	vendono	venderanno	venderebbero

	imperfect	perfect
io	vendevo	ho venduto
tu	vendevi	hai venduto
lui/lei	vendeva	ha venduto
noi	vendevamo	abbiamo venduto
voi	vendevate	avete venduto
loro	vendevano	hanno venduto

	present subjunctive	imperfect subjunctive
io	venda	vendessi
tu	venda	vendessi
lui/lei	venda	vendesse
noi	vendiamo	vendessimo
voi	vendiate	vendeste
loro	vendano	vendessero

past participle   venduto

gerund   vendendo

imperative   vendi, venda, vendiamo, vendete

pattern for regular verb ending in -ire
infinitive **dorm**ire *to sleep*
stem: dorm-

	present	future	conditional
io	dormo	dormirò	dormirei
tu	dormi	dormirai	dormiresti
lui/lei	dorme	dormirà	dormirebbe
noi	dormiamo	dormiremo	dormiremmo
voi	dormite	dormirete	dormireste
loro	dormono	dormiranno	dormirebbero

	imperfect	perfect
io	dormivo	ho dormito
tu	dormivi	hai dormito
lui/lei	dormiva	ha dormito
noi	dormivamo	abbiamo dormito
voi	dormivate	avete dormito
loro	dormivano	hanno dormito

	present subjunctive	imperfect subjunctive
io	dorma	dormissi
tu	dorma	dormissi
lui/lei	dorma	dormisse
noi	dormiamo	dormissimo
voi	dormiate	dormiste
loro	dormano	dormissero

past participle dormito

gerund dormendo

imperative dormi, dorma, dormiamo, dormite

pattern for regular verb ending in -ire, adding -isc

infinitive   **capire** *to understand*

stem: cap-

	present	future	conditional
io	capisco	capirò	capirei
tu	capisci	capirai	capiresti
lui/lei	capisce	capirà	capirebbe
noi	capiamo	capiremo	capiremmo
voi	capite	capirete	capireste
loro	capiscono	capiranno	capirebbero

	imperfect	perfect
io	capivo	ho capito
tu	capivi	hai capito
lui/lei	capiva	ha capito
noi	capivamo	abbiamo capito
voi	capivate	avete capito
loro	capivano	hanno capito

	present subjunctive	imperfect subjunctive
io	capisca	capissi
tu	capisca	capissi
lui/lei	capisca	capisse
noi	capiamo	capissimo
voi	capiate	capiste
loro	capiscano	capissero

past participle   capito

gerund   capendo

imperative   capisci, capisca, capiamo, capite

Around half of the verbs in the -ire group insert -isc. There's no way of predicting from the infinitive which they are; the most common are **capire** *to understand*, **finire** *to finish*, **preferire** *to prefer*, **spedire** *to send*, **costruire** *to build*, **pulire** *to clean*, **gestire** *to manage*.

reflexive verbs

The infinitive of reflexive verbs ends in **-si**: **chiamarsi** *to be called*, **alzarsi** *to get up*, **sposarsi** *to get married*.

These verbs follow exactly the same pattern of endings as regular **-are**, **-ere**, **-ire** verbs but also include **mi, ti, si, ci** or **vi** before the verb according to who/what is involved.

	present	perfect
io	mi alzo	mi sono alzato/a
tu	ti alzi	ti sei alzato/a
lei, lui/lei	si alza	si è alzato/a
noi	ci alziamo	ci siamo alzati/e
voi	vi alzate	vi siete alzati/e
loro	si alzano	si sono alzati/e

Mi, ti, si, ci, vi are also used with other verbs to convey *for/to oneself*:
Mi preparo un panino per il pranzo. *I make myself a sandwich for lunch.*
Si prende un anno di pausa. *She's taking a year out (for herself).*

avere or essere for past tense?

Most verbs form the perfect tense with the present tense of **avere** + the past participle of the main verb.
Reflexive verbs plus a range of other verbs, mainly relating to movement, use the present tense of **essere** instead of **avere** (page 70).
The same rules apply to the perfect, pluperfect, future perfect and past conditional.

questions

Italian doesn't use extra words like *do* and *does* in a question; you raise the pitch of your voice at the end so that it *sounds* like a question.

Aldo parte oggi. *Aldo leaves/is leaving today.*
Aldo parte oggi? *Is Aldo leaving today?*
Arriva in ritardo. *It's arriving late.*
Arriva in ritardo? *Is it arriving late?*
Capiscono. *They understand.*
Capiscono? *Do they understand?*

negatives

Do and *does* are not used in negatives. To say something negative, you simply put **non** in front of the verb.

Lavoro a Roma. *I work/I'm working in Rome.*
Non lavoro a Roma. *I don't work/I'm not working in Rome.*
Non capiscono. *They don't understand.*
Non capiscono? *Don't they understand?*
Hanno capito. *They understood. They have understood.*
Hanno capito? *Did they understand? Have they understood?*

In Italian, unlike English, both non and a negative word like **niente** nothing are used in the same sentence.
Non voglio niente. *I want nothing. I don't want anything.*
Maria non capisce nulla. *Maria understands nothing.*
Non c'è nessuno. *There's nobody here/there.*
Salvo non esce mai. *Salvo never goes out.*
Non è affatto prudente. *He's not at all careful.*
Questo colore non ci piace più. *We no longer like this colour.*
Non sa né cantare né suonare la chitarra. *He can neither sing nor play the guitar. He can't sing or play the guitar.*

In the perfect tense, some negative words go before the past participle, others after it, much like in English.
Non sono mai stato a Palermo. *I have never been to Palermo.*
Non abbiamo neanche/nemmeno cominciato. *We haven't even started.*
Non hanno ancora cenato. *They haven't yet had dinner.*
Non ho fatto niente/nulla. *I haven't done anything.*
Non hai visto nessuno? *Didn't you see anyone?*
Non abbiamo comprato né vino né birra. *We haven't bought wine or beer.*

irregular verbs

Not all verbs follow the regular patterns. **Essere** *to be*, is irregular in all tenses while many other widely used verbs are irregular in one, some or all their tenses.

present

andare *to go*: **vado, vai, va, andiamo, andate, vanno**
avere *to have*: **ho, hai, ha, abbiamo, avete, hanno**
dare *to give*: **do, dai, dà, diamo, date, danno**
dire *to say*: **dico, dici, dice, diciamo, dite, dicono**

dovere *to have to*: **devo, devi, deve, dobbiamo, dovete, devono**
essere *to be*: **sono, sei, è, siamo, siete, sono**
fare *to do, make*: **faccio, fai, fa, facciamo, fate, fanno**
potere *to be able to*: **posso, puoi, può, possiamo, potete, possono**
sapere *to know*: **so, sai, sa, sappiamo, sapete, sanno**
stare *to be*: **sto, stai, sta, stiamo, state, stanno**
tenere *to hold*: **tengo, tieni, tiene, teniamo, tenete, tengono**
uscire *to go out*: **esco, esci, esce, usciamo, uscite, escono**
venire *to come*: **vengo, vieni, viene, veniamo, venite, vengono**
volere *to want*: **voglio, vuoi, vuole, vogliamo, volete, vogliono**

imperfect

essere *to be*: **ero, eri, era, eravamo, eravate, erano**
bere *to drink*: **bevevo, bevevi, beveva, bevevamo, bevevate, bevevano**
dire *to say*: **dicevo, dicevi, diceva, dicevamo, dicevate, dicevano**
fare *to do/make*: **facevo, facevi, faceva, facevamo, facevate, facevano**
trarre *to pull*: **traevo, traevi, traeva, traevamo, traevate, traevano**
porre *to put*: **ponevo, ponevi, poneva, ponevamo, ponevate, ponevano**
produrre *to produce*: **producevo, producevi, produceva, producevamo, producevate, producevano**

+ other verbs with irregular infinitives ending in **-arre, -orre, -urre.**

future

essere *to be*: **sarò, sarai, sarà, saremo, sarete, saranno**
dare *to give*: **darò, darai, darà, daremo, darete, daranno**
fare *to do/make*: **farò, farai, farà, faremo, farete, faranno**
stare *to stay/be*: **starò, starai, starà, staremo, starete, staranno**

The following drop the first vowel of the future ending:
andare *to go*: **andrò, andrai, andrà, andremo, andrete, andranno**
avere *to have*: **avrò, avrai, avrà, avremo, avrete, avranno**
cadere *to fall*: **cadrò, cadrai, cadrà, cadremo, cadrete, cadranno**
dovere *to have to*: **dovrò, dovrai, dovrà, dovremo, dovrete, dovranno**
potere *to be able to*: **potrò, potrai, potrà, potremo, potrete, potranno**
sapere *to know*: **saprò, saprai, saprà, sapremo, saprete, sapranno**
vedere *to see*: **vedrò, vedrai, vedrà, vedremo, vedrete, vedranno**
vivere *to live*: **vivrò, vivrai, vivrà, vivremo, vivrete, vivranno**

A few verbs end in **-rrò, -rrai**, etc.
bere *to drink*: **berrò, berrai, berrà, berremo, berrete, berranno**
porre *to put*: **porrò, porrai, porrà, porremo, porrete, porranno**
produrre *to produce*: **produrrò, produrrai, produrrà, produrremo, produrrete, produrranno**
rimanere *to stay*: **rimarrò, rimarrai, rimarrà, rimarremo, rimarrete,**

rimarranno

tenere *to hold*: **terrò, terrai, terrà, terremo, terrete, terranno**

venire *to come*: **verrò, verrai, verrà, verremo, verrete, verranno**

volere *to want*: **vorrò, vorrai, vorrà, vorremo, vorrete, vorranno**

Verbs ending in **-care/-gare** add **-h-** before the endings:

cercare *to look for*: **cercherò**, etc.

spiegare *to explain*: **spiegherò**, etc.

conditional

Regular conditional endings are added to the future stem, e.g.

essere *to be*: **sarei, saresti, sarebbe, saremmo, sareste, sarebbero**

volere *to want*: **vorrei, vorresti, vorrebbe, vorremmo, vorreste, vorrebbero**

subjunctive present

essere *to be*: **sia, sia, sia, siamo, siate, siano**

andare *to go*: **vada, vada, vada, andiamo, andiate, vadano**

avere *to have*: **abbia, abbia, abbia, abbiamo, abbiate, abbiano**

dare *to give*: **dia, dia, dia, diamo, diate, diano**

dire *to say*: **dica, dica, dica, diciamo, diciate, dicano**

dovere *to have to*: **debba, debba, debba, dobbiamo, dobbiate, debbano**

fare *to do*: **faccia, faccia, faccia, facciamo, facciate, facciano**

potere *to be able to*: **possa, possa, possa, possiamo, possiate, possano**

sapere *to know*: **sappia, sappia, sappia, sappiamo, sappiate, sappiano**

stare *to be*: **stia, stia, stia, stiamo, stiate, stiano**

venire *to come*: **venga, venga, venga, veniamo, veniate, vengano**

volere *to want*: **voglia, voglia, voglia, vogliamo, vogliate, vogliano**

subjunctive imperfect

essere *to be*: **fossi, fossi, fosse, fossimo, foste, fossero**

Many verbs which are irregular in the imperfect indicative (page 191) use the same irregular stem for the imperfect subjunctive, adding regular **-ere** endings to it:

bere *to drink*: **bevevo** → **bev** → **bevessi ... bevessero**

dire *to say*: **dicevo** → **dic** → **dicessi ... dicessero**

fare *to do/make*: **facevo** → **fac** → **facessi ... facessero**

porre *to put*: **ponevo** → **pon** → **ponessi ... ponessero**

trarre *to pull*: **traevo** → **tra** → **traessi ... traessero**

produrre *to produce*: **producevo** → **produc** → **producessi ... producessero**

imperative

tu   **essere** *to be*: **sii**
         andare *to go*: **vai/va'**
         avere *to have*: **abbi**
         dare *to give*: **dai/da'**
         dire *to say*: **di'**
         fare *to do/make*: **fai/fa'**
         sapere *to know*: **sappi**
         stare *to stay/be*: **stai/sta'**

lei imperatives are identical to the **lei** present subjunctive, e.g.

         essere *to be*: **sia**
         andare *to go*: **vada**
         dire *to say*: **dica**
         venire *to come*: **venga**

voi   **essere** *to be*: **siate**
         avere *to have*: **abbiate**
         sapere *to know*: **sappiate**

past participle

essere *to be*: **stato**
bere *to drink*: **bevuto**
dire *to say*: **detto**
fare *to do/make*: **fatto**

morire *to die*: **morto**
nascere *to be born*: **nato**
offrire *to offer*, **soffrire** *to suffer*:
offerto, sofferto

In addition, many **-ere** verbs, e.g.

chiedere *to ask*: **chiesto**
chiudere *to close*: **chiuso**
correre *to run*: **corso**
decidere *to decide*: **deciso**
discutere *to discuss*: **discusso**
leggere *to read*: **letto**
mettere *to put*: **messo**
muovere *to move*: **mosso**
prendere *to take*: **preso**
scendere *to go down*: **sceso**
spendere *to spend*: **speso**

rimanere *to stay*: **rimasto**
rispondere *to reply*: **risposto**
rompere *to break*: **rotto**
scegliere *to choose*: **scelto**
scrivere *to write*: **scritto**
succedere *to happen*: **successo**
uccidere *to kill*: **ucciso**
vedere *to see*: **visto/veduto**
vincere *to win*: **vinto**
vivere *to live*: **vissuto**

numbers

numbers 1–99

0	**zero**	11	**undici**
1	**uno**	12	**dodici**
2	**due**	13	**tredici**
3	**tre**	14	**quattordici**
4	**quattro**	15	**quindici**
5	**cinque**	16	**sedici**
6	**sei**	17	**diciassette**
7	**sette**	18	**diciotto**
8	**otto**	19	**diciannove**
9	**nove**	20	**venti**
10	**dieci**		

- Zero translates *zero*, *nought*, *nil*, *love* (tennis) and *O* (telephone). The plural is **zeri: due zeri** *two noughts*.
- **Uno** changes to agree with its noun, like *a/an*: **un parco, un adulto, uno chef, una persona, un'idea.**

21	**ventuno**	31	**trentuno**
22	**ventidue**	32	**trentadue**
23	**ventitré**	33	**trentatré**
24	**ventiquattro**	34	**trentaquattro**
25	**venticinque**	35	**trentacinque**
26	**ventisei**	36	**trentasei**
27	**ventisette**	37	**trentasette**
28	**ventotto**	38	**trentotto**
29	**ventinove**	39	**trentanove**
30	**trenta**		

40	**quaranta**	70	**settanta**
50	**cinquanta**	80	**ottanta**
60	**sessanta**	90	**novanta**

41–99 follow the same pattern as 31–39:
quarantuno ... novantanove

numbers 100 +

100	**cento**	125	**centoventicinque**
101	**centouno**	150	**centocinquanta**
102	**centodue**	155	**centocinquantacinque**

110	centodieci	199	centonovantanove
120	centoventi	200	duecento
250	duecentocinquanta	900	novecento
300	trecento	999	novecentonovantanove
500	cinquecento		

Cento *a hundred* doesn't change in the plural: 500 **cinquecento**; but **mille** *a thousand* becomes -**mila**: 2 000 **duemila**, 5 000 **cinquemila**.

Thousands are separated either by a space or a full stop: 7 000 or 7.000.

1 000	mille	100 000	centomila
1 100	millecento	500 000	cinquecentomila
1 500	millecinquecento	1 000 000	un milione
2 000	duemila	2 000 000	due milioni
10 000	diecimila	1 000 000 000	un miliardo

Italian uses a comma where English has a decimal point:
L'inflazione annuale è dello zero v**i**rgola tre **per cento.** *Annual inflation is 0.3%.*
La banca prevede una cre**scita tra il due v**i**rgola cinque e il tre percento.**
The bank is predicting growth of between 2.5% and 3.0%.

first, second, third, etc.

1st	1°	primo	6th	6°	sesto
2nd	2°	secondo	7th	7°	s**e**ttimo
3rd	3°	terzo	8th	8°	ottavo
4th	4°	quarto	9th	9°	nono
5th	5°	quinto	10th	10°	d**e**cimo

From 11th onwards, you add -**<u>e</u>simo** to the cardinal number minus its final vowel:

11th	undic**e**simo	20th	vent**e**simo
12th	dodic**e**simo	50th	cinquant**e**simo
17th	diciassettesimo	100th	cent**e**simo

The only exception is 23, 33, 43, 53, etc., which keep the final **e**, but without its accent: 23 **ventitré**, 23rd **ventitre**e**simo.**

The endings of ordinal numbers used with a noun have to agree because they're adjectives:
il ventune**simo s**e**colo** *the twenty-first century*
la terza volta *the third time*
i secondi piatti *second (main) courses*
le prime donne *the first women*

answers

answers to checkpoints

checkpoint 1 page 24

1 Permesso; *2* lei; *3* molto lieto, lieto/a di conoscervi; *4* sono, non sono.
5 signore or dottore; *6* molte, mille. Prego, non c'è di che, si figuri;
7 commiserate; *8* Scusate; *9* dove abita? *10* ci vediamo stasera/dopo pranzo;
11 sei; *12* at any time; *13* figlia, nuora; *14* Accomodatevi; *15* autrice, traduttore,
traditrice; *16* they all work in education; *17* Di dove siete? *18* I am, they are

checkpoint 2 page 40

1 vero, giusto, no; *2* vive; *3* piscina, parco giochi, campo da tennis/bocce;
4 chi, quale, perché, che cosa, quando, dove, come, quanti, quanto;
5 Posso aiutarti/la/vi?; *6* ho sete, hanno freddo?, ha il raffreddore, ho lo
stomaco scombussolato; *7* mio nonno è vedovo: my grandfather is widowed,
le mie amiche sono gallesi: my (girl)friends are Welsh, mia cugina è bionda:
my cousin (f) is blonde, il mio vicino di casa è molto diligente: my neighbour
is very hard-working, mia suocera è gentilissima: my mother-in-law is really
kind; *8* pensavo, rispettavo; *9* calvo, testardo; *10* someone who spends money
like water; *11* Dove in Italia si trova?; *12* pessimo; *13* in, a; *14* insieme; *15*
ampio/stretto, collinare/piatto, immacolato/sporco, movimentato/tranquillo,
nuovo/vecchio; *16* sto imparando/studiando l'italiano.

checkpoint 3 page 52

1 microbiologo/stabilimento farmaceutico, meccanico/autofficina,
allenatore/palestra, giardiniere/vivaio, infermiere/studio medico; doganiere
= customs officer; *2* faccio; *3* lavoro qui da quindici anni; *4* meteorologo,
rheumatologist, ophthalmologist, mafia expert; *5* autista; *6* non fa differenza;
7 a tempo pieno, lavoratrice; *8* il mio/la mia partner lavora in proprio;
9 human resources, hotel sector, car industry, farm; *10* Qual è il suo ruolo?
11 voi, tu, lei, lui/lei; *12* factory manager; *13* gestiamo una fabbrica a Milano;
14 Sono responsabile del sito web in un'agenzia immobiliare: I'm in charge
of the website in an estate agency; *15* Ero (un) insegnante; *16* My grandfather
was a policeman.

checkpoint 4 page 66

1 Chiedo scusa; *2* Mi spiego? *3* admiration; *4* che; *5* come si dice crisis
in italiano? *6* troppo; *7* barboso; *8* capite you understand, caspita wow,
comunque however; *9* positive che sollievo, che gioia, the rest are negative;

10 ti/le dispiacerebbe spiegare? 11 cavolo, perciò, però, in breve; 12 Cosa vuol dire cartellino giallo? 13 per esempio; 14 piuttosto; 15 an accident; 16 in effetti; 17 beato/a te; 18 anzi; 19 This button is used for adjusting the contrast; 20 Ce l'ho sulla punta della lingua.

checkpoint 5 page 78

1 proibito, tenuto, sognato, accettato; 2 quando l'hai trovato? 3 l'altro ieri; 4 ho perso la valigia e il passaporto; 5 ammazzare avere, esistere essere, mangiare avere, nascere essere, morire essere, salire essere, viaggiare avere; 6 siamo andati/e in crociera l'anno scorso; 7 a fire, to trip, to meet, to swallow, instead; 8 Cos'ha fatto ieri? 9 ha soddisfatto, ha stupefatto; 10 quindici giorni fa: a fortnight ago, fra quindici giorni: in a fortnight's time; 11 leggere to read, rompere to break, aprire to open, vincere to win, aggiungere to add, mettere to put, spendere to spend; 12 mai: sei mai stato in Grecia? 13 where did you two meet; 14 they had/have imagined, she has/had gone out; 15 c'è stato un fraintendimento, c'è stata una reazione negativa; 16 earlier; 17 at the end of a fairy story: and they lived happily ever after

checkpoint 6 page 90

1 ogni tanto; di solito, normalmente; 2 pluperfect, imperfect; 3 essere to be; 4 eravamo; 5 mangiavano bene, facevamo tante fotografie; 6 quando viveva/abitava a Milano, il mio amico lavorava nelle pubbliche relazioni, il mio amico → la mia amica; 7 faceva caldo perché non funzionava l'aria condizionata, it was hot because the air conditioning wasn't working; 8 I am/I was daydreaming; 9 era; 10 da bambino/a, da studente; 11 stavo mangiando, I was just about to eat; 12 ogni sei mesi; 13 c'erano quattro campi da tennis; 14 there were/there have been 3 messages for Luigi; 15 ho conosciuto Anna quando avevo dodici anni; 16 stavo leggendo quando Laura è arrivata; 17 Mi piaceva lavorare da casa.

checkpoint 7 page 102

1 ortica nettle, the others are all insects; 2 ci piace molto/davvero la camera; 3 le piacciono i videogiochi? gli piacciono i videogiochi?/a loro piacciono i videogiochi? 4 non mi piace la folla; 5 you look a lot like Francesca; 6 mi è piaciuto; 7 preferiti, preferita, preferito, preferita, preferiti, preferite; 8 scusa(mi) il ritardo; 9 tu preferisci, lei preferisce, voi preferite; 10 gli piace correre/la corsa, a loro piace correre/la corsa; 11 mi dispiace molto, colpa mia; 12 affatto, per niente, per nulla; 13 sempre; 14 non le interessano le conseguenze; 15 migliore; 16 non ... per niente, poco, abbastanza, molto, moltissimo, da morire; 17 Non mi piace molto passare l'aspirapolvere o scaricare la lavastoviglie, io preferisco fare giardinaggio.

checkpoint 8 page 122

1 giovedì, sabato/maggio, giugno, luglio; *2* see you on the 13th/see you at 1 p.m; *3* compleanno, Natale, lavoro, viaggio, volo, fine settimana/weekend; *4* venticello/vento/burrasca, pioggerella/rovescio/pioggia; *5* Avete voglia di fare una passeggiata sulle scogliere? *6* purtroppo unfortunately; *7* the small hours, precise/in punto; *8* ricambio/ricambiamo gli auguri; *9* festival, stable, to climb, cliff; *10* potrei → potremmo; *11* noleggiamo let's hire, esploriamo let's explore, visitiamo let's visit, organizziamo let's organise, celebriamo let's celebrate; *12* fossi; *13* faceva freddo, era mite; *14* il giorno di Natale è il venticinque dicembre; *15* vi aspetterei se potessi; *16* Who knows?; *17* Grazie dell'invito; purtroppo ho già un impegno; *18* Magari! Ma non posso. Facciamo mezzogiorno lunedì il primo maggio?

checkpoint 9 page 136

1 I must/have to start straightaway, I ought to start straightaway; *2* Giorgio deve partire, vuole fare una foto di gruppo; *3* people you might know; *4* ho sempre voluto viaggiare; *5* potremo, dovrete, potranno; *6* vorrei imparare, dovrei imparare, devo imparare, voglio imparare, ho dovuto/dovevo imparare, posso imparare, potrei imparare; *7* Volevamo/Abbiamo voluto esplorare la zona circostante; *8* le dispiace se apro la finestra? *9* so, so, conosco, so, conosco; *10* where there's a will there's a way; *11* a lift to the station; *12* Rossi didn't manage to score/couldn't score; *13* scegliere, spiegare, scoprire, smettere, sognare; *14* volere bene = to love, ti voglio tanto bene; *15* sapere/indovinare, perdere/vincere, trascurare/curare, vietare/permettere, fingere to pretend; *16* dovresti → dovrai; *17* Dovevamo andare in crociera l'anno scorso ma abbiamo dovuto disdire la prenotazione.

checkpoint 10 page 150

1 ombra; *2* your opinion; a suo parere, Cosa ne pensa lei? *3* in secondo luogo; *4* 7.5%, 0.4%; *5* Bravo, siamo perfettamente d'accordo; *6* misunderstanding, on the same wavelength, rubbish, to show or demonstrate, to chat; *7* dato che, siccome, poiché, dal momento che; *8* is; *9* about 70, aged between 12 and 15; *10* ottavo, sedicesimo, ventiquattresimo; *11* Orlando, il più giovane; *12* what team you support; *13* centinaia; *14* Credi nei fantasmi? *15* abbiamo una divergenza di opinione; *16* tax evasion/tax avoidance; *17* sempre

checkpoint 11 page 164

1 chiudere/aprire, entrare/uscire, trovare/perdere, spingere/tirare, spegnere/accendere; dimenticare = to forget; *2* È il migliore che abbia mai mangiato; *3* Che ne dite di visitare Venezia? C'è Alessandro; *4* Ci sarà posto? Ci sarà da mangiare? *5* Mi raccomando; *6* dolore al polpaccio; *7* Offro io. Facciamo alla

romana. *8* have a rest/hurry up, si riposi/si sbrighi, riposatevi/sbrigatevi;
9 come si cambia/come si fa a cambiare/come faccio a cambiare la
password? *10* mancano i miei genitori, manca Sergio; *11* sono pieno come un
uovo; *12* gli fa male il torace, prende farmaci per la pressione alta; *13* cuoce,
cuocere, cuoce, cuociono; *14* Go out! uscire; *15* contiene frumento? *16* mi sa
dire cos'è successo/come si arriva al centro storico/se c'è qualche novità?
17 it's all over, we've reached the end/hit rock bottom

checkpoint 12 page 174

1 ci sentiamo presto; *2* it's a piece of furniture; *3* all of them are used;
4 it means in the cool/in prison; *5* hashtag, @, comma, full stop, brackets;
6 got a wrong number; *7* della; *8* fisso, la tastiera; *9* c'è/avete wifi libero?
10 chi, che, dove sei?, perdonami = forgive me; *11* devo/dovremmo/
potremmo scaricare le foto, Gianni scaricherà il file, hanno scaricato i file;
12 non dimenticare, non dimentichi, non dimenticate; *13* ho perso la mia
chiavetta, dobbiamo comprare un caricabatterie; *14* scriverò I will write,
googlerò I will google, torneremo we will return, condivideremo we will
share, manderanno they will send, scambieranno they will exchange;
15 è stato un piacere conoscerti/la/vi

answers to verb practice

verb practice 1 page 39

1   *a* sono, I'm divorced; *b* siamo, we're not English; *c* è, Cristina is very
      stubborn; *d* sono, Luca and his brother are twins; *e* siete, until when are
      you here? *f* è, the hotel is clean and comfortable; *g* sono, I'm not very
      religious; *h* è, Mr Bassani isn't in a relationship/isn't committed; *i* sono,
      they're extremely nice; *j* sei, Are you engaged?

2   *a* ho, ha, I have black eyes but he has blue eyes; *b* ha, Francesco is not
      sleepy; *c* ha, How old is Camilla?; *d* abbiamo, My wife and I have a
      weakness for chocolate; *e* hai, Are you 18 or 19?; *f* avete, You have three
      children, haven't you? *g* hanno, They have a tiny house in the centre;
      h ha, Are you hungry?

3   *a* Lei è canadese o americana? *b* Martina e Michela sono sorelle?
      c L'albergo ha una piscina? *d* Marco è gay, vero? *e* tu hai, lei ha, voi avete
      sete? *f* Ci sono campi da tennis?

verb practice 2 page 51

1   *a* aggiungi; *b* cambiano; *c* create; d dura; *e* mettiamo; *f* piange; *g* provo;
      h ripete; *i* salviamo; *j* succede

2   *a* dorme; *b* parte; *c* abolite; *d* pulisce; *e* finiscono; *f* fornisce;
     g garantiamo; *h* capisco

3   *a* si; *b* si; *c* ci; *d* si; *e* ti; *f* mi; *g* vi

verb practice 3 page 77

1   *a* tu hai guidato you drove/have driven; *b* voi siete usciti/e you went out;
     c lui ha baciato he (has) kissed; *d* io sono diventato/a I became/have
     become; *e* loro hanno creato they (have) created; *f* noi siamo stati/e we
     have been; *g* lei ha tagliato she (has) cut; *h* io ho mandato I (have) sent;
     i tu hai spiegato you (have) explained

2   *a* tu avevi guidato you had driven; *b* voi eravate usciti/e you had gone
     out; *c* lui aveva baciato he had kissed; *d* io ero diventato/a I had become;
     e loro avevano creato they had created; *f* noi eravamo stati/e we had
     been; *g* lei aveva tagliato she had cut; *h* io avevo mandato I had sent;
     i tu avevi spiegato you had explained

3   ammesso, commesso; permesso; riso, sorriso, diviso; fritto, corretto,
     eletto; colto, accolto, tolto; esteso, offeso, sceso

4   Ho lavorato fino a mezzogiorno. Sono andato/a in città dopo pranzo e
     ho visto Paolo. Ho fatto la spesa e ho speso troppo. Ho mandato una
     email a Salvatore e ho lasciato un messaggio per mia madre. Daniela è
     arrivata alle sei. Daniela era appena andata via e il bambino si era già
     addormentato quando mio padre ha telefonato.

verb practice 4 page 89

1   *a* tu volevi; *b* noi avevamo; *c* lei conosceva; *d* loro guardavano;
     e io prendevo; *f* noi discutevamo; *g* lui era; *h* voi meritavate

2   *a* prendeva; *b* andavo; *c* alzavo, faceva; *d* aveva, *e* preferivi; *f* controllava;
     g andavamo; *h* giocava, *i* mangiavate; *j* avevano

3   *a* Ero con Riccardo, eravamo in città e io sono caduto/a sul marciapiede.
     I was with Riccardo, we were in town and I fell on the pavement. *b* È nata
     nel 1984; da bambina viveva in Sicilia dove i nonni avevano una fattoria
     grande. She was born in 1984; as a child she lived in Sicily where her
     grandparents had a large farm. *c* Sei andato/a al villaggio dove tua madre
     andava con tuo padre? Did you go to the village where your mother
     used to go with your father?

verb practice 5 page 121

1   *a* tu risponderai you will reply; *b* loro andranno they will go; *c* voi
     prenderete you will take; *d* durerà it will last; *e* noi metteremo we will
     put; *f* lei dimenticherà you/she will forget; *g* io riuscirò I will succeed/

manage; *h* lui farà he will do/make; *i* noi arriveremo we will arrive; *j* succederà it will happen; *k* io sarò I will be; *l* tu avrai you will have

2   *a* tu risponderesti you would reply; *b* loro andrebbero they would go; *c* voi prendereste you would take; *d* durerebbe it would last; *e* noi metteremmo we would put; *f* lei dimenticherebbe you/she would forget; *g* io riuscirei I would succeed/manage; *h* lui farebbe he would do/make; *i* noi arriveremmo we would arrive; *j* succederebbe it would happen; *k* io sarei I would be; *l* tu avresti you would have

3   *a* future: you, he/she, it will depend; *b* present: you organise; *c* past: he/she, you phoned; *d* present: they're studying; *e* future: they will decide; *f* conditional: they would transform; *g* future: we will prefer; *h* conditional: we would prefer; *i* past: they (have) accused; *j* future: I shall continue

4   *a* iii; *b* vi; *c* viii; *d* i; *e* vii; *f* iv; *g* v; *h* ii

verb practice 6 page 135

1   volere: wanted to, would like to; potere: could, may, can, used to be able to; dovere: ought, was supposed to, must, should have, had to, used to have to

3   *a* lei deve, voi dovete; *b* noi vogliamo, tu vuoi; *c* loro devono, io devo; *d* lui può, io posso; *e* tu vuoi, loro vogliono; *f* io posso, noi possiamo; *g* tu devi, noi dobbiamo; *h* lei può, lui può; *i* io voglio, voi volete

4   future: *a* lei dovrà, voi dovrete; *b* noi vorremo, tu vorrai; *c* loro dovranno, io dovrò; *d* lui potrà, io potrò; *e* tu vorrai, loro vorranno; *f* io potrò, noi potremo; *g* tu dovrai, noi dovremo; *h* lei potrà, lui potrà; *i* io vorrò, voi vorrete

conditional: *a* lei dovrebbe, voi dovreste; *b* noi vorremmo, tu vorresti; *c* loro dovrebbero, io dovrei; *d* lui potrebbe, io potrei; *e* tu vorresti, loro vorrebbero; *f* io potrei, noi potremmo; *g* tu dovresti, noi dovremmo; *h* lei potrebbe, lui potrebbe; *i* io vorrei, voi vorreste

imperfect: *a* lei doveva, voi dovevate; *b* noi volevamo, tu volevi; *c* loro dovevano, io dovevo; *d* lui poteva, io potevo; *e* tu volevi, loro volevano; *f* io potevo, noi potevamo; *g* tu dovevi, noi dovevamo; *h* lei poteva, lui poteva; *i* io volevo, voi volevate

answers to questions on how to use a dictionary (page 106)

1   All of them except sardine

2   amica friend, barca boat, lago lake, pizzico pinch, profugo refugee; stanco tired, bianco white, largo wide, greco Greek; andare to go, pregare to pray, scaricare to download, negare to deny, pagare to pay

3   gioco game, giocare to play; elenco list, elencare to list

vocabulary builder

Nouns ending in **-o** are masculine and those ending in **-a** are feminine unless indicated otherwise. The gender of nouns ending in **-e** is included: **m, f** or **m/f**.

Adjectives are listed with their masculine singular ending.

Verbs are in the infinitive; irregular past participles (**pp**) are included.

A

able: to be able potere
absolutely assolutamente
absurd assurdo
to accept accettare
access accesso
accessory accessorio
accident incidente (m)
accommodation alloggio
according to secondo
accountant ragioniere/a (m/f)
actor attore/attrice (m/f)
to add aggiungere (pp aggiunto)
address indirizzo
to admire ammirare
to admit ammettere (pp ammesso)
adventure avventura
advice consiglio, consulenza
advisable consigliabile
to advise consigliare
affectionate affettuoso
afraid: to be afraid avere paura
after dopo
afternoon pomeriggio
again ancora
against contro
ago fa
agricultural agricolo
air traffic controller controllore di volo (m/f)
airport aeroporto
airy arioso
alcohol alcol (m)
alcoholic alcolico

all tutto
allergic allergico
to allow permettere (pp permesso)
almond mandorla
almost quasi
also anche
although benché
always sempre
amazed stupito
amazing eccezionale, splendido
amenity amenità
to amuse far ridere, divertire
amusing divertente
analyst analista (m/f)
anchovy alice (f)
ancient antico
and e, ed
ankle caviglia
anniversary anniversario
annoying fastidioso, seccante
to answer rispondere (pp risposto)
ant formica
antiquated antiquato
antique (adj) antico
anybody qualcuno, nessuno
anything qualcosa, niente
apologise scusarsi
to appear apparire (pp apparso), parere (pp parso)
appointment appuntamento
appropriate opportuno

archaeologist archeologo
archery tiro con l'arco
architect architetto
area zona
arm braccio (m): arms le braccia (f)
arms armi (f pl)
around circa
to arrange fissare
to arrive arrivare
art arte (f)
arthritis artrite (f)
article articolo
to ask chiedere (pp chiesto)
to assume assumere (pp assunto)
asthma asma
at a
to attach allegare
attachment allegato
to attack aggredire, assalire
attempt tentativo
to attend frequentare
aunt zia
Australia Australia
available disponibile
average medio
to avoid evitare

B

baby bambino
babysitter babysitter (m/f)
back dorso, schiena
backpack zaino, zainetto
badminton badminton (m)
balanced bilanciato,

equilibrato
balcony balcone (m)
bald calvo
to ban proibire
bank banca
banker banchiere (m)
banknote banconota
bargain affare (m)
barrister avvocato
basic spartano
basically sostanzialmente
basketball basket (m)
bath bagno
bathroom bagno
battery batteria,
pila: battery charger
caricabatterie (m)
to be essere, stare
(pp stato)
to be able to potere
to be necessary bisognare
beach spiaggia
bear orso
to beat sbattere
beautiful bello
because perché
to become diventare
bed letto
bee ape (f)
before prima
to begin cominciare
behind dietro
to believe credere
to bend piegare
beneficial benefico
benefits sussidio
better migliore (adj),
meglio (adv)
betting shop agenzia di
scommesse
between fra, tra
big grande
bike bici (f), bicicletta
binoculars binocolo (sing)
birth nascita
birthday compleanno
bit (a) un po'
black nero
to blame incolpare

block (of flats) palazzo
bloke tizio
blonde biondo
blood sangue (m): blood
pressure pressione (f)
blue azzurro, blu
to boil bollire
to book prenotare
booking prenotazione (f)
to boost promuovere (pp
promosso)
boot (footwear) stivale,
scarpone (m): walking/
ski boots scarponi da
trekking/da sci
to border with confinare
con
boring noioso
born: to be born nascere
(pp nato)
both entrambi
bottom fondo
bowl scodella
boy ragazzo
boyfriend ragazzo,
fidanzato, amico
break pausa
to break rompere (pp rotto)
breakfast colazione (f)
to breathe respirare
breeze venticello
bridge ponte (m)
bright vivace
broad ampio
brochure opuscolo
brother fratello
brother-in-law cognato
brown marrone, bruno
to browse guardare
to browse (IT) navigare
bruised contuso
builder costruttore (m)
bungee-jumping bungee-
jumping (m)
bunks letti a castello
burner fornello, fuoco
bus autobus (m)
bus stop fermata bus
bustling movimentato

busy occupato
busy (committed)
impegnato
but ma, però
butter burro
to buy comprare
by (date) entro

C
cake torta
to calculate calcolare
calendar calendario
to call chiamare
called: to be called
chiamarsi
calm sereno
camera macchina
fotografica
campsite campeggio
Canada Canada
to cancel annullare,
disdire (pp disdetto)
capable abile
capacious capiente
capsule capsula
car macchina, auto (f)
car park parcheggio
careful prudente
careless sbadato
carelessly sbadatamente
to carry portare
to carry on continuare
cash contante (m)
cash machine bancomat
(m)
castle castello
cat gatto
catastrophic catastrofico
to catch (train) prendere
(pp preso)
cathedral duomo,
cattedrale (f)
cause causa
to cause causare
to celebrate festeggiare
cellar cantina
central centrale
centre centro
certain certo
challenging stimolante

championships campionati (m pl)

chance opportunità

change cambiamento

to change cambiare

chaos caos (m)

characteristic caratteristico

to charge caricare

charge: in charge responsabile

charger caricabatterie (m)

charming incantevole

to chat chiacchierare

to chat online chattare

to check controllare

cheerful allegro

cheese formaggio

chef cuoco/a, chef (m/f)

chemist farmacista (m/f)

chemist's farmacia

chess scacchi (m pl)

childminder tata

chilled fresco

china vasellame (m)

chocolate cioccolato, cioccolata

to choose scegliere (pp scelto)

circumference circonferenza

to clamp down on dare un giro di vite su

to clarify chiarire

class classe (f)

to clean pulire

clean pulito

clear chiaro

clearly chiaramente

clever bravo, intelligente, astuto

cliff scogliera

climate clima (m), climatico (adj)

climate change cambiamento climatico

to close chiudere (pp chiuso)

cloud nuvola

cloudy nuvoloso

coeliac celiaco

coffee caffè (m)

cold freddo: to be cold avere freddo

to collapse crollare

colleague collega (m/f)

colour colore (m)

to come venire (pp venuto)

to come down scendere (pp sceso)

to come up salire

comfortable comodo

committment impegno

to communicate comunicare

community comunità

to commute fare il/la pendolare

compact compatto

companion compagno/a

to compare paragonare, confrontare

compass bussola

completely completamente

compliment complimento

to comprise comprendere (pp compreso)

computer computer (m)

computer scientist informatico

conference convegno

confident sicuro di sé

to confirm confermare

to confuse confondere (pp confuso)

confusion confusione (f)

congested trafficato

congratulations complimenti

to connect connettersi (pp connesso)

conservation conservazione (f)

construction costruzione (f)

consultant consulente (m/f)

contact contatto

to contain contenere

contents contenuti (m pl)

to contribute contribuire

convenient comodo, conveniente

to cook cuocere (pp cotto), cucinare

cook cuoco/a

cooker cucina

cooking cucina, cottura

cool fresco

corner angolo

correct corretto

to cost costare

cot lettino

cotton cotone (m)

cough tosse (f)

counsellor consulente (m/f)

country paese (m)

countryside campagna

course (meal) portata, piatto

course (study) corso

course: of course certo, naturalmente

court (sports) campo

cousin cugino/a

cover coperchio

to cover coprire (pp coperto)

cramped stretto

crazy pazzo, pazzesco

crèche baby parking (m), asilo nido

crockery stoviglie (f pl)

to cross attraversare

crowded affollato

crush: to have a crush on avere una cotta per

to cry piangere (pp pianto)

cuisine cucina

cultural culturale

culture cultura

cure cura

curiosity curiosità

curly riccio

currently attualmente

to cut tagliare
cybercrime crimine informatico

D

dance danza
to dance ballare
to dare osare
dark scuro
dark-haired moro
darling carissimo/a
data dati (m pl)
date data, appuntamento
dated antiquato
daughter figlia
daughter-in-law nuora
dawn alba
day giorno, giornata
to daydream fantasticare
dead morto
dear caro
to decide decidere (pp deciso)
to declare dichiarare
to decorate abbellire, decorare
deeply profondamente
to defeat sconfiggere (pp sconfitto)
defence difesa
to degenerate degenerare
degree (°C/F) grado
degree (academic) laurea
dehydrated disidratato
to delay ritardare
delegate delegato/a
to delete cancellare
deli gastronomia
delicate delicato
delightful incantevole
democracy democrazia
demonstration dimostrazione, manifestazione
dentist dentista (m/f)
to depart partire
to depend dipendere (pp dipeso)
dependable serio
depressing tetro

depth profondità
to descend scendere (pp sceso)
to describe descrivere (pp descritto)
description descrizione (f)
design disegno
designer grafico, stilista (m/f)
desktop computer computer (m) fisso
detached indipendente, monofamiliare
detail dettaglio
to detest detestare
devastating devastante, sconvolgente
to develop sviluppare
diabetic diabetico
to die morire (pp morto)
diet dieta
different diverso
difficult difficile
dilapidated decrepito
to dine cenare
dining room sala da pranzo
dinner cena
director direttore (m)
dirty sporco
disabled disabile
disagreeable antipatico
to disappear sparire
disappointed deluso
disappointing deludente
disaster disastro
disco discoteca
discount sconto
to discover scoprire (pp scoperto)
discrimination discriminazione (f)
disease malattia
dish piatto
dishwasher lavastoviglie (f)
to distribute distribuire
diversity diversità
divorced divorziato
DIY fai da te (m)

to do fare (pp fatto)
doctor medico, dottore(ssa)
dog cane (f)
dogsbody tuttofare (m/f)
double doppio
to doubt dubitare
doubt dubbio
down giù
to drain scolare
to draw (sketch) disegnare
to draw (tie) pareggiare
dreadful malissimo, pessimo
dream sogno
to dress vestirsi
dress vestito
to drink bere (pp bevuto)
to drive guidare
driver autista (m/f)
driving licence patente di guida (f)
drizzle pioggerella
to drop lasciare cadere
drop goccio
to drown annegare, affogare
drug droga
drug addict tossico:
drug addiction tossicodipendenza
dry secco, arido
dryer (clothes) asciugatrice (f), asciugabiancheria
during durante
to dust spolverare
dust polvere (m)

E

each ogni
ear orecchio
early presto
earthquake terremoto
easily facilmente
east est (m)
Easter Pasqua
to eat mangiare
economy economia
to edit modificare

effect effetto
effective efficace
egg uovo (m): eggs uova (f pl)
emperor imperatore (m)
employment occupazione (f)
to empty svuotare
end fine (f)
energy energia
engineering ingegneria
England Inghilterra
English inglese
to enjoy godere
to enjoy oneself divertirsi
enough abbastanza
to enter entrare
entrance hall ingresso, atrio
environment ambiente (m)
equal pari
equal opportunities pari opportunità
equipped attrezzato
to eradicate eradicare
to escape scappare
especially soprattutto
essentially effettivamente
estate agent/agency agente (m)/agenzia immobiliare
eternal eterno
etiquette galateo
EU UE: Unione Europea
European europeo
euthanasia eutanasia
even anche
evening sera, serata
event evento
every ogni: every so often ogni tanto
evidently evidentemente
exact esatto
to exaggerate esagerare
example esempio
to exceed superare
excellent eccellente, ottimo
to exchange scambiare,

scambiarsi
exercise esercizio
exhibition mostra
to exist esistere
expensive caro
experience esperienza
to expire scadere
to explain spiegare
exploration esplorazione (f)
to explore esplorare
exquisite squisito
extensive esteso
external esterno
extraordinary straordinario
extravagant stravagante
extreme estremo
extremism estremismo
eye occhio

F
fabric tessuto
fabulous favoloso
face viso, faccia
facilities attrezzature (f pl)
factory fabbrica
to faint svenire (pp svenuto)
faithfully: Yours faithfully Distinti saluti
fake falso, contraffatto
to fall cadere
false falso
family famiglia
famous conosciuto, famoso
fan (sports) tifoso
fan (ventilation) ventilatore (m)
fantastic fantastico
far lontano: as far as fino a
farm fattoria
farmhouse casale (m)
fascinating accattivante
fashion moda: designer stilista (m/f)
fastening chiusura
fat grasso
father padre
father-in-law suocero

favourite preferito
to fear avere paura di, temere
fear paura
feast abbuffata
to feed dare da mangiare a
to feel sentire
female femmina
ferry traghetto
festival festa, sagra
fever febbre (f)
few pochi/e
few: a few alcuni/e
fiancé/e fidanzato/a
field campo
fight lotta
to fight combattere
to fill riempire
to fill (form) compilare
finance finanza
to find trovare
to find out scoprire (pp scoperto)
finger dito (m): fingers dita (f pl)
to finish finire
fire incendio, fuoco
fire fighter pompiere (m/f)
fireplace camino, caminetto
first primo
first aid pronto soccorso
fish pesce (m)
flat appartamento
flat (adj) piatto
flavour sapore (m)
flight volo
flood alluvione (f)
floor pavimento
floor (storey) piano
flower fiore (m)
flu influenza
fly mosca
to focus on concentrarsi su
fog nebbia
to follow seguire
food cibo

food poisoning intossicazione alimentare (f)
foot piede (m)
football calcio
footballer calciatore (m)
for per, da
to forbid vietare
forehead fronte (f)
to forget dimenticare
fork forchetta
fortnight quindici giorni
fortunate fortunato
fortunately fortunatamente
forward: to look forward non vedere l'ora
free libero, (no cost) gratis
freedom libertà
fresh air aria fresca
fridge frigo(rifero)
friend amico/a
friendly cordiale
frog rana
from da
fruit frutta
full pieno
full-bodied (wine) corposo
fundamentalism fondamentalismo
funny comico, divertente, buffo
fur pelliccia
furnished arredato

G
gallery galleria
garage box (m), garage (m)
to garden fare giardinaggio
garden giardino
garden centre vivaio
gardener giardiniere (m)
gay gay
gender equality parità dei sessi
general generale
generally generalmente
generous generoso

genetic genetico
to get off scendere (pp sceso)
to get on salire
to get up alzarsi
girl ragazza
girlfriend ragazza, fidanzata, amica
glass bicchiere (m)
glasses (vision) occhiali (m pl)
global warming riscaldamento globale
glove guanto
to go andare
to go back (ri)tornare
to go down scendere (pp sceso)
to go in entrare
to go out uscire
to go up salire
goal (sports) gol (m)
gold oro
golf course campo da golf
good buono, bravo
goodbye arrivederci
gourmet buongustaio
government governo
grandchild nipote (m/f)
granddaughter nipote
grandfather nonno
grandmother nonna
grandson nipote
grape uva
graphic designer grafico
great grande: GB Gran Bretagna
great-grandfather bisnonno
great-grandmother bisnonna
greedy ingordo, goloso
green verde
greeting augurio, saluto
greetings card biglietto di auguri
grey grigio
gross schifoso
ground terra

group gruppo
to grow (up) crescere
to guarantee garantire
to guess indovinare
guest ospite (m/f)
guide guida
gym palestra
gymnastics ginnastica

H
to haggle contrattare
hair capelli (m pl)
half metà, mezzo (adj)
hall entrata, vestibolo
ham prosciutto
hand mano (f): hands mani (f pl)
handbag borsetta
handsome bello
handy pratico
hanger attaccapanni (m), gruccia
hangover postumi di una sbornia (m pl)
to happen succedere (pp successo)
happily allegramente
happy allegro
hard duro
hardworking diligente
hat cappello
to hate odiare
hateful odioso
to have avere
to have to dovere
hazel nocciolo
he lui
head testa, capo
headteacher preside (m/f)
health salute (f)
to hear sentire
heart cuore (m)
to heat (ri)scaldare
heat calore (m)
heating riscaldamento
heatwave ondata di caldo
height altezza
hello buongiorno, (telephone) pronto
helmet casco

to help aiutare
help aiuto
her la, lei, suo
herbalist's erboristeria
here qui: here is/are ecco
hiccups singhiozzo
to hide nascondere
(pp nascosto)
hill collina
hilly collinare
him lo, lui
to hire noleggiare
his suo
historian storico
historic(al) storico
history storia
hobby passatempo
holdall borsone (m)
holiday soggiorno, vacanza
holistic olistico
hollow vallata
home casa, domicilio
homeopathic omeopatico
homesickness nostalgia
di casa
hood cappuccio
to hope sperare
horrendous orrendo
horrible orribile
horse cavallo
hospital ospedale (m)
to host ospitare
host ospite (m/f)
hot caldo: to be hot avere
caldo
hour ora
house casa
housework faccende
domestiche (f pl)
how che: how lovely che
bello
how many? quanti/e?
how much? quanto/a?
how? come?
however comunque, però
to hug abbracciare
hug abbraccio
huge enorme, stragrande
human umano

humid umido
hungry: to be hungry
avere fame
to hurt avere/fare male
hurt ferito
husband marito
hypermarket ipermercato

I
I io
i.e. cioè
idea idea
ideal ideale
to identify identificare
identity theft furto
d'identità
idiot cretino, scemo
if se
to ignore ignorare
ill ammalato
ill: to be ill stare male
illegal abusivo,
clandestino
illness malattia
immediately subito
important importante
to impose imporre
(pp imposto)
imposing grandioso
impressive
impressionante
to improve migliorare
in a, in
included compreso,
incluso
inconvenience disturbo
inconvenient
sconveniente
to increase aumentare
incredible incredibile
independent
indipendente
individual individuo
inevitably inevitabilmente
informally informalmente
information informazioni
(f pl)
injured ferito
insensitive insensibile

inside dentro
instant attimo, istante
instructor istruttore,
istruttrice
insurance assicurazione
(f)
intelligent intelligente
intense intenso
to interest interessare
interesting interessante
interior interiore (m)
interior designer
arredatore, arredatrice
internal interno
to introduce presentare
to investigate indagare
to invite invitare
Ireland Irlanda
Irish irlandese
to iron stirare
iron ferro da stiro
irresponsible
irresponsabile
is è
island isola
isolated isolato

J
jacket giacca, giacchetta
job lavoro
to joke scherzare
joke scherzo, barzelletta
journalist giornalista (m/f)
journey viaggio
jumper maglione, maglia

K
key chiave (f): (IT) tasto
to key in digitare
keyboard tastiera
to kill uccidere (pp ucciso)
kilometre chilometro
kind gentile
to kiss baciare
kiss bacio, bacione (m)
kitchen cucina
knee ginocchio (m): knees
ginocchia (f pl)
knife coltello
to know (facts) sapere

to know (person/place) conoscere

L

lack mancanza
to lack mancare
laid-back rilassato
lamb agnello
land terreno
landscape paesaggio
language lingua
lanky allampanato
laptop portatile (m)
large ampio, grande
to last durare
last (final) ultimo
last (previous) scorso
late tardi, (behind time) in ritardo
to laugh ridere (pp riso)
to launch lanciare
law legge (f)
lawyer avvocato
lazy pigro
to learn imparare
least minimo: at least almeno
leather cuoio, pelle (f)
to leave lasciare
lecturer docente
left sinistra
leg gamba
legal legale
to legalise legittimare
length lunghezza
lesbian lesbica
less meno
letter lettera
level livello
lid coperchio
to lie mentire
to lie down sdraiarsi
life vita
lifeguard bagnino/a
lift ascensore (m)
lift (ride) passaggio
light luce (f)
light (weight) leggero
to like piacere (a) (pp piaciuto)

like come
likely probabile
linguistic linguistico
link collegamento
liquid liquido
list elenco, lista
to listen ascoltare
little piccolo
to live abitare, vivere
lively vivace, animato
to load caricare
lobster aragosta
local locale
long lungo
to look after curare, occuparsi di
to look at guardare
to look for cercare
to lose perdere (pp perso)
loss smarrimento
lot: a lot of molto
lounge salone, soggiorno
to love amare, volere bene
luckily fortunatamente
lucky fortunato, beato
to lunch pranzare
lunch pranzo
luxurious lussuoso
luxuriously lussuosamente

M

mad matto, pazzo
magnificent magnifico
mainly principalmente
to maintain mantenere
to make fare (pp fatto)
male maschio
to manage to riuscire a
manager direttore (m)
manageress direttrice
many molti/e
map mappa, pianta, piantina
marathon maratona
marine marino
marriage matrimonio
married sposato: to get married sposarsi
to marry sposare
martial arts arti marziali (f pl)

marvellous meraviglioso
massage massaggio
masterpiece capolavoro
to match abbinare
match (sport) partita
maximum massimo
maybe forse, magari
me me, mi
meal pasto
mean meschino
to mean volere dire, significare
meat carne (f)
medal medaglia
media studies scienze (f pl) della comunicazione
medication farmaco
medicine medicina
medieval medioevale
meditation meditazione (f)
medium-sweet (wine) amabile
to meet incontrare: meet up incontrarsi
meeting incontro
memory stick chiavetta USB
message messaggio
microwave microonde (m)
midday mezzogiorno
midnight mezzanotte
migration migrazione (f)
mild mite
mill mulino
minimum minimo
minister ministro
minute minuto (n, adj): minutes (meeting) verbale (m)
to miss mancare
mist foschia
to mistake sbagliare
to mix mescolare
mobile phone cellulare (m), smartphone (m), telefonino (m)
model modello/a
modern moderno

moment attimo, momento
month mese (m)
more più
moreover inoltre
morning mattina
mosquito zanzara
most il più
mother madre
mother-in-law suocera
mountain montagna
mountaineering alpinismo/scalata
mountainous montuoso
mouse topo: (IT) mouse (m)
moustache baffi (m pl)
mouth bocca
moving emozionante
mud fango
muddy fangoso
muggy afoso
municipal municipale
museum museo
music musica
musician musicista (m/f)
mussel cozza
must: to have to dovere
my mio

N

naïve ingenuo
name nome (m)
nanny (childminder) tata
narrow stretto
nasty sgradevole, antipatico
national nazionale
nationality nazionalità
naturally naturalmente
nature natura
nautical nautico
navy blu
near vicino
nearly quasi
necessary necessario: it's necessary bisogna
need bisogno: to need avere bisogno
to neglect trascurare
neglected trascurato

to negotiate negoziare
neighbour vicino/a di casa
neither... nor né ... né
nephew nipote
nettles ortiche (f pl)
never mai
new nuovo
New Zealand Nuova Zelanda
news notizie (f pl)
newspaper giornale (m)
next prossimo
next to accanto
nice simpatico
niece nipote
night notte (f), notturno (adj)
nightclub locale notturno (m)
nightmare incubo
nobody nessuno
noon mezzogiorno
north nord (m)
nose naso
nothing niente
now ora, adesso, attualmente
nuclear deterrent deterrente nucleare
nurse infermiere/a
nursery (children) asilo nido
nursery (plants) vivaio
nut noce (f), nocciola

O

object oggetto
to observe osservare
occasion occasione (f)
occasionally ogni tanto
odd curioso
of di
of course senz'altro, certo
to offer offrire (pp offerto)
office ufficio
office worker impiegato/a
often spesso, frequentemente
OK d'accordo, va bene

old vecchio
olive oliva
olive tree olivo
omelette frittata
on su
one-off irripetibile
only solo, soltanto
open aperto: open air all'aperto
to open aprire (pp aperto)
opening apertura
opera musica lirica
opinion punto di vista: in my opinion secondo me
opportunity opportunità
opposite di fronte a
optimistic ottimistico
or o, oppure
order ordine (m)
to organise organizzare
original originale
originally originalmente
other altro
our nostro
outside fuori
outskirts periferia (f sing)
oven forno
overweight sovrappeso
to owe dovere
own proprio: on one's own da solo/a
owner proprietario/a
oyster ostrica

P

packet pacchetto
padlock lucchetto
pain dolore (m)
painkiller antidolorifico
to paint dipingere (pp dipinto)
to paint (decorate) imbiancare
painting pittura, quadro
pair paio
palace palazzo
pale spento, (colour) chiaro
pan padella, pentola
parachuting

paracadutismo
paragliding parapendio
parcel pacchetto
parents genitori (m pl)
to park parcheggiare
park parco
parmesan parmigiano
part parte (f)
partially parzialmente
participate partecipare
partner compagno/a, partner
party festa
passion passione (f)
password password (f)
path sentiero
patient paziente (m/f)
pavement marciapiede (m)
to pay (for) pagare
peace pace (f), tranquillità
peaceful tranquillo
peacefully tranquillamente
peach pesca
penguin pinguino
pepper pepe (m)
perfect perfetto
perfection perfezione (f)
perfectly perfettamente
perhaps forse, magari
period periodo
person persona
personal personale
pessimistic pessimistico
petite minuto
to phone telefonare
photo foto (f), fotografia
physically fisicamente
picturesque pittoresco
piece pezzo, pezzettino
pink rosa
pitch (sports) campo
pity peccato
place posto, luogo: to take place avere luogo
plain ordinario
to plan progettare
plate piatto
to play (instrument)
suonare
to play (sport, game) giocare
please per favore/piacere
to please piacere a
pleasure piacere (m)
plumber idraulico
plump in carne, grassoccio
pocket tasca
point of view punto di vista
police polizia, carabinieri
police officer agente di polizia (m/f), poliziotto
police station questura
polite educato
politician politico
politics politica
to pollute inquinare
polluted inquinato
pollution inquinamento
pool piscina
poor povero
position posizione (f)
possibility possibilità
postman postino
pot pentola
potato patata
potholing speleologia
to pour versare
practical pratico
practically praticamente
precise preciso
precisely precisamente
to prefer preferire
preferably preferibilmente
pregnancy gravidanza
pregnant incinta
prehistoric preistorico
to prepare preparare
to present presentare
press stampa
to pretend fingere (pp finto)
price prezzo
principal principale
printer stampante (f)
problem problema (m)

product prodotto
profession professione (f)
professional professionale
profit guadagno
programmer programmatore, programmatrice
to promise promettere (pp promesso)
property proprietà
proprietor proprietario/a
to protect proteggere
proudly orgogliosamente
puppy cucciolo
pure puro
purse portafogli(o), borsetta
to put mettere (pp messo)

Q
quality qualità
quantity quantità
to quarrel litigare
quarter quarto
quick rapido
quickly rapidamente, velocemente
quiet tranquillo
to quit smettere (pp smesso)
quite abbastanza

R
racism razzismo
rain pioggia
to rain piovere
rape stupro
to rape violentare
rapidly velocemente
rarely raramente
rash (adj) impetuoso, audace
rash (n) eruzione cutanea (f)
rate tasso: birth/death rate tasso di natalità/ mortalità
rather piuttosto
raw crudo
to reach raggiungere

(pp raggiunto)
to read leggere
ready pronto
real vero
really davvero, veramente, proprio
reason motivo
reasonable ragionevole
to receive ricevere
recent recente
recipe ricetta
to recommend raccomandare
to recount raccontare
recyclable riciclabile
to recycle riciclare
red rosso
to reduce ridurre (pp ridotto)
refinement raffinatezza
refugee profugo, rifugiato
refund rimborso
to refurbish ristrutturare
to refuse rifiutare
region regione (f)
regional regionale
regularly regolarmente, abitualmente
to reject rifiutare
relationship rapporto
relaxing rilassante
relief sollievo
to remember ricordare, ricordarsi
to remind ricordare
remote remoto
to remove togliere (pp tolto)
renewable rinnovabile
to rent prendere in affitto
to replace sostituire
to reply rispondere (pp risposto)
reply risposta
to report denunciare, fare una denuncia
reputation reputazione (f)
request richiesta
researcher ricercatore, ricercatrice

to resemble rassomigliare a
reservation prenotazione (f)
resident residente (m/f)
resource risorsa
to respond rispondere (pp risposto)
responsible responsabile
to rest riposarsi
restaurant ristorante (m)
to restore restaurare
result risultato
to resume riprendere (pp ripreso)
retired in pensione
to return ritornare, tornare
to reward ricompensare
rich ricco
ridiculous ridicolo
right diritto
right (direction) destra
right: to be right avere ragione
rightly giustamente
risk rischio
to risk rischiare
road strada, stradale (adj)
robbery rapina
robust robusto
rock roccia, scoglio, sasso
rocky roccioso
room stanza, sala, locale (m), camera
room temperature temperatura ambiente
rose rosa
rosé rosato
rosemary rosmarino
round rotondo
rowing canottaggio
rubbish rifiuti (m pl)
rude maleducato
rugby rugby (m)
rule regola
to run correre: run the marathon correre la maratona
rural rurale

rush hour ora di punta
rustic rustico

S
sad triste
safe sicuro
to sail fare la vela
sailing vela
salary stipendio
salt sale (m)
salty salato
same stesso
sandy sabbioso
sauce salsa, sugo
saucepan pentola
to say dire (pp detto)
scientist scienziato/a
scooter motorino
to score segnare
score (game) punteggio
Scotland Scozia
screen schermo:
screensaver salvaschermo
scruffy sciatto
sea mare (m)
seafood frutti di mare (m pl)
seafront lungomare (m)
to search (for) cercare
to season insaporire, condire
secret segreto
sector settore (m)
security sicurezza
security guard sorvegliante (m/f)
to see vedere (pp visto)
to seem sembrare, parere (pp parso)
to sell vendere
semi-detached bifamiliare
seminar seminario
to send inviare, mandare, spedire
sensitive sensibile
serious grave, serio
to serve servire
service servizio
to settle down sistemarsi
several parecchi

to sew cucire
sexism sessismo
shade ombra
shady ombreggiato
shape forma
to share condividere
(pp condiviso)
shirt camicia
shoddy scadente
shoe scarpa
shop negozio
shop assistant
commesso/a
short basso, corto, breve
shoulder spalla
to shout sgridare
to show mostrare
show spettacolo
shower doccia
shower (rain) acquazzone
(m)
to shut chiudere (pp
chiuso)
shy timido
side lato (n), laterale (adj)
side effects effetti
collaterali (m pl)
signal segnale (m)
silence silenzio
silk seta
silver argento
to simmer sobbollire
simple semplice
simply semplicemente
sin peccato
sincerely: Yours sincerely
Distinti saluti
singer cantante (m/f)
single singolo
sister sorella
to sit down sedersi
size (clothing) taglia,
(shoes) numero
to skate pattinare
skating pattinaggio
ski sci
to ski sciare
skin pelle (f)

to sleep dormire
sleeve manica
slim snello
small piccolo
smart elegante
smell odore (m)
to smile sorridere
(pp sorriso)
snack boccone (m)
snail lumaca
snow neve (f)
to snow nevicare
so dunque, quindi, così
sofa divano: sofa-bed
divano-letto
soft morbido
solicitor avvocato
solid massiccio
something qualcosa
sometimes qualche volta
son figlio
son-in-law genero
soon fra poco: as soon as
possible prima possibile
sorry mi dispiace
south sud (m)
spa terme (f pl)
space spazio
spacious spazioso
sparkling (wine) spumante
to speak parlare
special speciale
speciality specialità
spectacular spettacolare
speech discorso
to spend spendere
(pp speso)
to spend (time)
trascorrere (pp trascorso)
spicy aromatico, piccante
splendid splendido
spoon cucchiaio
sport sport (m)
to sprain slogarsi
to squabble litigare
square (shape) quadrato
square (public place)
piazza

squash (game) squash (m)
stair scalino
to start cominciare
station stazione (f)
to stay stare, restare,
rimanere (pp rimasto),
alloggiare
steep ripido
step passo: stair scalino
stepdaughter figliastra
stepson figliastro
still ancora, sempre
to stir mescolare
stockbroker
intermediario/a,
finanziario/a
stocky tarchiato
stomach stomaco
stone pietra
to stop fermare, smettere
(pp smesso)
storm tempesta,
temporale (m)
straight diritto, etero
straight (hair) liscio
straightaway subito
streetwise scaltro
stressed stressato
stressful stressante
strong forte
struggle lotta
stubborn testardo
student studente (m/f)
to study studiare
stupid scemo, sciocco,
stupido
style stile (m)
stylish elegante
subject (email) oggetto
suburb periferia
to succeed riuscire
suddenly subito
suede scamosciato
to suffer soffrire
(pp sofferto)
to suggest suggerire
suitable adatto
summer estate (f)

sun sole (m)
sunburn scottatura
sunglasses occhiali da sole (m pl)
sunny soleggiato
sunset tramonto
superb meraviglioso, stupendo, eccezionale
superior superiore
supermarket supermercato
supper cena
to support sostenere
to support (team) tifare per
sure certo, sicuro
surely sicuramente
surgeon chirurgo
surgery studio medico
surname cognome (m)
surprise sorpresa
surrounding circostante (adj)
survey sondaggio
sustainability sostenibilità
to swallow ingoiare
sweater maglia, maglione (m)
sweatshirt felpa
sweet dolce
to swim nuotare
swimming nuoto
swimming pool piscina
to switch off spegnere (pp spento)
to switch on accendere (pp acceso)
symptom sintomo

T
table tavola, tavolo
tablet (IT) tablet (m)
tablet (med.) pastiglia, compressa
to tackle affrontare
tactful discreto
tactless indelicato
to take prendere (pp preso)
talented abile

to talk parlare
tall alto
to taste assaggiare, provare
taste gusto
tasting degustazione (f)
tax imposta, tassa
to teach insegnare
teacher maestro/a, professore(ssa)
team squadra
teaspoon cucchiaino
tedious barboso
to telephone telefonare
telephone telefono
television televisione (f), tivù (f)
to tell dire (pp detto)
temperature temperatura, febbre (f)
temple tempio
tender tenero
tennis tennis (m)
terrace terrazza, terrazzo
terraced a schiera
terrific mitico
terrorism terrorismo
than di, che
that quello
the il, la, l', lo, i, le, gli
theft furto
their loro
them li, le, loro
then poi
therapeutic terapeutico
there là, lì, ci
there are ci sono
there is c'è
therefore dunque, quindi
they loro
thin magro
thing cosa
thingy coso, aggeggio
to think pensare
this questo/a
thoughtful premuroso
thrilling emozionante
throat gola
to throw buttare

to tidy up mettere in ordine (pp messo)
tie cravatta: bow tie cravatta a farfalla
to tie legare, allacciare
to tie (draw) pareggiare
tight stretto
tight-fisted tirchio
time ora, tempo, volta
timetable orario
tiny minuscolo
tired stanco
toast brindisi (m)
today oggi
together insieme: to get together riunirsi, vedersi (pp visto)
tomorrow domani
too anche, troppo
too many troppi/e
too much troppo
tooth dente (m)
torch torcia
totally totalmente
tour escursione (f)
tourism turismo
touristic turistico
towards verso, in direzione di
towel asciugamano
tower torre (f)
town città
town hall municipio
trade commercio
traditional tradizionale
traffic traffico
traffic lights semaforo (sing)
tragic tragico
to train allenarsi
train treno
trainer (person) allenatore, allenatrice
trainers scarpe da ginnastica (f pl)
training allenamento
to translate tradurre (pp tradotto)
transport trasporti (m pl)

trash rifiuti (m pl)
to travel viaggiare
travel agent agente di viaggi (m/f)
treasure tesoro
to treat trattare
treatment trattamento
tree albero
triathlon triathlon (m)
to trip inciampare
trousers pantaloni (m pl)
true vero
truly veramente
truth verità
to try provare
to turn girare
twilight crepuscolo
twin beds letti gemelli
type tipo

U
ugly brutto
UK Regno Unito
uncle zio
under(neath) sotto
to understand capire
underwater subacqueo
unemployment disoccupazione (f)
unexpected imprevisto, inatteso
unforgettable indimenticabile
unfortunate sfortunato
unfortunately purtroppo, sfortunatamente
university università
unless a meno che
unpleasant antipatico, spiacevole
unrepeatable irripetibile
until fino a
up su
to update aggiornare
us noi, ci
USA Stati Uniti
to use usare
useful utile
uselessly inutilmente
user name nome utente (m)

usual solito
usually di solito, normalmente
utility room bagno di servizio

V
validity validità
value valore (m)
various vario
vegetable verdura
version versione (f)
very molto
vicar parroco
victim vittima
victory vittoria
view vista, panorama (m)
village paese (m), paesino, villaggio
vine vite (f)
vinegar aceto
vineyard vigna, vigneto
violence violenza
to visit visitare
volleyball pallavolo

W
wage stipendio
waist vita
waist-bag marsupio
waistcoat gilet (m)
to wait aspettare
waiter cameriere
waitress cameriera
to wake svegliare
to wake up svegliarsi
Wales Galles (m)
to walk camminare, passeggiare
walk passeggiata
to walk (e.g. a dog) portare a passeggio
walking boots scarponi (m pl) da trekking
wall muro
wallet portafogli(o)
to wallpaper tappezzare
walnut noce (f)
to want desiderare, volere
war guerra

wardrobe armadio
to wash lavare, lavarsi
washable lavabile
washing bucato
washing machine lavatrice (f)
wasp vespa
to watch guardare
water acqua
way modo
we noi
wealth ricchezza
to wear indossare, portare
weather tempo
weather forecast previsioni (f pl), meteo
website sito internet/web
wedding matrimonio
week settimana
weekly settimanale
weight peso: to lose weight dimagrire
weight lifting sollevamento pesi, pesistica
weird bizzarro
well bene, allora
wellbeing benessere (m)
well-equipped ben attrezzato
well-kept ben tenuto
west ovest (m)
what che
what? (che) cosa?
when(?) quando(?)
where(?) dove(?)
which che
which? quale?
white bianco
who, whom che
who? chi?
wholemeal integrale
why(?) perché(?)
widow/er vedova/o
width larghezza
wife moglie
Wi-Fi wifi (m)
willingly volentieri
to win vincere (pp vinto)

wind vento
window finestra
windsurfing windsurf (m)
wine vino
winner vincitore
winter inverno, invernale
(adj)
to wish augurare
wish augurio
with con
to withdraw (cash)
prelevare
without senza
woman donna

to wonder chiedersi (pp
chiesto)
wonderful meraviglioso
wonderfully a meraviglia
wooded boschivo
wool lana
to work lavorare
work lavoro
world mondo, mondiale
(adj)
to worry preoccuparsi
worse peggiore (adj),
peggio (adv)
wrist polso

to write scrivere
(pp scritto)

Y
year anno
yellow giallo
yes sì
yesterday ieri
you tu, lei, voi
young giovane
your tuo, suo, vostro
youth giovinezza

Z
zip cerniera